*The
Complete
Bond Book*

The Complete Bond Book

**A GUIDE TO
ALL TYPES
OF FIXED-INCOME SECURITIES**

David M. Darst

McGRAW-HILL BOOK COMPANY

*New York   St. Louis   San Francisco   Auckland   Düsseldorf
Johannesburg   Kuala Lumpur   London   Mexico   Montreal
New Delhi   Panama   Paris   São Paulo
Singapore   Sydney   Tokyo   Toronto*

Library of Congress Cataloging in Publication Data

Darst, David M., date.
  The complete bond book.

  Includes index.
  1. Bonds.   2. Securities.   3. Interest and
usury.   I. Title.
HG4651.D37   332.6'32   75-8889
ISBN 0-07-017390-7

    67890   BPBP   784321098

*The editors for this book were W. Hodson Mogan and Lester
Strong, the designer was Naomi Auerbach, and the production
supervisor was Teresa Leaden. It was set in Baskerville
by University Graphics, Inc.*

It was printed and bound by The Book Press.

With love and homage to C.D.E.W.D.

Contents

Preface

The coverage of this book is uniquely broad. It includes information on how to analyze, purchase, and sell U.S. government and Federal Agency securities, corporate bonds and preferred stocks, tax-exempt securities, short-term money market securities, and international securities. These various securities, taken together as a group, are generally referred to as *fixed-income securities*. The value of this book to the investor stems from its usefulness in (1) analyzing one's own investment objectives and ranking them in order of importance, (2) critically judging and investing in the type of security most consistent with the investor's aims, (3) deriving maximum profit from the investment alternative chosen, and (4) switching from one investment to another when the appropriate conditions argue for such a transaction.

In the unsettled economic conditions such as we have recently experienced, it is essential to obtain sound investment advice, particularly in bonds and other fixed-income securities; yet it has been difficult for the average investor to find a clear and concise guidebook on the full range of investment possibilities in this area. This book fills that need and at the same time provides many specific suggestions on how to manage one's fixed-income portfolio to achieve maximum yields, while keeping risks to a level specified by the investor. Throughout the book, the emphasis is on encouraging the investor to think independently and form sound opinions and investment strategies on his own, using the ideas contained here as a vehicle to this end.

This book is intended for individuals who have portfolio capital of between $5,000 and $5 million to invest on their own and who want to earn higher yields. These monetary parameters encompass a wide variety of men and women, all having a common goal of seeking higher income and stability in their investments, yet each also having a unique set of circumstances and investment objectives. One large segment of readers consists of individuals with $10,000 to $500,000 to invest and would include anyone who has earned a sum of capital and wants to make it earn money—with minimal risks of loss. This group is interested in keeping the money they have been able to accumulate and most likely are concerned with safety as they approach the investment process.

Another set of readers for whom safety is a major concern would include the average smaller investor with perhaps $5,000 to $25,000 in savings accounts. These individuals are seeking to earn a higher return on their assets to keep up with the rising cost of living. Still another group of investors may have the resources to place a portion of their assets in a broader range of securities in order to earn increased income. This group might typically comprise moderate to very wealthy individuals who manage their own investments, which amount to $500,000 to $5 million and up. These persons might be retired corporate executives or entrepreneurs who have sold their companies for stock or cash and who want to handle the reinvestment of the proceeds themselves.

Finally, a sizable readership segment includes the financial officers of smaller- and medium-sized companies, as well as investment counselors and securities brokers who manage money on a full- or part-time basis but who have not had much recent investment experience in bonds and other fixed-income securities. Throughout this book, both female and male investors are being referred to whenever the pronoun "he" is used for the sake of brevity.

Most investors in the asset range described here have a tendency to invest in a certain security without having formulated their own personal investment objectives, investment time horizon, income requirements, and other aims. This book assists the investor in setting objectives in an organized fashion, and once the objectives have been formulated, the book helps the investor rank and set an order of priority for his goals. *The Complete Bond Book* is unique in this feature.

The average investor is usually not at all discriminating in the selection of investments. Often, the investor buys whatever has been recommended by a friend or broker, without analyzing the security beforehand. In many cases, this recommendation may have been inappropriate or may have been even the exact opposite of what the investor should have done. The worksheets and information tables in this book help the investor to evaluate quickly yet thoroughly any possible fixed-income investments. As far as is known, this is the only investment guide which actively involves the investor in this manner.

Other books do not teach the investor to take the broad view of how and why interest rates move up or down, while simultaneously explaining the specifics (including how to save on commissions) of buying each type of fixed-income security. This book covers both general concepts and practical details, including a framework for analyzing the macro- and microeconomic factors influencing any particular investment situation.

In preparing this book, I have been fortunate in being able to call upon the accumulated wisdom and experience of numerous individuals, organizations, and academic institutions. In particular, the libraries and research departments of the 12 Federal Reserve district banks have been especially helpful. I am grateful to Sidney Homer and Martin Liebowitz, authors of *Inside the Yield Book,* for some of the ideas on bond price fluctuations expressed in the latter part of Chapter 3. Additionally, Henry H. Fowler, H. R. Young, Richard L. Menschel, Michael H. Coles, George M. Van

Cleave, George M. Ross, Robert L. Edelblut, Jr., Susan B. Fitzpatrick, W. Blair Garff, Robert M. Kock, Charles G. Reynolds, Donald P. Sheahan, and Richard B. Worley offered numerous constructive comments and suggestions on various parts of the book. A final word of thanks should go to San. K. Flesch, S. R. Squires, E. Robert Wassman, and Ole Skaarup for their continued encouragement and wise counsel on this project. It is hoped that many investors of all types will be able to profit from this book, now and over a long period of years.

D. M. D.

How to Get Started

In the interests of those investors who would like some suggestions and practical advice both on how to approach this book and on how to approach the investment process, the following pointers may be useful:

1. The investor should first conduct a *personal finances review* to determine whether family responsibilities, debt obligations, yearly income, and capital position will permit him to begin a systematic investment program in fixed-income securities. There is no minimum or maximum amount needed to start investing, but the investor should be sure that any amounts devoted to investments are not excessive in relation to his personal financial position.

2. Second, the investor should quickly *read the Introduction* to this book in order to obtain some sense of fixed-income markets— their scope, their advantages, and their limitations.

3. Third, the investor might begin to *make himself aware of the current developments* in fixed-income securities by reading articles on this subject in the newspapers and financial periodicals mentioned in Chapter 15.

4. Fourth, the investor should begin to *take stock of his personal*

investment objectives and biases, using the worksheet in Chapter 2 to aid him in this effort.

5. Fifth, the investor should *skim the Table of Contents* of this book to learn what is contained in each chapter. Chapters 1 to 5 are a general introduction to the principles and specifics of fixed-income securities and interest rates, Chapters 6 to 11 review specific types of securities, Chapter 12 is a quick summary of much of the information in Chapters 6 to 11, and the last three chapters are for more advanced forms of investing.

6. Sixth, the investor should *read Chapters 3, 4, 5, and 12* (the last of which contains information charts on all types of fixed-income securities), with particular attention to the worksheets at the end of Chapters 4 and 5.

7. Seventh, the investor should *think about the type of security he wants to buy* at this moment in time and make plans to *select a securities brokerage firm and/or commercial bank* through which his transactions can be executed. The comments on this point in Chapter 15 may be of some help, and even if the investor currently has a firm to help him with securities trades, he may wish to re-evaluate the firm at this time.

8. Eighth, the investor should *read the chapters relating to the securities he is considering purchasing.* If the investor is undecided, he should read Chapters 6 through 11. If the investor wants to read still more about the security in question, he should check the suggested sources of further information in Chapter 15 and ask his broker to obtain other materials germane to the subject for him.

9. Ninth, many investors will at this point want to purchase a certain security. It is recommended that they *read any parts of the book which they have not finished* before doing this.

10. Tenth, the investor is now *ready to purchase the issue which he believes best fits his objectives.* Again, it is recommended that the investor subject the security to the questions contained in the worksheet at the end of Chapter 4, and the investor should begin a program of carefully monitoring his investments, particularly in view of the expected pattern of interest rates. In this effort, the investor should find the worksheet at the end of Chapter 5 to be of help.

ONE

Introduction

Purpose and Scope of the Book

The purpose of this book is to help individuals with $5,000 to $5 million, as well as small- and medium-sized corporations, judge and effectively invest in *securities bought primarily to earn steady income from regular interest and dividend payments*. Such securities include an extremely broad range of investment possibilities, most of which are set forth in the list below:

U.S. Treasury bills	U.S. Treasury bonds
U.S. Treasury notes	Federal Agency bonds
Federal Agency notes	Government-sponsored bonds
Government-sponsored notes	World Bank bonds
Tax-exempt notes	Tax-exempt bonds
Bankers' acceptances	Corporate bonds and notes
Certificates of deposit	Preferred stock
Repurchase agreements	Convertible bonds
Commercial paper	Convertible preferred stock
International bills and notes	International bonds
Eurocurrency instruments	Fixed-income funds

Each of the above categories contains several distinct types of securities, further expanding the number of investment alternatives to choose from. This book helps the investor learn about each of these securities so that he can decide which fit his own needs and objectives most appropriately.

The first part of the book, Chapters 2 through 5, shows the investor how to formulate personal investment objectives and then presents a brief description of the fundamentals of interest rates and yields. The second part of the book, Chapters 6 through 12, then leads the investor into a specific review of guidelines for successful investing in each major type of fixed-income security—short-term and long-term, taxable and tax-exempt, domestic and international. In the third and final part of the book, Chapters 13 and 14 show the investor how to adapt his portfolio to varying interest rate conditions and other investment goals.

Why Individual Investors Are Interested in Fixed-Income Securities

In the absence of an all-inclusive term for such a wide variety of securities, many professional investors have begun calling them *fixed-income securities,* because the interest rate or dividend payments on these securities are fixed at the time they are initially offered to investors, even though the exact *yield* derived from these securities changes according to the price paid to acquire them. In this book, we will also use the term fixed-income securities when we wish to describe the entire group of investments which one might purchase to earn a certain yield.

While large investment institutions such as insurance companies and bank trust departments have taken advantage of recently high interest levels by putting their money into fixed-income securities, the average individual investor has not done so because of a general lack of knowledge about this area. During the past 25 years, if a person had between $5,000 and $5 million to invest, most of the advice given to this prospective investor concerned common stocks. Bonds and other fixed-income securities were often neglected because they seemed passive and unexciting.

Now, more and more individual investors are becoming aware of profitable investment opportunities in fixed-income securities, because (1) inflation has severely eroded consumers' purchasing power, forcing individuals to seek additional sources of income; (2) during the 1960s and early 1970s, the performance of stock prices proved to be volatile and in many cases extremely disappointing; and (3) interest rates currently offer very attractive returns compared with those of other periods in our country's history.

This new consciousness of profit possibilities in the fixed-income area was dramatically evidenced by individual investors' large purchases of U.S. Treasury 8½ percent bonds and 8¾ percent notes in a massive government financing during May of 1974. Yet investing properly in that offering was by no means an easy task. The average individual faced many critical choices. Should he buy the 25-year bonds, the 4¼-year notes, or the 25½-month notes? Which securities would change most in price if interest rates rose or fell? How did minimum purchase requirements for certain of these securities affect the investment decision? Should the investor instead have bought short-term securities of the Federal Home Loan Banks, which were then yielding 9.10 percent? What yields were available from medium- and high-grade corporate or municipal bonds? These questions, and many others, underscore the need for some practical guidance in the formulation and execution of a fixed-income investment strategy over a period of time.

Some Paradoxes Inherent in Fixed-Income Securities Markets

Gaining a true understanding of what is available and how all these securities work is vitally necessary, particularly since the best move for one investor may *not* necessarily be appropriate for another. Finding the right road to profit is further complicated by some of the paradoxes inherent in fixed-income securities markets, some of which are described in the following paragraphs.

Fixed-income securities are incredibly *diverse,* with literally thousands of issues of different maturities, quality ratings, coupons, forms, and prices to choose from. Yet with few exceptions, all these securities react in the *same* way to a change in the overall level of interest rates—though in varying degrees, as we shall see in Chapters 3 and 4.

Fixed-income securities are thought to be *safe, stodgy,* and *conservative,* but many issues can undergo *sizable price changes,* both up and down, when interest rates shift. Moreover, fixed-income securities purchased on margin are among the most *speculative* investment vehicles available to an individual investor. Another form of speculation can be found in those fixed-income securities which pay very high rates of interest because of their *low quality.*

Fixed-income investing is generally reputed to draw upon some of the most *advanced, complex,* and *esoteric* portfolio techniques developed to date, in which high-powered computers are pushed to their capacity. By the same token, once the fundamentals of fixed-income securities are understood, the *average investor can successfully manage his own portfolio,* by either choosing a strategy which needs a minimum of day-to-day attention or taking an active trading involvement with his holdings.

To the outsider, the fixed-income securities markets appear *narrow* and *unchanging,* with little of the direct connection to the "real world" offered by stock prices' reactions to corporate earnings, political developments, and other factors. In truth, bonds, notes, bills, and other fixed-income securities are in a *constantly changing state,* mirroring current governmental, financial, economic, social, psychological, political, and international events, as well as investors' *expectations* about the future in each of these areas.

While *institutions* have been the principal investors in fixed-income securities, actually most of them are usually acting on behalf of *individuals* who in one way or another have supplied the institution with funds. This can take many forms—individuals' placing their money on deposit at a commercial bank or savings and loan institution, paying insurance premiums, or contributing to pension, profit-sharing, or union trust funds.

One final paradox involves the use of *apparently simple language but with different meanings* to describe specialized facets of fixed-income securities markets. For instance, "par" in the fixed-income securities world does not refer to one's golfing prowess. It means $1,000 principal amount of a fixed-income security. Similarly, "flower bonds" do not have lilacs, roses, and other flora imprinted on the certificates—they are Treasury obligations which are given a special break by the Internal Revenue Service in the settlement of federal estate taxes. "Sallie Mae," "Ginnie Mae," and "Fannie Mae" are by no means three sisters in a gospel-singing group. Rather, each is the nickname for a specific government agency designed to assist a certain sector of the economy—the Student Loan Marketing Association, the Government National Mortgage Association, and the Federal National Mortgage Association, respectively. Also, *one word can have several different meanings,* depending on its specific usage. For example, the word "spread" might refer to a yield spread, an underwriting spread, or a price quotation spread (these terms will be explained more fully in the next few chapters).

As in many other fields of endeavor, before one can achieve success in investing, it is first necessary to understand the language and comprehend the big picture. Helping the individual investor see the big picture and understand the terminology is one of the objectives of this book.

Six Key Objectives of the Book

What else does this book aim to accomplish?

Profit   First and foremost, this book is intended to help the investor make money by improving the total return generated from his fixed-income securities holdings—whether these securities represent his entire portfolio or just a portion of his total investments of all types. Profit gains can be achieved through employment of the tactical and strategic guides described throughout the book.

It should be pointed out that this book cannot *guarantee* anyone a profit. Nevertheless, the book seeks to help the investor significantly improve his chances for profitable investing by showing him how to limit his losses when the fixed-income securities markets are declining in price (yields rising) and how to augment his gains when these markets are experiencing a price uptrend. For example, if the investor is able to improve his overall return by 2 percentage points per annum on an investment of $10,000, this means $200 additional profit will accrue to this particular investor *each year*. On a portfolio of $100,000, an improvement of 2 percentage points per annum translates into $2,000 more each year.

Avoidance of losses Avoiding mistakes and losses is just as important as the profit objective, but not quite the same. The investor must be sensitive to the risks, as well as the rewards, of each type of fixed-income security. Risks include *credit risks,* where the issuer will not be able to repay the interest on, or principal of, the security when it comes due. Another form of risk is *price risk,* which occurs if the securities held have fallen in price when the time comes to sell them (or risen in price, if the securities were sold and a decision is then made to buy them back). Still another type of risk is *liquidity risk,* which can take place when it takes an abnormally long time (and sometimes greater-than-usual price concessions) to effect a desired transaction. Throughout the book, the emphasis is on foreknowledge of all possible risks, in order to minimize mistakes and avoid unpleasant surprises.

Perspective and knowledge While we assume some prior awareness of the absolute basics, such as the difference between a bond (a certificate representing the issuer's promise to repay a certain sum of money plus interest, if any, on specified dates) and a stock (a certificate representing ownership and thus the right to share in profits and losses), this book provides an introduction to, and an overview of, fixed-income securities markets in their entirety.

This broad scope helps the investor discover, organize, and compare investment opportunities against the full range of fixed-income alternatives. The information and knowledge afforded by this book are oriented toward teaching the reader numerous concepts, tactics, and strategies of investing *in general,* as well as the *specific* features and uses of each type of fixed-income security.

Practicality and skepticism This book emphasizes the practical rather than the academic aspects of investing. In this sense, it might be compared to a car owner's manual and road map, which show how to operate the car and where to go, instead of a service guide, which describes the detailed workings of an automobile's engine, transmission, and steering mechanism. For those who do want to explore certain areas in greater depth, Chapter 15 reviews sources of more detailed information and ways of keeping informed about fixed-income securities. Every chapter contains specific examples, comments, and advice designed to help the investor approach the investment process from a pragmatic standpoint.

We also hope to impart to the reader a sense of healthy skepticism which will lead him to be demanding not only in the choice of investments but also in the selection of firms and people to execute his transactions. In addition, the investor will be encouraged to question what he reads and hears and to think about the implications which an action or event might have for interest rates in general and for his own securities portfolio in particular. It is also hoped that this tendency to ask questions and anticipate the future will lead to an ability to take advantage of major price movements in fixed-income securities markets and thus open up the possibility of capital gains to boost the investor's overall return.

Reference and investment tool This book is intended not only to aid the investor in *initially* forming sound investment rules to apply in good and bad market environments, but also to be of assistance as a reference guide in adapting one's investment principles *over a period of years* in a variety of economic and financial conditions. The worksheets in Chapters 4, 5, and 14, as well as the information charts in Chapter 12, can aid the investor in evaluating specific investments and shifting his portfolio, year in and year out, into the most favorable sector of the fixed-income securities markets. The examples used throughout this book employ a variety of interest rates to emphasize the general applicability of the techniques described, at any yield level. In addition, some tax pointers are provided, but the investor should always check the tax treatment of any specific transaction with properly qualified tax counsel or with the Internal Revenue Service.

Guide to special situations For the more venturesome investor, parts of various chapters of this book are devoted to special types of fixed-income investments, their advantages, and their disadvantages—fixed-income mutual funds, convertible bonds, convertible preferred stock, and short- and long-term international fixed-income securities, denominated in dollars and in foreign currencies. This book discusses, but does not treat in detail, those non-marketable investment vehicles which return a fixed-income. These include savings accounts at commercial banks or savings and loan institutions, annuities, and the various forms of real estate investments. Finally, while tax questions are reviewed throughout the book, the tax advice given should be treated only as general guidelines. Any complicated or uncertain tax situations should be checked with the investor's accountant or tax lawyer, or directly with the Internal Revenue Service, as mentioned earlier.

TWO

Setting Personal Investment Objectives

The starting point in successful investing should be careful consideration and definition of one's own investment objectives. Unless the investor organizes his goals, it is extremely difficult, if not impossible, to choose the most appropriate security which matches his specific needs and capital position. Furthermore, the objective-setting process can be a very valuable discipline in helping the investor avoid investment errors and portfolio losses.

On the following pages, a fixed-income securities Investment Objectives Worksheet is provided to help survey the investor's own status and requirements in such areas as income needs, safety, maturity, taxation, capital position, and money inflow. At the end of each section in the worksheet, brief comments have been inserted to guide the investor in his self-analysis. If some of the terms used in

9

the worksheet are not entirely clear now, they will begin to make more sense after the next few chapters have been read.

On a regular basis, the investor should refer to the Investment Objectives Worksheet in order to reexamine his own investment position and revise his objectives accordingly. Needless to say, whenever the investor's family situation, employment status, income level, or capital position changes, a reassessment of investment goals and objectives is in order, and utilizing this worksheet in conjunction with the worksheets at the end of Chapters 4, 5, and 14 and the information charts at the end of Chapter 12 will aid the investor in selecting the most appropriate investment to meet his requirements.

WORKSHEET: FIXED-INCOME SECURITIES INVESTMENT OBJECTIVES

1. Income Factors

Since income is one of the primary reasons for investing in fixed-income securities, it is helpful for the investor to determine exactly how important current income is in his own situation. This will be influenced by such things as age, the investor's level of fixed monthly and yearly expenses and their timing, family responsibilities, and current income from all other sources (salary, bonus, commissions, and so forth), as well as the *degree of fluctuation* in his annual income. For example, current income from investments may be of paramount importance to a retired couple, while it may not have the same significance for someone already in a high-income tax bracket or for a young couple setting aside a specific amount of money to pay their children's college expenses at some future date. The retired couple may desire a stable and relatively high rate of current income from their fixed-income investments. On the other hand, the high-tax-bracket individual or the couple planning for college expenses may prefer to obtain part of their investment return in the form of capital gains and therefore accept a somewhat lower rate of current income to obtain this feature. Often, a higher level of current income on a security is earned by sacrificing quality or by purchasing a security with a long maturity, but these characteristics can also increase the investor's risks of capital losses. The investor should remember that extraordinarily high yields normally have a "hidden" cost associated with them.

1. *Income factors*

(Circle one number in each category.)

A. Do I need to earn large amounts of current income from my portfolio?	*Low current income needs*				*Moderate current income needs*			*Substantial current income needs*
	1		2		3		4	5
B. Do I prefer to obtain a part of my investment return in the form of short- or long-term capital gains?	*Capital gains very important*				*Capital gains of moderate importance*			*Capital gains of little importance*
	1		2		3		4	5
C. Can I accept variability of income as interest rates fluctuate?	*Stable income desired*				*Some variability acceptable*			*Wide income fluctuations acceptable*
	1		2		3		4	5

Total Score = _____

COMMENT: A low numerical score might indicate that the investor should invest in lower-coupon securities selling at a discount to par, whereas a high score might argue in favor of high-coupon bonds.

2. Safety Factors

For the average investor, the safety of each investment should be carefully evaluated so that he knows exactly how certain it is that the timely repayment of principal and interest will be accomplished. Generally speaking, the smaller the investor's portfolio, and the less time he has to investigate and review his holdings' creditworthiness and susceptibility to large price fluctuations, the more he should emphasize quality and safety in choosing investments. As will be seen in later chapters, safety can be measured in many ways and in numerous gradations of quality. Nevertheless, investors who are concerned about safety should select only those securities which can withstand the most difficult of economic and financial circumstances. If the investor pursues an investment strategy of a somewhat higher degree of risk in order to increase the possibility of higher returns, such as investing on margin, he should exercise special care and diligence in reviewing his investments frequently.

2. *Safety factors*

(Circle one number in each category.)

A. Am I financially able and emotionally willing to sustain losses in my portfolio, either in fact or on paper?	*Try to avoid all losses*		*Can accept some losses*		*Able to sustain sizable losses*
	1	2	3	4	5
B. How much time per month can I spend reviewing my securities holdings, studying alternative investments, and making portfolio changes?	*Less than 2 hours per month*		*Between 5 and 10 hours per month*		*More than 20 hours per month*
	1	2	3	4	5
C. How much of a sacrifice in quality will I make to obtain a higher yield on my portfolio?	*Little sacrifice in quality*		*Moderate sacrifices in quality*		*Willing to accept very low quality for higher yields*
	1	2	3	4	5
D. Will I invest my funds in a longer maturity issue to gain more yield, even though this means greater exposure to price fluctuation?	*Never*		*Occasionally*		*Frequently*
	1	2	3	4	5
E. Am I willing to borrow money (invest on margin) to add to my own funds in the hope of achieving greater-than-average gains, even though this can expose me to greater-than-average losses?	*Never willing to invest on margin*		*Sometimes willing to invest on margin*		*Frequently willing to invest on margin*
	1	2	3	4	5

Total Score = _____

COMMENT: A low numerical score might indicate that the investor should stick to U.S. government and other top-rated securities, whereas a high score may point to a willingness to assume greater risks in pursuit of greater-than-average gains.

3. Maturity Factors

The time span over which the investor can invest his funds has a direct impact on the maturity options of the security selected. At the same time, however, Chapter 3 demonstrates that interest rate changes influence the price behavior of long-term securities differently than that of short-maturity issues. In addition, Chapter 13 contains a detailed method of deciding on the maturities of specific investments, depending upon the investor's estimate of the future level and direction of interest rates. Although maturity considerations may seem unimportant when the investor is choosing a specific security, this feature can often be the most significant determinant of the overall return (income plus capital gains) earned from an investment.

3. *Maturity factors*

(Circle one number in each category.)

A. When do I need my money back?	*Within 1 year*				*Between 3 and 7 years*			*After 10 years*
	1		2		3		4	5
B. Will I need all my money at one time in the near future?	*All money needed at one time*				*About half of money needed at any one time*			*Only a small portion of funds needed at any one time*
	1		2		3		4	5
C. Are my funds being invested to satisfy known future outlays (such as college expenses) or as a current reserve to meet unexpected needs?	*Invested as current reserve to meet unexpected needs*				*Part for current reserve and part for known future outlays*			*Invested to satisfy known future outlays*
	1		2		3		4	5
D. How do I expect interest rates to move during the next 6 to 18 months?	*Sharply upward*				*Flat to unchanged*			*Sharply downward*
	1		2		3		4	5

Total Score = _____

COMMENT: A low numerical score might indicate that the investor should invest in securities which are maturing in the near to intermediate term, whereas a high score might permit the investor to tie up his funds in longer-maturity securities.

4. Taxation Factors

Tax factors should not be an overriding influence on the investment process, but the investor should be aware of his current and future tax brackets at the federal, state, and local levels in order to maximize his investment yields on an aftertax basis. Since some securities are exempt from income taxes at one or more taxation levels, it is advantageous to examine every investment's yield after all taxes before making any commitments.

4. *Taxation factors*

(Circle one number in each category.)

	Low tax bracket		Intermediate tax bracket		High tax bracket
A. What is my present marginal income tax bracket at the federal level?	1	2	3	4	5
B. What is my present marginal income tax bracket at the state level?	1	2	3	4	5
C. What is my present marginal income tax bracket at the local level?	1	2	3	4	5
	Downward		Same		Upward
D. If my marginal tax bracket in any of the above categories is expected to change in the near future, how will it change? (Remember that one's income tax bracket can change because of a a change in income level or because of a change in tax rates!)	1	2	3	4	5

Total Score =_____

COMMENT: A low numerical score might indicate that tax-exempt securities offer little benefit, in terms of aftertax income, to the investor, whereas a high score might alert the investor to explore tax-exempt investment possibilities and to emphasize capital gains, tax-swapping techniques, and other means of reducing total taxable income.

5. Capital Position and Money Inflow Factors

The less capital and income the investor has when beginning an investment program, the more important it is for him to exercise caution in his investment program, since losses in any one investment can have a much greater percentage impact on his portfolio. The investor should remember that if he suffers a capital loss of *25 percent* of his portfolio and is left with 75 percent of his original investment, he must achieve a gain of *33 percent* (25 ÷ 75 equals 33 percent) merely to get even with his earlier position. Several of the chapters in this book point out ways of avoiding or minimizing losses in principal due to rising interest rates. The higher the investor's money inflow, the greater the opportunity for him to purchase securities whose return is concentrated in the form of capital gains as opposed to current income. At all times, the investor with small amounts of money coming in and with a relatively small capital position should not invest any monies which might be needed for unforeseen contingencies in difficult-to-dispose-of securities.

5. *Capital position and money inflow factors*

(Circle one number in each category.)

A. How much money do I have to invest?	$5,000– $25,000		$100,000– $250,000		Over $1 million
	1	2	3	4	5
B. How much money will be coming in to invest in the future?	Small amounts ($1,000 and up)		Moderate amounts ($10,000– $100,000)		Large amounts (over $250,000)
	1	2	3	4	5
C. How regularly will money be coming in for future investment?	Irregularly		Frequently but not regularly		Regularly
	1	2	3	4	5
D. Can I subdivide my portfolio according to specific investment objectives?	Very difficult to subdivide portfolio		Some subdivision possible		Large enough to permit easy subdivision
	1	2	3	4	5

Total Score = _____

COMMENT: A low numerical score might indicate that the investor should avoid investments for which commissions or service charges will significantly lower the actual realized return, whereas this will generally not have much influence on the investor with a high score in this category. A high score might also indicate more possibilities for diversification into a variety of fixed-income investments of varying maturities.

6. Summary and Ranking of Factors

After the investor has filled out the sections of the Investment Objectives Worksheet relating to income, safety, maturity, taxation, and capital position and money inflow, it is worthwhile to review all these factors together in order to determine the relative importance of each area to the investor. Although this exercise entails a good deal of subjectivity, it nevertheless helps the investor grasp his investment situation *as a whole*. For instance, income may be of primary importance, with safety only a secondary consideration. On the other hand, maturity or taxation factors may be paramount for some investors. When the investor has ranked each series of factors in order of importance, from 1 equals most important to 5 equals least important, it is also helpful to assign a percentage weighting to each area in order to quantify exactly how important each factor is in his overall investment strategy. If the investor assigns roughly equal weightings to each of the five areas (roughly 20 percent to each factor), this implies that one factor or another might be changed slightly on a particular investment without significantly altering its possible appeal to the investor. Conversely, if the investor assigns a 50 percent weighting to one factor (such as safety), this implies that he is unwilling to compromise in this area, even if benefits in other areas would be obtained by relaxing these standards.

6. *Summary and weighting of factors*

Area	Score	Ranking in order of importance (1–5)	% Weighting for each area
Income	_____	_____	_____
Safety	_____	_____	_____
Maturity	_____	_____	_____
Taxation	_____	_____	_____
Capital position and money inflow	_____	_____	_____
Total Score	_____	Total % Weighting	100%

COMMENT: A low numerical total might indicate that in most, but not necessarily all, cases the investor should stick with fairly conventional investments which do not demand a great deal of supervision. On the other hand, a high total score tends to permit greater latitude in choosing securities. The rankings and weightings do not permit easy generalizations. Rather, they are to help the investor better assess the *relative* importance of each factor compared with the others. In the chapters to come, we will discover what a powerful influence these weightings can exert in selecting the specific fixed-income security which is best suited to an investor's requirements.

THREE

How Interest Works

Since the primary purpose of investing in any type of fixed-income security is to earn a given rate of interest, or yield, it makes sense to explore (for some readers, this may be more of a review than a new exploration) what is comprised in the rate of return from a fixed-income investment. While the idea of interest seems simple and obvious, this concept is nevertheless full of subtleties and subcategories which, when understood in a bit more depth, will be of significant value in analyzing specific securities and investing for profit.

How Fixed-Income Securities Pay Interest

Fixed-income securities can pay interest in either of two ways. First, the security can be issued to the investor at a discount from the amount which will be paid off at maturity (the date the debt falls due). This is similar to borrowing $100 from a friend who lends $90 in return for a promise to repay $100 in some agreed upon time period. Another name for this practice is *discounting,* and the resulting *non-interest-bearing* certificates generally have a short maturity, ranging from 5 days up to 1 year. These securities include U.S., Canadian, and British *Treasury bills;* the *discount notes* of several govern-

18

ment agencies; and *commercial paper.* At one time or another, many investors have no doubt run across or heard of discounted securities of over 1 year's maturity—*U.S. Series E savings bonds,* which currently run for 5 years and 10 months.

On the other hand, *U.S. Series H savings bonds* have a maturity of 10 years and earn interest in the second and perhaps more commonly known way by generating yield through the payment of interest at regular intervals; that is, in the case of the Series H savings bonds, interest is paid by check every 6 months until the securities come due. These are called *interest-bearing* securities. Because these bonds are *fully registered* in the name of the owner as to both principal and interest, the interest check and final repayment of principal are sent automatically to the registered owner of the securities, thus providing protection from loss or theft.

Contrasting with registered securities are *bearer* securities, which are considered to be owned by the person who has them in his possession. Since the issuer of bearer securities will generally not know where to send the interest payments, bearer certificates usually have coupons attached which can be clipped off and presented directly to the issuer or its designated payment agent to collect the interest.

Whether in bearer or registered form, the majority of interest-bearing securities, such as most taxable corporate and governmental bonds and notes, pay interest every 6 months (semiannually). Some securities pay interest annually (most Eurobonds and notes of the Farmers Home Administration), quarterly (preferred stocks), and even monthly [Government National Mortgage Association (GNMA) modified pass-through securities]. The yields from interest-bearing securities are normally converted to a *semiannual equivalent basis* to facilitate comparison with returns offered by the most common type of payment, semiannual. A few interest-bearing securities, such as bank *certificates of deposit* and short-term *tax-exempt notes,* pay interest not semiannually but at the time the principal is paid back. More detailed explanations of the specific features of each of the securities mentioned above will come in later chapters.

Most bonds and other fixed-income securities are of $1,000, $10,-000, and sometimes higher minimum denominations, though $100 and $500 denominations, referred to as *baby bonds,* or *small pieces,* are also seen from time to time. Where possible, it is best for the investor to avoid small pieces and *odd-lot* amounts (which are amounts less than the common unit of trading for a specific type of security), since it is difficult to find buyers for these smaller denominations when the investor wants to sell them. If the securities will definitely be held until maturity, holding smaller denominations is less of a problem. Sometimes, small denominations of a particular security may be combined with other small pieces of the same security and *interchanged* into larger denominations, but this is not always the case. The investor should check this interchangeability feature carefully before making any small purchases which may be traded before final maturity of the securities.

How Fixed-Income Securities Pay Back Principal

How do issuers of fixed-income securities pay off the principal of their obligations? Often, short-term borrowers will simply issue new securities to *refund,* or "roll over," maturing debt. Long-term issues may be retired in one or a combination of the following ways. First, the issuer can wait until the time the bonds come due and pay back the principal in a "balloon payment" (all of the issue at once) from cash reserves or from the proceeds of newly issued bonds. The formal name for bonds which mature all at once is *term bonds.* Second, *serial bonds* pay back the principal by scheduling portions of the issue to come due in installments during the life of the issue. Because of their varying maturities and yields, serial bonds are usually quoted on a percentage yield basis rather than on a dollar price basis. Third, the security may be structured to require the issuer to operate a *sinking fund* designed to retire a part or all of the issue by the final maturity date. Bonds chosen for sinking-fund redemption are usually selected by lottery. Although the issuer has to pay at least par or a premium over par for bonds called in for redemption, if the bonds happen to be trading at below par (called trading at a *discount*), the issuer may buy them in the open market in order to satisfy sinking-fund requirements.

One final way fixed-income securities can be paid off is through a *call,* or redemption of the entire issue for repayment prior to maturity. This may occur when interest rates have dropped substantially from levels at which the securities were originally issued. The issuer thus saves interest payment expenses by issuing a new, lower-coupon security to retire the original high-coupon bond. Needless to say, early redemption is not popular with investors, since their bondholdings which are paying a high rate of interest (and probably trading above par, or at a *premium*) are being replaced by securities which will pay a lower rate of interest. In periods of tight money (high interest rates), bond issuers thus often have to provide assurance that they will not refund the bonds being issued for 5 or 10 years. These assurances are needed not only to attract investors to buy the securities but also to help the issuer raise money at somewhat lower interest rates than would have to be paid if the security did not have this feature, which is termed *call protection*. This call protection feature, plus the fact that the issuer generally has to pay a premium over par for bonds which are called, serves to protect the investor somewhat in the event of falling interest rates. For this reason, when investigating a new or existing security during a period of high interest rates, the investor should find out if the security has call protection, and if so, for how long. Also, when purchasing a security, the investor should compare the purchase price to the current and future minimum call price on the issue. If the purchase price is above the call price when the bond becomes callable, the investor may be forced to give up his high-yield investment in favor of a security with a lower yield.

How Fixed-Income Securities Prices Are Quoted

Most fixed-income securities prices are quoted in percentages-of-par value (usually $1,000). For example, a price of 80 for a $1,000 par-value bond or note means 80 percent of $1,000, or $800. Similarly, a price of 110½ means 110.5 percent of $1,000 or $1,105. When the security sells at a price above par, it is said to be selling at a *premium,* and when it is below par, it is trading at a *discount.* As was mentioned earlier, some securities, such as many short-term bill issues of the U.S. Treasury and almost all tax-exempt bonds, are quoted on a *yield basis* rather than in percentage-of-par terms. Thus, the investor might hear "180-day bankers' acceptances are currently offered at

7.5 percent," or "State of New Jersey bonds can be purchased on a 5.10 percent basis," or "Treasury bills maturing on August 8 of this year can be bought at a 5.96 percent yield." In the chapters on U.S. government securities and tax-exempt securities, the investor will learn how to figure out dollar prices when the issue is quoted on a yield basis.

The Meaning of Yield: Yield to Maturity versus Current Yield

Exactly what is meant by the term "yield," and how are yields derived and calculated? Yield is a relatively straightforward concept, with a few nuances and shades of meaning which must also be understood in order to evaluate alternative investments properly. For example, when a 20-year $1,000 bond is issued with a 7.5 percent coupon, the bondowner will receive a total of $75 in interest on this security each year for 20 years, at which time the $1,000 is also paid back. The *current yield* on this security is calculated by dividing the dollar amount of the annual interest received ($75) by the current dollar price of the bond ($1,000, assuming the new bond is issued at par), to give $75 ÷ $1,000, or a 7.5 percent current yield.

The *yield to maturity* is a measure of the annual return on the investment until the security comes due, and this figure takes into account the amount paid for the bond, the interest rate, and the length of time to maturity. If the bond in our example were purchased at a price of $1,000, the yield to maturity would also be the same as the current yield, or 7.5 percent. The yield to maturity on a security is different from the current yield whenever the price paid for the security is different from the security's par value ($1,000).

The reason an investor might pay more or less than $1,000 in the marketplace for a $1,000 par-value bond relates to the security's coupon rate (in our case, a 7.5 percent coupon is attached to the 20-year bond) as it compares with the overall level of interest rates for securities of a similar maturity. In Chapter 5, we will look at the major factors causing interest rates in general to move upward to downward.

For the moment, however, let us assume that, for whatever reason, 2 years after the original 7.5 percent 20-year bond was issued, the general level of long-term interest rates has risen and a new bond is brought to market with a final maturity date the same as the one on the original bond. Since 2 years have passed from the time the first bond was issued, this means that the second bond has an 18-year maturity. Because interest rates have risen, the second bond is issued with a coupon of 8.5 percent. Holders of the first bond, or people who are considering the purchase of the first bond, can now obtain a similar security which returns $85 per year in interest income, rather than $75 per year. Since the coupon rate on a bond is generally fixed for the duration of the bond's life, the only way the $75-interest-paying bond can stay competitive with the one paying $85 (or 8.5 percent annually) is by declining in price—so that by paying *less than $1,000* per bond for the 7.5 percent coupon issue, the investor's yield is greater than 7.5 percent.

At a price of 88¼ ($882.50 per $1,000 bond), the *current yield* of the first bond is $75 ÷ $882.50, or 8.52 percent, which should theoretically bring it into line with rates currently offered by similar new issues having an 8.5 percent coupon. However, the investor should remember that bonds are paid off at par ($1,000) at maturity, and if an investor were to buy the 7.5 percent coupon bond at a price of 88¼, he would receive par for those same bonds in 18 years' time. Somehow, the yield to maturity should take this gain in value into account and reflect the fact that the additional money (11¾ points, or $117.50 per $1,000 bond) is returned not during the life of the bond but after 18 years, at maturity.

Complicated arithmetic formulas have been devised to allow for the time-value-of-money principle (which says that $1 received *now* is worth more in present value terms than $1 received at some point in the *future*), in arriving at the right price to pay for a bond with a 7.5 percent coupon when similar bonds are being currently issued at 8.5 percent coupon rates. This "right price" takes into account the gain in principal amount of the bond at maturity as well as the coupon rate relative to current coupon rates. Fortunately for investors, these calculations have been done for many combinations of coupons, maturities, and interest rate levels, and the results have been grouped together in *bond yield tables,* or interest tables.

Checking in the interest tables, we find that a 7.5 percent coupon 18-year bond has an 8.5 percent yield to maturity at a price of around 90¾, or $907.50. The reason that this price is above our rough estimate of 88¼ for the 7.5 percent coupon bonds to give a yield to maturity equal to the 8.5 percent coupon bonds purchased at par is that some of the yield to maturity comes in the form of the gain in value when the investor who paid 88¼ today receives 100 in 18 years' time. At a price of 90¾, a 7.5 percent coupon bond has a *current yield* equal to $75 ÷ $907.50 = 8.26 percent. The difference between the current yield on these bonds (8.26 percent) and the yield to maturity (8.5 percent) is directly attributable to the gain in value at maturity. It should also be apparent from the foregoing discussion that if an investor had purchased the 7.5 percent bonds when they were originally issued at par and then held onto them for the 2-year period when interest rates were rising, he would suffer a capital *loss* if the bonds had to be sold when other similar 18-year maturity securities were yielding 8.5 percent. We will come back to price gains and losses shortly.

The same process works in reverse when interest rates *decline* from the interest levels in effect when the 7.5 percent bonds were initially issued. If we had purchased our 7.5 percent 20-year securities and then had seen interest rates decline after 2 years to the 7 percent level, we would notice that our bonds pay $75 in interest each year, while new and substantially similar bonds pay only $70. Obviously, investors will bid the price of the 7.5 percent bonds up until their yield to maturity is 7 percent. The yield tables tell us that a 7.5 percent coupon 18-year-maturity bond yields 7 percent to maturity at a purchase price of 105 ($1,050 per $1,000 bond). At 105, the current yield is 7.14 percent, which is *higher* than the yield to maturity because the yield to maturity must now take into consideration the eventual *decrease* to par, or capital *loss,* at maturity of a bond bought at a premium above par (the investor paid 105 for the bonds and receives back only 100 from the issuer at final maturity).

This discussion contains some very important conclusions which bear repeating for the investor in fixed-income securities:

1. Unless the investment is held until final maturity, the investor assumes possible *price risk* (the chance of capital loss or gain) whenever he buys bonds or any other fixed-income securities. Exceptions are U.S. Series E and H savings bonds, which may be redeemed by the Treasury (not sold to other investors) at or above the original

purchase price, regardless of interest rate fluctuations. As we will see later on in this chapter, the specific degree of price risk, or risk of principal loss, depends on several factors.

2. When interest rates *rise,* fixed-income securities *fall* in price. When interest rates *fall,* fixed-income securities *rise* in price. This is a most important, and basic, point to remember.

3. When a fixed-income security is purchased at a *premium* over par value, current yield is *greater* than yield to maturity. When a fixed-income security is purchased at a *discount* from par value, current yield is *less* than yield to maturity.

To sum up, the total yield derived from a fixed-income security investment comes from three sources: (1) the actual coupon rate, relative to the price paid for the security; (2) the decline in principal value (also called *amortization*) or the rise in principal value (also called *accumulation,* or *accretion*) from the price paid for a security and the par value received at maturity, if the fixed-income security was purchased at a level above or below par; and (3) the assumed reinvestment of the interest payments received each year at the rate of yield at which the bond was purchased. This means, for instance, that if a bond is said to have a 7.5 percent yield to maturity, the arithmetic formula which produced this yield calculation assumes that every 6 months during the remaining life of the bond, when the semiannual interest check is received, it is reinvested at a 7.5 percent interest rate. Because interest rates fluctuate, and because many investors *spend* their interest payments rather than reinvest them, the "true" yield to maturity generally varies from the arithmetic "formula" yield to maturity. This third contributor to the total yield produced by a fixed-income investment is often overlooked, but it should be kept in mind in the case of long-term high-coupon bonds purchased at a price which yields a high rate of yield to maturity, since this "reinvestment" component of yield can be a significant contributor to the total yield in these situations.

Using Interest Tables

Interest tables permit the investor to find the yield to maturity of a security at various purchase prices. For example, the investor might want to know the yield to maturity of a 7.5 percent coupon bond

TABLE 3-1 Sample Interest Table for a 7.5% Semiannual Coupon Rate

Current bond price	Time remaining to maturity					
	1 year	2 years	5 years	10 years	15 years	20 years
95	12.99%	10.33%	8.76%	8.24%	8.08%	B 8.01%
96	11.86	9.75	8.50	8.09	7.96	7.90
97	10.74	9.18	C 8.24	7.94	7.84	7.80
98	9.65	8.61	7.99	7.79	7.73	7.70
99	8.56	8.05	7.75	7.64	7.61	7.60
100	7.50	7.50	7.50	7.50	7.50	7.50
101	6.45	6.96	7.26	7.36	7.39	7.40
102	5.42	6.42	7.02	7.22	7.28	7.31
103	4.40	5.89	6.78	7.08	7.17	7.21
104	3.40	5.36	6.55	A 6.94	D 7.06	7.12
105	2.41	4.85	6.32	6.80	6.96	7.03

with 10 years remaining to maturity if he pays 104 for the bond. First, the pages in the interest tables which treat 7.5 percent coupon bonds should be located. Table 3-1 is taken from the 7.5 percent coupon page of a book of interest tables.

It should be noted that Table 3-1 is considerably abbreviated from the interest tables an investor will generally. refer to, which will contain considerably more maturities (sometimes even broken down by months, rather than years) and considerably more bond prices (often broken down by eighths or quarters of a point).

Returning to our question, to find the yield to maturity of 7.5 percent bonds with 10 years to maturity if they are purchased at a price of 104, first the price row for 104 is located and then, looking in the 10-year maturity column, we find that they intersect at a yield of 6.94 percent to maturity (see the circle marked "A" above). Now the investor should try another one. What is the yield to maturity of a 7.5 percent coupon bond with 20 years left to maturity if it is bought at a price of 95? The investor should come up with an answer of 8.01 percent (the circle marked "B" in the table).

Interest tables can be used for another purpose—to find the price change which takes place when interest rates rise or fall. For example, what is the approximate price change on a 7.5 percent coupon issue with 5 years left to maturity if interest rate levels rise from 7.5 to 8 percent? To find the answer, (1) locate the 7.5 percent coupon page, (2) look for the 5-year maturity column, and (3) scan up and down the column until a yield to maturity level of around 8 percent is located. We can see that at a price of 98 the yield to maturity of a 7.5 percent coupon issue with 5 years to maturity is 7.99 percent, and at a price of 97 the yield to maturity on the same issue is 8.24 percent. (See the circle marked "C" in the table.) Since 7.99 percent is very close to an 8.00 percent yield to maturity, 98 can be used as a close approximation of the price if interest rate levels in general should rise to 8 percent. When interest rates were at 7.5 percent, the 7.5 percent coupon issue was trading at par, or 100; with the rise of 50 basis points in interest rates from 7.50 to 8.00 percent (a *basis point* is one one-hundredth of a percentage point, or 0.01 percent), the securities dropped by 2 *points* (different from basis points) from 100 (or $1,000 per bond) to 98 (or $980 per bond) to bring this issue's yield into line with the general level of interest rate yields.

The investor should try another example of this use of interest tables to make sure he is familiar with how to find price changes using the tables. If the investor buys a 7.5 percent 16-year coupon issue at par (100) today, when interest rates are at the 7.5 percent level, what will the bond price be in 1 year's time (it will then have *fifteen* years to maturity), if long-term interest rates have declined from the 7.5 percent level to the 7 percent area? Looking in the 15-year column we see that at a price of 104 the bonds yield 7.06 percent to maturity, and at a price of 105 they yield 6.96 percent to maturity (see the circle marked "D" on the table). By the process of interpolation, one finds that the bonds will be trading at a price of 104½ ($1,045 per bond) if interest rates have declined from 7.5 to 7 percent in 1 year's time.

In practice, fewer investors and securities dealers are using the interest tables, since many of the small calculators now offered on the market have a feature which performs yield to maturity and related calculations. Nevertheless, it is worthwhile for the individual investor to have a grasp of how yield tables are constructed and what they mean. Many different types of interest tables are published by the Financial Publishing Company, located at 82 Brookline Ave.,

Boston, Mass. 02215, and by writing to them the investor can obtain a catalog of interest tables available for purchase.

Factors Which Influence the Degree of Price Fluctuation of Fixed-Income Securities

There are three primary factors which determine the inherent degree of price fluctuation proneness of fixed-income securities— the *maturity*, the *coupon rate*, and the actual *level of interest rates* from which the fluctuation begins. Each of these factors can influence the degree of price fluctuation of a fixed-income security on its own or in combination with one of the other two factors; but to understand how each factor works separately, in the examples on the following pages we will always keep two of the three factors constant, while focusing on each factor in its turn. The investor should be aware, however, of the fact that *all* these factors can be different for one security as compared with another and that while one factor may cause a greater degree of price fluctuation, another factor may partially or even completely counterbalance this and thus cause a *lesser* degree of price fluctuation. Finally, it should be mentioned that other technical factors, such as the relationship between the supply of, and demand for, a particular security, may also influence the degree of price fluctuation. These other elements of price fluctuation will be treated in Chapter 4.

As we examine how the maturity, the coupon rate, and the level of interest rates can influence the degree of price fluctuation of fixed-income securities, we will observe what happens when securities prices are falling (a 100-basis-point, or 1 percent, *rise* in interest rates) and when prices are rising (a 200-basis-point, or 2 percent, *decline* in interest rates). The magnitude of the price fall was consciously made different from the magnitude of the price rise to give the investor a feeling for what happens under a variety of interest rate fluctuations. Similarly, the coupon rates, maturities, and interest rate levels in the examples have been arbitrarily chosen to illustrate general principles. What is most important for the investor is to gain some intuitive awareness of how certain aspects of a fixed-income security can influence its magnitude of price fluctuation when interest rates change.

Maturity   Table 3-2 shows what happens to fixed-income securities of various maturities when interest rates move up or down. It can be observed that for a given change in interest rates *the longer the time remaining to maturity for a security, the greater the price fluctuation which will occur.*

Thus, we can see in the table that when interest rates rise from 7 to 8 percent, a 7 percent coupon issue with 1 year remaining to maturity will decline by 1 percent in its principal value (the circle marked "A" in the table), whereas if the same 7 percent coupon issue had 20 years remaining to maturity, it would decline by 10 percent in its principal value (circle "B"). This same degree of greater price fluctuation holds true when interest rates are declining. If interest rates decline from 7 to 5 percent, an investor holding a 7 percent coupon security with 6 months left to maturity will experience a price rise of 0.88 percent in its principal value (circle "C" in the table), while an investor holding the same coupon security with 10 years to maturity would show a price increase of 15.5 percent in the principal amount of the bond. It should be mentioned that, past a certain point, all very long maturity bonds tend to fluctuate virtually equally in price for a given change in interest rates. For example, a

TABLE 3-2   Price Fluctuations for Various Maturities   (7% coupon rate)

Time to maturity	Falling securities prices (rising interest rates)			Rising securities prices (falling interest rates)		
	Price @ 7%	Price @ 8%	% Change	Price @ 7%	Price @ 5%	% Change
6 mo	100	99½	−0.50	100	100⅞	C +0.88
1 yr	100	99	A −1.00	100	101	+1.00
2 yr	100	98⅛	−1.88	100	103¾	+3.75
5 yr	100	96	−4.00	100	108¾	+8.75
10 yr	100	93¼	−6.75	100	115½	D +15.50
20 yr	100	90	B −10.00	100	125⅛	+25.13

25-year bond will usually fluctuate almost the same in price as a 60- or 100-year bond.

The implication of this phenomenon leads to one of the fundamental rules of fixed-income securities investing: *If interest rates are expected to rise, the investor should own short-maturity securities, and if interest rates are expected to fall, the investor should own longer-maturity securities.*

Coupon rate In Table 3-3, we can see that for a particular basis-point change in interest rates *the lower the coupon rate on an issue, the more widely it will fluctuate up and down in price.* Conversely, *the higher the coupon rate on a fixed-income security, the less it will fluctuate for a specific basis-point change in interest rates.*

As can be seen in the table, when a 20-year maturity bond with a 4 percent coupon undergoes an interest rate rise from 7 to 8 percent, its price falls by 11.3 percent (the circle marked "A" in the table), while a bond of the same maturity and an 8 percent coupon falls in price by 9.5 percent in principal amount (circle "B") for an equivalent rise in market interest rates. A lower-coupon security also moves faster percentagewise on the upside. If a 4 percent 20-year bond moves from a 7 percent yield to maturity to a 5 percent yield to maturity, it gains in price by 28.7 percent (circle "C"), but an 8 percent 20-year bond gains only by 24.4 percent (circle "D") for the same shift in interest yields.

This brings us to another general principle for fixed-income

TABLE 3-3 Price Fluctuations for Various Coupon Rates (20-year maturity bonds)

	Falling securities prices (rising interest rates)				Rising securities prices (falling interest rates)			
Coupon rates, %	Price @ 7%	Price @ 8%		% Change	Price @ 7%	Price @ 5%		% Change
4	68	60⅜	A	−11.3	68	87½	C	+28.7
5	78⅝	70⅜		−10.5	78⅝	100		+27.1
6	89⅜	80¼		−10.0	89⅜	112½		+25.8
7	100	90⅛		−9.8	100	125⅛		+25.1
8	110⅝	100	B	−9.5	110⅝	137⅝	D	+24.4

securities investing: *If interest rates are expected to rise, it is better to own securities with a high coupon, and if interest rates are expected to fall, it is better to own securities with a low coupon.* An important sidelight to this principle is the fact that, in a period of falling interest rates (rising fixed-income securities prices), lower-coupon securities not only move faster in price but are also much less likely to be called by the issuer, because they *already* will have been paying a low rate of interest vis-à-vis their par value.

Actual level of interest rates Table 3-4 shows that *the higher the absolute interest rate level from which a certain percentage change in interest rates takes place, the more widely securities prices will fluctuate.* The reverse is also true—if a certain percentage change in interest rates takes place, starting from a low level of interest, securities prices will fluctuate less widely.

In each of the examples in Table 3-4 we have assumed that a basis-point change equal to 10 percent of the original yield occurred (for example, 4.0 percent plus 40 basis points, or 4.4 percent in the falling securities prices environment, and 4.0 percent minus 40 basis points, or 3.6 percent in the rising securities prices scenario). We can see that when a 6 percent coupon 20-year bond moves from a 5.0 percent yield to maturity to a 5.5 percent yield to maturity, the price change of the bond is − 5.8 percent (circle "A" in Table 3-4), while if the same security moves from an 8.0 percent yield to maturity to an 8.8 percent yield to maturity, the price decline of the bond is steeper, −8.0 percent (circle "B" in the table). When bond prices are rising, if our hypothetical 6 percent coupon 20-year to maturity bond moved from a yield to maturity of 4.0 percent to a yield to maturity of 3.6 percent, the price gain of the bond is +5.3 percent (circle "C" in the table), but if the same bond underwent a change in yield to maturity from 8.0 percent to 7.2 percent, the percentage price gain in the bond's principal amount is even greater, +9.0 percent (circle "D" in the table).

Thus, if interest rates *rise* by a certain percentage amount in basis-point terms from their original levels, the investor is better off (he experiences less of a price decline) if the rise starts from a low original yield level instead of from a high original yield level. How-

TABLE 3-4 Price Fluctuations from Various Interest Rate Levels (for a 6% coupon 20-year bond; in each case, a basis-point change equal to 10% of original yield occurs)

Falling securities prices					Rising securities prices				
Original yield, %	Price	New yield, %	Price	% Change	Original yield, %	Price	New yield, %	Price	% Change
4.0	127¼	4.4	121⅛	−4.9	4.0	127¼	3.6	134	C (+5.3)
5.0	112½	5.5	106	A (−5.8)	5.0	112½	4.5	119⅝	+6.3
6.0	100	6.6	93	−7.0	6.0	100	5.4	107¼	+7.3
7.0	89¼	7.7	82⅞	−7.3	7.0	89¼	6.3	96½	+8.1
8.0	80⅛	8.8	73⅞	B (−8.0)	8.0	80⅛	7.2	87⅜	D (+9.0)

ever, if interest rates *drop* by a certain percentage amount in basis-point terms from their original yield levels, the investor is better off (more of a price increase) if the drop starts from a high original yield level than if the decline starts from a low original yield level.

The investor should remember that when any two, or even all three, of the above factors—maturity, coupon rate, and absolute level of interest from which the interest rate change starts—operate in opposite directions, the impact of each factor on the total price change in principal amount of the security will be strengthened or weakened depending on what is happening to the other factors. Therefore, before making a particular fixed-income investment, the investor should try to assess which factor (or factors) will carry the most weight in influencing the relative instability or stability of the security's price. In general, everything else being equal, *a shorter-maturity higher-coupon security starting from low to moderate interest rate levels will swing less rapidly up or down in price than a longer-maturity lower-coupon security starting from high interest rate levels.* The final section at the end of the next chapter contains a worksheet to aid the investor in evaluating possible investments in specific fixed-income securities, and at the end of Chapter 5 a worksheet designed to help the investor evaluate the general interest rate environment has been included.

FOUR

Why Different Fixed-Income Securities Have Different Yields

Up to this point, whenever we have talked about interest rates, we have usually referred to "the general level of interest rates." It is very important to realize, however, that not all types of fixed-income securities will be yielding the same rate of interest at a particular moment in time. When we say, for example, that "interest rates are currently at the 7 percent level," exactly what do we mean? Are we referring to *long-term* interest rates (rates on securities maturing in at least 7 years, but generally much longer), *intermediate-term* interest rates (covering securities which have from 1 to 7 years to maturity), or *short-term* interest rates (yields on securities maturing in less than 1 year)?

The problem can become even more complicated. Did our statement about interest rates describe a 7 percent interest rate on *newly issued* securities or securities which have already been trading in the secondary market for a period of time (so-called *seasoned* issues)? Which securities were we referring to? Did we mean *U.S. government securities, Federal Agency obligations, tax-exempt issues,* or *corporate securities?* Even more subcategories exist. Corporate bonds, for instance, are further subdivided into utility, railroad, and industrial categories. Within each of these classifications, there are top-quality, intermediate-quality, and low-quality issues.

It should be apparent that we have to be more specific when we talk about interest rate levels, since each particular security has features which may cause the interest on that security to be different from the interest yield on another security. Just how specific one has to be will depend on the investor's purpose. The investor may merely want to know in general terms how all longer-term corporate bond prices have been trending recently, and so his question might be phrased, "What has been the recent pattern of long-term corporate rates?" On the other hand, if the investor is contemplating the purchase or sale of a specific security, he might ask, "What is the 3-month U.S. Treasury bill rate compared to the 6-month rate?" or, "How are 25-year seasoned high-quality utility bond rates relative to newly issued medium-quality industrial bond rates of the same maturity?" Take heart, it is not as complicated as it sounds!

The Meaning of Yield Differentials, or Yield Spreads

The yield differences between varying types of fixed-income securities are called *yield differentials,* or *yield spreads.* Yield spreads should be distinguished from the other types of spreads encountered in fixed-income securities parlance—for example, the *quotation spread* between the bid and offered prices of a market quotation given by a fixed-income securities dealer (more information on quotation spreads is contained in Chapters 6 to 11). Yield spreads come up whenever we compare the yields available on one type of fixed-income security with that of any other type. One might hear that "the yield spread between highest-quality industrial bonds and highest-quality tax-exempt bonds is currently 250 basis points (2.5 percent)," or "the yield spread between 1-year U.S. government issues and 1-year Federal Agency securities is 16 basis points (0.16 percent)." In fact, many professional fixed-income securities investors devote a great deal of time to watching for possible changes in the normal yield spreads between many types of issues. They are looking for what they consider *overpriced* situations, where they might *sell* securities they own, and *underpriced* securities, which could be *purchased* at what the investor feels are bargain prices. In Chapter 14 we will return to this type of portfolio improvement activity as it relates to the individual investor.

What, then, are some of the factors which determine the different rates of interest on a specific fixed-income security and which thus cause yield spreads to exist between various types of securities? While reviewing each of the factors listed in the following paragraphs, we briefly assume that all the other factors are kept the same while we focus on the feature being analyzed. In practice, however, each factor may influence, and be influenced by, other factors. For this reason, issuers and investors do not consider each factor separately; rather, they look at the security in its entirety and try to come up with the characteristics *differentiating* it from similar securities. This helps the prospective investor to decide whether the security should be higher, lower, or the same in price as its fixed-income security cousins. In reviewing all these factors on the following pages, the investor should primarily attempt to obtain a general feeling as to how each feature, by its presence or absence, contributes to or detracts from the total worth of a security.

The Manner and Frequency of Interest Payments

To start at the very beginning, we should list the manner and frequency with which interest is paid as a factor determining the interest rate on a fixed-income security. Some short-term securities calculate yield based on a 360-day year rather than a 365-day year. If we receive 8 percent on an investment every 360 days rather than every 365 days, the actual annualized interest is slightly higher than the stated interest; to be exact, it is $^{365}/_{360}$ equals $^{73}/_{72}$, or $^{1}/_{72}$ higher.

Also, as was mentioned in the previous chapter, many short-term securities are discounted from the principal value received at maturity, and their return comes from the gradual increase to par value during the life of the short-term issue. A stated 6 percent *discounted* interest rate actually earns higher than 6 percent, since the 6 percent is paid back not on an investment of par but on an outlay of par *less* 6 percent (the investment is thus $100 - 6 = 94$). In 1 year's time, $60 interest on a $940 investment works out to 6.38 percent yield, not 6 percent.

Similarly, since most bonds pay interest semiannually, bond yield calculations usually assume that the bondholder receives his interest payments on a timely basis every 6 months. However, a majority of Eurobonds pay interest once rather than twice a year, and so the prospective Eurobond buyer should be aware that the effective semiannual yield equivalent of an 8 percent coupon Eurobond is less than 8 percent—approximately 7.84 percent, in fact. On the other hand, GNMA pass-through certificates pay interest monthly rather than semiannually, and so an 8 percent stated yield on a GNMA certificate, assuming an average maturity of 12 years, actually works out to 8.13 percent.

Maturity

The second factor influencing the yield on a security is its maturity (the investor should recall that in the last chapter we discussed the influence of maturity on the degree of price fluctuation which a fixed-income security will undergo for a certain change in the over-all level of interest rates, whereas in this section we are looking at how the maturity influences the rate of interest paid on a security at a particular interest rate level). In all probability, one might charge a friend a higher rate of interest on a personal loan which extends for 2 years than on a loan which lasts for only 6 months. Similarly, on average during the past century, short-term interest rates for both corporate and governmental securities have been lower than the corresponding long-term rates. Even though both short-term rates and long-term rates generally move in the same direction over time, the yield differentials between short- and long-term rates can vary substantially. For example, in the 10-year period from 1964 to 1974, long-term high-quality utility bonds, on average, yielded 401 basis points (4.01 percent) more than 1-year Treasury bill rates; yet in January of 1966, these same bonds yielded only 24 basis points (0.24 percent) more than the 1-year Treasury bills.

In addition, during certain time periods, short-term rates have been *higher* than intermediate-term and long-term yields. In the past decade, this situation occurred during parts of 1966, 1968–1969, and in 1973–1974. It should be mentioned that short-term interest rates usually exhibit much wider swings than long-term rates, since the same dollar price change in the prices of short- and long-term issues produces a larger fluctuation in the *yields* of short-maturity obligations than in the yields of long-term debt. The relationship between short-term and long-term rates (called the *term structure of interest rates*) and the way in which the investor can study this relationship to his advantage *(yield curve analysis)* will be explored further in Chapter 13.

Generally, the investor should look for a higher interest return on long-term securities than on short-term securities. However, the difference between long-term and short-term securities' yields can vary substantially, particularly in a period of large interest rate movements, such as that experienced during the 1969–1974 period.

Quality

Quality considerations also have a significant impact on a security's yield. A lower-quality issue tends to sell at a lower price and thus offers a higher yield than a similar issue of higher quality. (A description of the various quality rating categories of the major rating services, including Moody's and Standard & Poor's, is contained in Chapters 8, 9, and 10.)

The following is an example of how quality affects yield. In December of 1974, the Carnation Co. 8.5 percent sinking fund debentures due in 1999, carrying the highest-quality rating from both Moody's (Aaa) and Standard & Poor's (AAA), were yielding 8.90 percent to maturity, while another similar bond, the Pfizer Inc. 8.5 percent sinking-fund debentures due in 1999, which were substantially similar to the Carnation Co. 8.5s in every respect except rating—they were rated AA by Moody's and Standard & Poor's—were selling at a lower price and a higher yield to maturity, 9.53 percent. This 63-basis-point difference in yield (10.63 percent) has at times been wider or narrower and can be almost entirely attributed to the difference between the quality rating on the two bonds.

Similar gradations of quality, and yield differentials owing to quality factors, exist in the short-term end of the fixed-income securities markets. In the second week of November 1973, a period of fairly high short-term interest rates, an investor intending to put his money to work for a 6-month period of time would have had the investment possibilities shown in Table 4-1, among others (if the investor is unsure as to the meaning of the securities listed below, they will be explained in Chapter 8):

TABLE 4-1 Short-Term Investment Possibilities as of November 1973

Security	Effective annualized bond equivalent yield, %
6-month U.S. Treasury bills	8.12
6-month FNMA discount notes	8.40
6-month bankers' acceptances	8.50
6-month certificates of deposit	8.75
6-month dealer-placed commercial paper	9.50

The securities in Table 4-1 are arranged according to *perceived* quality ranking, with U.S. Treasury bills, which are considered to be riskless from a credit standpoint, at the top of the list. FNMA discount notes, which fall into the Federal Agency category, are seen as being almost as safe as Treasury bills, and safer than a bankers' acceptance, which is backed by the credit of the bank accepting the instrument as well as the specific transaction which gave rise to the acceptance. Certificates of deposit, backed directly by the bank issuing the certificate, come next, and finally, commercial paper of corporations strong enough to borrow on their name alone. By referring to Table 4-1 it should be apparent that the highest-quality security (Treasury bills) gives the lowest yield and that the yields on each type of short-term security increase slightly for each slight step-down in perceived quality ranking from the previous category.

A security which is rated lower than another similar security is considered as having somewhat more risk, however small, of a default in the timely payment of interest or principal (or both). Quality ratings measure *credit risk* but do not judge interest rate risk, i.e., the risk that a security will decline in price because of a rise in interest rates. Roughly 25 percent of the *dollar value* of corporate bonds have the highest rating, triple-A. About 30 percent are rated double-A, 35 percent carry the A rating, and approximately 10 percent are judged to have ratings below the A level. In the tax-exempt area, excluding obligations of states, roughly 2 percent of the bonds carry the triple-A rating, 19 percent are classified double-A, 45 percent have an A ranking, and about 34 percent are lower than A quality or are not rated.

Many criteria go into the formulation of quality ratings, including (1) the amount and composition of any other existing debt of the issuer, (2) the stability of the issuer's cash flows, (3) the ability of the issuer to meet scheduled payments of interest and principal on its debt obligations, (4) asset protection, and (5) management ability. For noncorporate issuers, other criteria are also considered. A municipality would also be rated, among other things, according to (1) its local tax base, (2) the level of existing debt relative to this base, and (3) the variability of existing tax revenues.

We should mention a few points relating to the effect which quality ratings have on yield levels of a particular fixed-income security. Yield spreads between high-quality and low-quality issues can narrow or widen according to the degree of investors' choosiness about quality at a given moment in time. In periods of real or imagined economic difficulty, such as occurred in 1970 and 1974, investors tend to sell lower-rated bonds and buy high-quality issues, with the result that yields on low-quality securities rise relative to higher-quality issues. In prosperous times, investors may pay a bit less attention to quality differences and seek out the higher yields available on lesser-quality securities. This tends to narrow the yield spreads between issues of various quality ratings. For example, in 1970 when investors were concerned about possible corporate bankruptcies, Baa-rated newly issued industrial bonds yielded as much as 3.1 percent more than Aaa-rated newly issued industrial bonds. In 1972 and 1973, after fears of bankruptcies had subsided, Baa industrial bonds generally yielded only 0.75 percent more than Aaa industrial issues.

Since only nine rating classifications are used to judge a very large number of debt securities, it should be remembered that within each quality rating some issues will undoubtedly rank higher than others. Thus, a bond might be called "a strong double-A credit," or another issue might be referred to as "a weak A credit," to more finely differentiate the particular issue within its rating category. Some-times, the rating agencies will rate a bond issue differently, and a *split rating* will result. This also implies that security quality ratings can be changed over a period of time, as an issuer's financial strength improves or deteriorates. When a rating change occurs, the security may adjust in yield, by a small amount if investors anticipate the change or sometimes by a larger amount if the revised rating comes as a surprise to most investors.

For these reasons, the investor should be aware of possible ratings changes in the securities he holds or is thinking of buying. As a matter of portfolio policy, it is virtually always better to compromise one's maturity or liquidity criteria and *not* to be lax in one's credit criteria. It is preferable to forgo those extra few basis points in yield if any doubts *whatsoever* exist that the issuer will be able to pay back interest and principal when they become due. It is not worth it to risk one's entire investment in order to eke out a bit more income.

Liquidity

The liquidity, or marketability, of a fixed-income security influences the rate of interest it pays and the yield spreads between it and other securities. Marketability is made up of two elements—the *volume* of securities which can be bought or sold at one time without signifi-cantly affecting its price and the *amount of time* needed to complete a desired transaction. All factors being equal, the less marketable and easily tradable a security is, the higher yield (lower price) it carries relative to other more liquid securities. A highly liquid security can be purchased or sold in large amounts over a very short time period, while an illiquid issue is one which takes time or price concessions (or both) to effect a trade of even moderate size. "Price concessions" refer to having to accept a noticeably lower price than the current market quotations if you are a seller of securities or having to pay higher-than-normal prices over the current market quotations if the investor is a buyer.

U.S. government obligations, particularly Treasury bills, are issued and traded in hundred million and even billion dollar amounts and are generally accepted as being among the most liquid of fixed-income securities. Nevertheless, at times certain maturities of Treasury bills will exhibit temporary periods of illiquidity because of an imbalance of supply or demand. The investor should always find out how marketable a security is *before* it is purchased. If the funds to be invested in the security might be needed on short notice, the best policy is probably to give up a little bit of yield and invest in liquid, easily tradable issues.

Some evidence of the fact that investors tend to demand higher yield returns for less-marketable securities is provided by looking at the difference between interest rates on publicly offered and privately issued A-rated industrial bonds. *Private placements* are long-term issues sold directly to a small number of institutional investors. They are normally bought with an intention of holding the issue until maturity, and secondary market sales of private placements do not occur frequently because there is no established trading market for them. Except under very unusual circumstances, private placements carry higher yields than publicly traded securities of equal quality and maturity, primarily because of their lack of liquidity.

Returning to publicly traded securities, a key factor affecting the marketability of an issue is its absolute size. In general, the greater the dollar amount and number of securities outstanding, the greater the trading activity and liquidity of the issue. For example, corporate bond issues of less than $30 million in size are often difficult to trade into or out of easily and quickly, particularly as time passes from the original date of issuance and the bonds move into more permanent investors' portfolios to be held until maturity, thereby substantially reducing the floating supply which could be traded back and forth. When possible, if the liquidity of a particular issue is not known, it is helpful to inquire as to the number and type of likely long-term institutional holders and how active these and other holders are in trading the particular security. Sometimes, if the issue is listed on a major national securities exchange, it aids the marketability of small transactions.

Seasoned versus New Issues

Whether a security is a new issue or has been traded in the market for a period of time (i.e., become "seasoned") will affect the size of the yield spread between issues of otherwise similar characteristics.

The amount of the yield spread attributable to this factor can vary significantly, from no yield differential to a yield spread of 50 basis points or more in some instances, depending on the absolute level of interest rates. Generally speaking, the higher the overall rate of interest on fixed-income securities, the higher the yield spread that newly issued securities will have to pay over seasoned issues of the same type.

Especially when interest rates are relatively high (fixed-income securities prices low), securities underwriters, who purchase a new issue from the issuer for subsequent resale to the public, do not want to find themselves holding a large inventory of unsold bonds which might decline in price if interest rates moved higher. Thus, they tend to structure the price of the new offering to make the upcoming issue a bit more attractive than older issues from a yield standpoint, in order to attract buying interest and make for a successful underwriting.

Another related reason for new issues to yield more than seasoned securities during a high-interest-rate environment is that the cost of borrowing money to finance underwriting and trading inventories for the dealers is higher than usual, giving added impetus to the underwriters' desire not to have to hold the newly issued securities in their own inventories for too long a time period.

A final, more subtle reason for this type of spread situation to develop in periods of high interest rates relates to taxation. As was shown in the previous chapter, when the overall level of interest rates moves up, prices of already outstanding, seasoned bonds go to a discount from par value, and the lower the coupon, the deeper the discount. Since the difference between this discount (if the investor buys a seasoned issue after it has gone to a discount) and the par value which will be received at maturity is a capital gain rather than ordinary income, a portion of the actual yield to maturity received by the investor in a seasoned issue (which is trading at a discount) will be taxed at capital gains rates, which are lower than the rates on ordinary interest income. Because part of the total yield to maturity is thus subject to somewhat of a tax advantage (the greater the discount, the greater the tax advantage), investors tend to bid up the prices of discount seasoned issues somewhat in order to shelter part of the yield from the higher taxes. A lower pretax yield can be accepted (i.e., a higher price can be paid) on the seasoned bond to gain a return after taxes which is equivalent to the interest on the new bond issued at or close to par. All of the yield to maturity on the latter security is in the form of interest income and subject to possible call at some point in the future should interest rates decline. Lower-coupon bonds which are selling at a sizable discount from par in a period of high interest rates are not as likely to be called in for redemption if interest rates fall, since the issuer would achieve only a slight interest savings on the low-coupon securities. As a result, the yield to maturity on low-coupon discount bonds is considered less likely to be "called away" from the investor than a yield to maturity coming entirely or substantially from a high coupon. It should be mentioned that a large portion of corporate bonds are bought for pension funds and other nontaxable investors, and thus these tax advantages are not applicable to this investor group.

Call Protection Features

As mentioned in the preceding paragraph and in Chapter 3, certain long-term securities can be redeemed, or called, prior to their regularly scheduled maturity. While a great majority of all tax-exempt state and local government securities are noncallable, some U.S. government bonds, as well as many corporate bonds and preferred stocks, are callable at some point during the life of the security.

Investors normally do not like this callability feature, because bonds are most often called after interest rates have fallen in order that new bonds can be issued at the lower rates of interest. The specific term for this practice of calling an issue merely for the purpose of immediately reissuing new bonds at a lower rate of interest is *refunding*. Technically, a *redemption*, or *call*, might be for refunding purposes or for any other reason, such as the simple reduction of total debt. Some bond issues are redeemable, or callable, but *not* if the proceeds are used for refunding purposes. Since the term "call" is more all-inclusive, it is used in this book, but investors should be aware of the difference between a call and a refunding.

When a bond is called, rather than benefiting from the original high coupon, the investor has to reinvest the money he receives back from the issuer at a much lower rate of interest. For this reason, in periods of high interest rates, bonds which carry call protection (also known as a *deferred-call feature*) for a certain number of years are more attractive to investors than current-coupon (as distinguished from lower-coupon bonds issued earlier in a lower-interest-rate environment) securities which have no call protection.

In a high-interest-rate environment, if an investor wishes to lock up high yields on long-term securities and obtain call protection for a period of time longer than the standard 5 or 10 years, he might purchase low-coupon issues selling at a deep discount from par and hold them to maturity. Since a large part of a deep-discount security's total yield to maturity represents the gain from the low, discounted purchase price to par at maturity, and not from high-interest income, it is relatively insulated from the threat of redemption. However, the investor should remember that the combination of low-coupon long-maturity securities bought at a high absolute level of interest rates can cause wider price fluctuations (in an upward as well as in a downward direction) than practically any other fixed-income security configuration, and so caution must be exercised when buying low-coupon long-maturity deep discounts in a high-interest-rate environment.

Thus, a deferred-call feature on an issue can cause an interest rate spread, or differential, to develop vis-à-vis a similar issue with no deferred call or one which is currently callable. The size of the interest rate spread varies according to investors' expectations about the magnitude and timing of future interest-rate movements. Generally speaking, when interest rates are high and expected to fall, all other factors being equal, bonds with call protection will carry higher prices (and consequently will sell at lower yields) than bonds which have no call protection and which could be redeemed immediately. In high-interest-rate conditions, for example, utility bonds with 5-year call protection have yielded up to 50 basis points (0.50 percent) less than similar bonds which were currently callable.

Whether a bond is callable immediately after it is issued or after a deferred period, redemption of a bond usually involves the payment of a premium over par value (typically 1 year's interest payments) by the issuer, the size of the premium which must be paid if the bonds are called scaling down toward par as the issue gets closer to maturity. A 30-year 7 percent coupon bond issue, for example, might have a deferred-call period (in which it is noncallable) for the first 5 or 10 years of its life, becoming callable at 107 for the next 5 years, 106 for the 5 years after that, and so on until the last 5 years, when the issue might be callable at 101 or perhaps even at 100 (par). On issues with a deferred-call feature, some investors compute the *yield to first call,* which assumes the bondholder receives par plus the call premium in the first year the issue becomes callable.

If interest rates are low and expected to rise, the value of call protection decreases, since corporations and governmental issuers will not redeem their debt only to reissue bonds with higher coupons than before. When such conditions exist, the yield spread narrows between callable securities and substantially similar securities with call protection. Investors are not willing to pay higher prices (cause lower yields) on bonds for protection against call when they think there is little chance the securities will be called. An example of this is that in periods of low interest rates which were expected to rise, bonds with a deferred-call feature have often sold *at the same yields* as similar bonds which were currently callable.

Sinking-Fund Provisions

Another factor which affects fixed-income securities prices and causes yield differentials to develop between securities with this feature and those without it is whether the issue has a *sinking fund.* A sinking fund is generally used by corporations to retire all or part of a security issue prior to its maturity. The sinking fund is operated by the bond's *trustee,* who acts to protect the interests of the broad group of investors who hold the security. The corporation periodically pays cash to the trustee, who may either (1) call in a certain number of bonds by lot through a special sinking-fund call privilege or (2) buy the bonds in the open market (if their market price is below the sinking-fund call price).

Sinking funds can take several forms. Some issues permit the corporation to pay the trustee in the form of bonds (which might have been purchased by the issuer in the open market earlier in the year) rather than in cash. The amount of bonds required to be bought back or retired through operation of the sinking fund may be a fixed amount each year, or in some cases the bond may allow for variable annual sinking-fund payments. Because the operation of a sinking fund reduces the weighted average life of the bond issue outstanding, some investors may also compute a yield to weighted average life, which uses the average maturity of the bonds outstanding of an issue rather than the final maturity of the bonds which have not been purchased by the sinking fund.

Compared with similar issues which do not have a sinking fund, a bond with a sinking fund can be of value to the bondholder in two additional ways. First, the sinking fund reduces the investor's risk, to a degree, by reducing the total amount of debt outstanding of the company. Second, as long as the bonds are trading below their sinking-fund call price, the buying of bonds to satisfy sinking-fund requirements tends to support somewhat the market price of the bonds and also acts to decrease the supply available for trading each year. Balanced against these benefits, the investor should keep in mind the possibility that the bonds he is holding may be called by lot for the sinking fund if they are selling above the sinking-fund call price.

Convertibility

If a bond or preferred stock is convertible into a stated number of shares of common stock of the corporation issuing the security, this can cause substantial yield differentials between a convertible issue and a "straight," or nonconvertible, security of the same or similar companies. For example, in March 1971, the Pennzoil Company sold $75 million worth of straight (nonconvertible) debentures due in 1996 with an $8\frac{3}{8}$ percent coupon, while at the same time Pennzoil issued $50 million worth of convertible subordinated debentures due in 1996 with a $5\frac{1}{4}$ percent coupon.

Why does the convertible security of a company carry a much lower coupon (and thus exhibit such a wide yield spread) versus a similar straight bond of the same company? The reason stems from the fact that investors are willing to accept less interest from the company in order to be able to share in any substantial rise in the

price of the company's common stock. This ability to participate in a
meaningful price rise in the stock price derives from the privilege
the convertible-security holder has of converting the bonds (or
convertible preferred stock, as the case may be) into common stock.
The size of the yield spread between the straight and convertible
securities of the same company is subject to many influences, including the perceived "glamour" and growth prospects of the company's
industry and the issuer itself, as well as the overall level of straight
bond interest rates. The more attractive the common stock underlying the convertible is believed to be by investors, the more they will
think of the convertible security as common stock rather than debt,
and the lower the coupon rate will be relative to the coupon which
would be attached to a straight, nonconvertible issue of the company
at that same moment in time.

Virtually all convertible securities allow the issuer a call privilege,
which is generally utilized to force holders of the convertible to
convert into common stock, if the price of the common stock does in
fact go up. For example, if a $1,000 bond were initially offered to
investors when the price of the common stock was $10 per share,
each bond might be convertible into 100 shares of stock. After 1
year, if the common were to move up to $15 per share, the bond
would then be worth 100 × $15 = $1,500, or in bond language, 150.
The company may have a call feature on the bond allowing the issue
to be redeemed at a price of 107. By announcing that the bonds will
be called at 107, the company can force conversion. Conversion will
occur because holders will take action which produces 150 rather
than accepting 107 when the company announces the call. After the
bonds have been converted into common stock, the investor can
continue to hold the common stock or sell the stock and reinvest the
money elsewhere. If the price of the common stock drops in price,
however, the convertible securities will also fall in price, though their
fixed yield from the interest coupon provides some price support on
the downside (as they take on more *debt* characteristics than *equity*
characteristics). The amount of price support which develops
depends, among other factors, on the convertible security's coupon
relative to the overall level of interest rates. The lower the coupon on
the convertible, the more the bond might fall in price (in a period of

moderate-to-high interest rates) to reach its theoretical *bond invest-ment value,* which would happen if the common stock fell sharply in price.

It should be mentioned that because issuing corporations usually view convertible securities as future *common stock* rather than debt, convertibles are generally *subordinated* to other straight debt of the issuer. Thus, convertible securities normally carry a debt quality rating at least one notch lower than straight debt of the same company. Convertible securities will be discussed more in the chapter on corporate bonds, Chapter 10.

Income Taxation

The varying tax rates on income produced from different sources also cause yield differentials to occur between otherwise similar securities.

The securities of state, county, city, and local governments, and many of their special agencies (called *tax-exempt,* or *municipal,* securities, even though strictly speaking a "municipality" refers to a city or town and not a state government) are exempt from federal income taxes and often from any state or local income taxes (and sometimes even property taxes) of the locality which issues the securities. Because of this tax-exempt feature, municipal securities can pay a lower rate of interest and still be competitive, *on an aftertax basis,* with normally taxable fixed-income securities for taxable investors. A married couple earning income of $30,000 per year can buy a tax-exempt security yielding 4.0 percent, and the couple will receive the same *aftertax* income as if they had bought a fully taxable investment yielding 6.56 percent, or 256 basis points more than the tax-exempt security.

For corporations and taxpayers in higher tax brackets, the difference in yields on tax-exempt securities and fully taxable issues is even greater. Thus, for issues of substantially similar quality and maturity, the income tax exemption feature causes municipal securities to trade at yields anywhere from 50 to 350 basis points (or more) *less* than fully taxable issues, with the actual yield spread depending on the absolute level of interest rates (see the interest rate chart in Chapter 10) and other factors.

At high absolute levels of overall interest rates, the demand for short- and long-term credit is strong, and so commercial banks (which are large investors in municipals because of municipal issues' tax-exempt status) *sell* municipal securities out of their portfolios to raise additional funds to lend to their best borrowing clients. This is one reason why municipal interest rates may rise faster than fully taxable securities' yields, thus narrowing the spread between yields on tax-exempt and fully taxable securities. When credit demands subside and interest rates decline somewhat, commercial banks tend to buy tax-exempt securities again, causing their yields to drop and the yield spread between taxable and tax-exempt securities to widen.

Currency of Issue

If the investor is considering the purchase of a fixed-income security denominated in a currency other than dollars, the particular currency of the issue will affect the yield differential between that security and a security of similar maturity and quality denominated in dollars. Generally speaking, the yield to maturity on a foreign currency issue will reflect (1) the demand of investors buying the issue, (2) interest rate and money market conditions within the foreign country in whose currency the issue is denominated, and (3) whether the currency of the issue is expected by investors to be *revalued* or *devalued* relative to the investor's own currency.

If the currency is expected to be *devalued* compared to external currencies, foreign investors will demand *higher* yields on the issue, to compensate them for any loss expected to be incurred if the currency is in fact devalued relative to the investor's home currency. This situation prevailed in the United Kingdom during 1973 and 1974 when internal money market pressures within Britain, combined with investors' fears that the British pound would be devalued, caused U.K. Treasury bills to yield up to 12.85 percent and U.K. Treasury long-term bonds to yield 15.00 percent and more, substantially in excess of government securities' yields in other major countries with the same degree of credit tightness in their markets as the United Kingdom.

On the other hand, if the currency is expected to be *revalued* compared to external currencies, yields on fixed-income securities will be *lower* (and prices thus higher) than on similar securities denominated in another currency not expected to be revalued. This was demonstrated throughout 1973 and the first half of 1974 when United States corporations' long-term issues denominated in dollars yielded an average of 8.5 percent, while the long-term issues of United States corporations which were denominated in Swiss francs yielded an average of 6.0 percent, primarily because investors thought the Swiss franc would be revalued vis-à-vis the United States dollar.

Psychological and Fundamental Considerations

A final, but nevertheless very important determinant of interest rate differentials is investor psychology, which can often have a temporary (or even long-lasting) impact on the yields available on one type of fixed-income security relative to another. All other things being equal, an unfavorable fundamental or psychological development for a specific issue, or a specific sector of the fixed-income security markets, can cause prices to fall and yields to rise on this particular issue or sector relative to other issues or sectors of similar quality and maturity.

For example, after the oil embargo in October of 1973 caused widespread fears of gasoline shortages and forced many states to adopt various forms of gas allocation measures, the tax-exempt revenue bonds of toll road, bridge, and tunnel projects declined rapidly in price (yields rose rapidly), since investors felt that people would be driving less and thus paying fewer tolls, thereby impairing the ability of toll road, bridge, and tunnel authorities to generate sufficient revenues to meet interest and principal payments on their bond issues. As a result of this sell-off of these types of bonds, yield differentials between toll road, bridge, and tunnel project bonds and the other sectors of the tax-exempt market widened substantially from historical relationships. Similarly, the energy crisis psychology of late 1973 and early 1974 helped higher-grade railroad bonds to improve in price and narrow the wide yield spreads between rail issues and other corporate bonds, which had existed since 1970 when some railroads' financial difficulties caused investors to sell all railroad bond issues, raising yields on railroad securities compared with utilities, industrials, and finance company issues.

Often, psychological reactions are overdone and eventually self-correcting. The task of the investor should be to gauge not only the truth and extent of unfavorable news about an issue or sector of the fixed-income securities market but also *the reactions of other investors* to the unfavorable developments. Even though the actual impact of certain news may be only slight on a company or industry's earning power and ability to repay interest and principal, *if other investors believe* the development will have adverse consequences, they will sell the securities anyway and cause interest yields to rise. The investor should try to separate short-term psychological reactions from longer-term, truly fundamental changes affecting a company or sector of the fixed-income securities market. If the investor is unsure as to whether certain news will positively or negatively impact certain securities he holds or is interested in, it might be wise to look at another area of the market for making an investment.

By way of reviewing some of the points made in this chapter and the preceding chapter, and in order to help the investor evaluate prospective fixed-income securities investments, an Evaluation Worksheet of Points to Consider in Investing in Specific Fixed-Income Securities has been included on the following pages. It is hoped that the investor will not only review it briefly when first reading this book but also refer to this worksheet frequently when buying or selling any type of fixed-income investments.

WORKSHEET: POINTS TO CONSIDER IN INVESTING IN SPECIFIC SECURITIES

Note: In many of the questions which follow, the investor will be able to find out the information he needs on his own; but for several of the questions, to obtain the answer it will be necessary to ask for professional advice from a securities broker, banker, or any other individual who is familiar with fixed-income securities.

POINT 1: *How does the security pay interest?* _____

COMMENT: If the security being evaluated is a non-interest-bearing discounted security based on a 360-day year, its yield may have to be adjusted upward (Chapters 6 and 8 show how to do this) to make it comparable with interest-bearing securities based on a 365-day year.

POINT 2: *How often does the security pay interest?* _____

COMMENT: If the security does not pay interest semiannually, the investor should find out what the semiannual yield equivalent of the security is in order to better compare it with yields as they are commonly quoted on a semiannual basis. Yields on securities which pay interest more frequently than semiannually (such as monthly) will have to be adjusted upward to put them on an equivalent basis as semiannual yields, while yields on securities which pay interest less frequently than semiannually (such as annually) will have to be adjusted downward to put them on an equivalent basis with semiannually paying securities.

POINT 3: *Is the security available in registered or bearer form?* _____

COMMENT: If the security is registered, interest and principal payments will be sent automatically to the investor, at whatever address he specifies to the issuer's paying agent. If the security is in bearer form, the security should be safeguarded as carefully as cash; it is the responsibility of the investor to collect his interest and principal when they become due.

POINT 4: *In what minimum denominations does the security come?* _____

Are smaller denominations of this security easily tradable, and can small pieces be combined with other small pieces to obtain larger-denomination securities? _____

COMMENT: If the security's smaller denominations are not combinable with other small denominations to obtain larger-denomination securities, and if the small denominations are not easily marketable, the investor should think very carefully about his possible cash needs before buying the security, and he should possibly be prepared to hold on to the security until its final maturity to avoid reducing his effective yield through the acceptance of price concessions if the security were sold before maturity.

POINT 5: *What are normal commissions on the security?* _____
What odd-lot charges and extra fees, if any, are charged for dealing in less than the standard unit of trading for the security? _____

COMMENT: Particularly when smaller amounts of money are involved, the commissions, odd-lot charges, and other fees (such as custodial fees) can reduce the effective yield earned by the security, often by a substantial amount.

POINT 6: *What is normal (and odd-lot) settlement on the security?*
_____

COMMENT: Before buying or selling a security, the investor should find out how much time there is after the purchase or sale for the securities to be paid for or delivered. This can be of importance when buying one type of security and selling another, because if each has different settlement periods, the investor may be short of money (or else his money may be left idle, earning no interest). Also, odd-lot transactions sometimes have different settlement periods than round-lot transactions.

POINT 7: *Does payment for the security have to be made in Federal funds or in clearinghouse funds?* _____

COMMENT: The investor should be aware of the difference between Federal funds and clearinghouse funds. *Federal funds* are deposits in, or checks drawn on, Federal Reserve Banks. These funds are immediately available to the recipient of the funds or the check, and they have come into more frequent use in recent years for settlement involving short-term fixed-income securities. Federal funds are also actively traded among commercial bank members of the Federal Reserve System, in order to satisfy weekly reserve requirements (more on this in Chapter 5). *Clearinghouse funds* represent ordinary checking deposits (also called demand deposits) at commercial banks, and money presented in this form may take one or more business days to be credited to the recipient of the check. If payment for a particular fixed-income security is required in Federal funds, the investor may have to obtain a special check for this purpose from his commercial bank or else submit his clearinghouse funds check a few days in advance of the due date for payment, in order that the check can clear and Federal funds can be released for payment to whoever sold the security to the investor.

POINT 8: *How will the principal on the security be paid back?*

_____

Does the security have a sinking fund, and if so, how does it operate?

_____

COMMENT: On long-term securities especially, there is some merit to, and prudence in, having a sinking fund to retire part or all of an issue before its final maturity, but the investor should be aware that, particularly if the market price of the security is above par, some or all of his securities could be called in by lot for sinking-fund purposes.

POINT 9: *Are the securities callable, and if so, when and at what price?*

_____

COMMENT: If the fixed-income securities are callable, the investor should realize that his investment might be redeemed (now, if they are currently callable; in the future, if there is a deferred-call feature on the securities) by the issuer. This should be taken into account at all times, especially when buying securities at a price above the call price, since the investor may lose out if interest rates fall and the issuer decides to call the securities at the call price. Fixed-income securities with call protection may sell at a higher price and lower yield than securities without call protection.

POINT 10: *What is the current yield, and the yield to maturity of the security, compared with the security's coupon rate?* _____

COMMENT: When a fixed-income security is purchased at a premium over par value, current yield is less than the coupon rate and greater than the yield to maturity. When a fixed-income security is purchased at a discount from par value, current yield is greater than the coupon rate and less than yield to maturity. If the security is purchased exactly at par value, current yield is equal to both the coupon rate and the yield to maturity.

POINT 11: *What is the maturity of the security?* _____

COMMENT: As was seen in Chapter 3, a fixed-income security's maturity can vastly influence its tendency to fluctuate widely in price, with longer-maturity securities tending to fluctuate more widely in price than short-maturity securities. If interest rates are expected to rise, the investor should own short-maturity securities, and if interest rates are expected to fall, the investor should own longer-maturity securities.

POINT 12: *What is the actual coupon rate of the security?* _____

COMMENT: The coupon rate on a fixed-income security also influences how widely the security will fluctuate in price for a given change upward or downward in interest rates, with lower-coupon issues fluctuating more widely in price than higher-coupon issues. If interest rates are expected to rise, the investor should own securities with a high coupon, and if interest rates are expected to fall, it is better to own securities with a low coupon.

POINT 13: *What is the current level of interest rates?* _____

COMMENT: Chapter 3 also showed that the higher the absolute interest rate level from which a certain percentage change in interest rates takes place, the more widely a security's price will fluctuate. This implies that the investor may want to exercise a bit more cautious approach when investing in a high-interest-rate environment as compared with a low-interest-rate environment.

POINT 14: *What is the quality rating of the security?* _____
How does the security compare in quality with other securities of the same quality rating? _____
Is there any possibility that the quality rating will be changed in the foreseeable future? _____

COMMENT: The investor should always check out the quality of whatever fixed-income security he is buying *before* the purchase is made. At the same time, he should try to ascertain how it compares with other securities of the same quality classification and determine whether this security might be upgraded or downgraded in quality at some point during the life of the security. Unless the investor can afford to sustain the loss of all or a sizable portion of his funds, or if there is any doubt about the creditworthiness of a particular investment, low-quality issues should be avoided.

POINT 15: *How does the yield on the security under evaluation compare with yields of other securities (1) of similar quality but different maturities and (2) of similar maturity but different quality ratings, now, versus the average of the past 5 years?* (1) _____ (2) _____

COMMENT: Although we will treat the subject of taking advantage of changing yield spreads due to quality or maturity differences (or both) at greater length in Chapter 14, the investor should be aware of the fact that the highest-quality securities will sell at higher prices (lower yields) than lower-quality issues in one type of market environment rather than in another type of market environment. The relative attractiveness of higher-quality shorter-maturity securities vis-à-vis lower-quality longer-maturity issues will vary, and the more active investor must examine this changing relationship to find opportunities for buying and selling securities at the most attractive prices.

POINT 16: *How liquid and easily tradable is the security?* _____

COMMENT: If a fixed-income security is not very liquid and trades inactively, the investor must be prepared to pay higher prices when buying the security (except if bought on the initial offering of the issue), and to receive lower prices when selling the security, both of which conditions adversely affect its yield. Less actively traded securities should therefore offer higher yields to the investor to compare with securities which trade freely, with a minimum of price concession and time delay involved in executing a transaction.

POINT 17: *If the issue is a seasoned security, is there an equivalent security being initially offered which carries a somewhat higher yield?*

_____

COMMENT: The higher yield offered by newly issued securities compared with seasoned securities generally apply to a greater extent in periods of high interest rates.

POINT 18: *If the security is a convertible security, how does the conversion price of the shares into which the security is convertible compare with the market price of the stock?* _____

COMMENT: When the common stock price is trading near or above the conversion price of the shares, the convertible fixed-income security will act like common stock, moving upward as the stock price moves upward. If the common stock price is trading below the conversion price of the shares, the convertible may act like a bond, and as the stock price moves further downward, the convertible will tend to sell on its bond features, with its coupon causing it to trade like other fixed-income (nonconvertible) securities with the same coupon rate. Convertible securities usually are lower-rated than straight-debt securities of the same issuer.

POINT 19: *What is the taxability of interest income from the security at the federal, state, and local levels?* _____

COMMENT: Tax-exempt securities should be compared with taxable securities yields on an aftertax equivalent basis. Often the investor will find that, after the payment of income taxes, he is better off owning a tax-exempt security, though in periods of very tight money tax-exempt securities' yields may rise relative to taxable issues. As shown in Chapter 6, the fact that U.S. government securities' interest income is not taxable at the state and local levels can enhance their attractiveness to investors in a locality of high state and local taxes.

POINT 20: *If the issue is denominated in a currency other than dollars, what is the outlook for the currency?* _____

COMMENT: As the large foreign exchange trading losses of several major banks during 1974 have shown, it is dangerous and difficult to attempt to forecast with accuracy what a foreign country's currency will be worth at some future point. If a currency is expected to be devalued, fixed-income securities denominated in that currency will tend to sell at higher yields than other securities of similar features but not denominated in that currency. On the other hand, if a currency is expected to be revalued, fixed-income securities denominated in that currency will tend to sell at lower yields than similar securities not denominated in that currency.

POINT 21: *Are any major psychological or fundamental changes likely to affect yields on the security?* _____

COMMENT: The investor should be aware of how fundamental changes or perceived changes in the attractiveness of particular securities or sectors of the fixed-income securities markets can affect yields and prices, positively and negatively.

FIVE

Major Influences on the Level and Direction of Interest Rates

To achieve success in investing in fixed-income securities, it is help-ful to have a basic understanding of the major influences on the level and direction of interest rates. Since 1900, interest rates have ranged from a low of between 0.5 to 2.5 percent up to 9 to 13 percent in recent times, with many fluctuations in between. Figure 5-1 shows the fluctuations in several long- and short-term interest rates since 1900.

As mentioned in Chapter 3, interest rate changes are highly important to investors because (1) they can directly cause fixed-income securities' prices to change; (2) they have an impact on the total yield returns available to investors putting new funds into fixed-income securities; and (3) they can thus cause fixed-income securities to appear relatively more or less attractive than alternative types of investments, such as the stock market, savings accounts, or real estate holdings.

Yet accurately forecasting the level and direction of interest rates is extremely difficult. Even full-time professional economists and fixed-income security portfolio managers, armed with computers and other sophisticated analytical techniques, do not have anything even approaching a perfect record in predicting interest rates, and there are often substantial differences of opinion among them as to which way interest rates will go and how far. All too frequently the professionals' prognostications are proven incorrect, either because a seemingly minor point which later turned out to be significant was neglected, or because certain past trends were projected forward and were expected to continue in the future, whereas in fact the trends changed.

Another reason it is so hard to anticipate changes of interest rates is that it is necessary for one not only to forecast data and events correctly, but also to have the *intuition* which is essential in weighting numerous considerations differently at different points in time. The *interrelatedness* of the many influences on the level and direction of interest rates complicates the forecasting task even further. A final perplexing and exasperating twist is caused by a continuing debate over whether changes in interest rates are a *cause or effect* of certain monetary policy actions.

In our analysis, we will aim at a logical, common sense approach to

FIGURE 5-1. *Long- and short-term interest rates. (By permission of the Board of Governors of the Federal Reserve System.)*

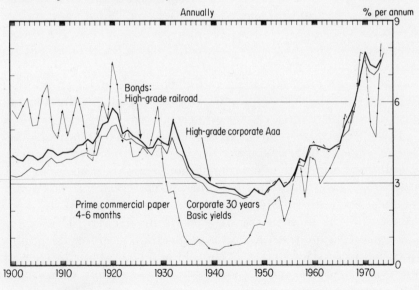

understanding what causes interest rates to move. Our practical rather than academic approach will concentrate on seeing the big picture. Instead of trying to guess every small fluctuation in interest rates, we will endeavor to acquire a feeling of how interest rates may trend in a broad sense. In reading this chapter, the investor should try to develop a wide perspective of how things fit together in the interaction of supply and demand forces to arrive at a particular level of interest rates. As a generalist, it is impossible to become and remain completely knowledgeable about the intricacies of each topic under discussion. Our overview of the fundamental reasons behind interest rate changes will focus in large part on information which is readily available to the individual investor, such as figures published in the newspaper each week on the reserve condition of commercial banks.

Since interest rates are really the price of money, or stated another way, the cost of obtaining credit, we will tackle the problem of finding out what causes interest rates to change and to what degree by examining those factors which influence the supply of and demand for money and credit. As we do this, we should keep in mind that *supply* and *demand* forces for money and credit often interact and overlap with one another. For example, individuals would be considered to *supply* credit whenever they deposit money in a savings account or buy fixed-income securities, but they would also be considered to use, or *demand,* credit when they borrow to purchase a home or a new car. In fact, many consumers do both at once, supply credit and demand credit. Throughout our economy, it is not easy to tell which comes first, the supply side or the demand side of the equation for money and credit.

As we proceed with our analysis, we should keep in mind the fact that psychological factors in the marketplace for money and credit will often determine the direction of interest rates for a specific type of security, even though such movements may apparently contradict the facts currently at hand. All markets tend to anticipate future events, and the investor has to learn to do likewise. The factors causing today's interest rates to be at a certain level may be important, but just as important is consideration of what the level of interest rates will be after 6 months, 1 year, 5 years, or even longer periods of time. It is the job of the investor to try to discern which forces will cause interest rates to move, and to what levels. Through all this, it is important to separate broad, long-lasting trends from short-term or even seasonal fluctuations.

It should be remembered that interest rates do not necessarily follow a uniform pattern in each of the many sectors of the fixed-income markets—long-term, short-term, domestic, international, governmental, corporate, taxable, tax-exempt—the sectors and subdivisions are numerous. For example, the market for long-term money (usually referred to as the *capital* market) is different from the market for short-term funds (also called the *money* market). The money market is the focal point for Federal Reserve Board monetary policy execution. It thus becomes important to monitor money market developments, since they are often a reliable barometer of Federal Reserve intentions and an indicator of developing pressures in short-term securities prices. In addition, the yields on short-term money market securities frequently have an impact on the yields of intermediate- and longer-term issues, and through them, on capital market interest rates.

Short-term and long-term interest rates can move up and down together, but they can also diverge, as was the case in the early 1960s when the Federal Reserve Board, through "Operation Twist," carried out actions to *lower* long-term interest rates in order to stimulate business borrowing and promote economic growth, while at the same time it was taking measures to *raise* short-term interest rates to prevent funds from flowing outside the United States and thus hurting our balance-of-payments situation.

We will now examine factors influencing the *supply* of credit, after which we will look at the equation from the *demand* point of view.

The Supply of Money and Credit

Banks and the Federal Reserve System   The Federal Reserve System is perhaps the single most powerful and direct influence on the level and direction of interest rates. In its key role as the nation's central bank, the Federal Reserve regulates the growth of money and credit by influencing their availability and cost. Approximately 5,800 national and some state member banks, in 12 Federal

Reserve districts around the country, account for close to 80 percent of all commercial bank deposits and assets. The Federal Reserve Board of Governors, in Washington, D.C., coordinates and supervises the activities of the District Federal Reserve Banks and performs many services for its member banks, including check collection, the maintenance of a teletype network for transferring funds, and the issuance and handling of paper money. The Federal Reserve System also assists the U.S. Treasury and governmental agencies by acting as depository for their money, by receiving and delivering government securities sold to the public, and by paying interest coupons on government issues. The principal policy-making group of the Federal Reserve System is the Federal Open Market Committee (FOMC), which is made up of the seven governors of the System, the president of the New York Federal Reserve, and four other Federal Reserve district presidents.

The primary function of the Federal Reserve is to adjust the money supply and to influence the cost of money in order to provide monetary conditions favorable to the attainment of the following four objectives: (1) to promote full employment, (2) to maintain stability in the general price level, (3) to foster sustainable growth rates in economic activity, and (4) to promote equilibrium in the country's balance of payments. The Federal Reserve Board has numerous tools at its disposal to achieve these sometimes elusive objectives, many of which directly or indirectly influence interest rates through their effect on member banks' reserves.

Member bank reserves and the Federal funds rate   How and why does a change in a member bank's reserve position have an impact on the money supply and interest rates? We will digress for a moment to review, through a very simplified example, how banks can expand the money supply.

Banks can expand the money supply by making loans to corporations and individuals. These loans usually show up as credits in the borrower's checking account at the bank which extended the loan. In order to meet possible demands for withdrawals by depositors, Federal Reserve member banks are required by law to keep a minimum reserve, either as cash in the bank's own vaults or in the form of a deposit at the District Federal Reserve Bank, equal to a specified percentage of total deposits.

For example, if the reserve requirement were 10 percent, $100 must be set aside as reserves for every $1,000 in deposits. The bank's ability to expand deposits (by making new loans to borrowers) is limited by its total level of reserves. With a 10 percent reserve requirement, if the bank had $120 in reserves and $1,000 in deposits, it could expand deposits in the amount of $200 ($120 *divided* by 10 percent equals $1,200, minus $1,000, gives $200 as the amount of new deposits which can be created by loaning money to borrowers), thus adding an additional $200 to the money supply. Through several different types of maneuvers which can affect member banks' ability to expand the money supply, the Federal Reserve can control overall monetary growth and thus influence the cost of obtaining credit (the level of interest rates).

Every Wednesday, member banks are required to bring their reserve accounts at the Federal Reserve up to prescribed levels. Some banks may have deficiencies in their reserve accounts, while other banks may have surplus reserves. A bank with a shortfall in required reserves can fill the gap by (1) borrowing money directly from the Federal Reserve, at the so-called *discount rate,* or (2) borrowing reserves from other member banks which have surplus reserves that week in the *Federal funds* market. Because banks do not like to be continually borrowing from the Federal Reserve to meet their reserve requirements when they have a deficiency, the Federal funds market is the more commonly used alternative for meeting a gap in the required reserve position.

The rate of interest on these interbank loans of excess reserve money is called the *Federal funds rate,* and because it reflects instantaneous pressures in the supply of and demand for bank reserves, it is a sensitive indicator of the level and direction of interest rates over the near term. The Federal funds rate is published daily in the newspaper, and it is worth direct and continuous observation by the investor in fixed-income securities. A high or rising Federal funds rate for a period of time usually indicates a strong degree of tightness in excess reserves and, consequently, a *firmer tone* to interest rates (higher interest rates), whereas a low or falling Federal funds rate over a period of time indicates that banks are not in as great a need for reserves, with *easier* (lower) interest rates in the offing.

In watching the Federal funds rate, several points should be kept in mind. The first is that the Federal funds rate is very volatile and can fluctuate widely from hour to hour and from day to day, particularly on Wednesdays, when banks are quickly moving around in the money market and adjusting their reserve positions to meet required levels. Because vault cash and reserves held at the Federal Reserve Banks do not earn interest for banks, the surplus banks (banks having a surplus over reserve requirements) often want to lend these reserves to another bank for 1 to 2 days, or even longer. Also, seasonal and weekly patterns (the Federal funds rate tends to be higher on Thursdays and Fridays, but lower on Wednesdays, with wide savings) should be taken into account when looking at the Federal funds rate level on any given day. This underscores the need to watch the Federal funds rate for a period of time to get a sense of the *underlying trend* of the rate—upward, downward, or sideways (no change from previous levels)—and only in this way will the investor develop better insight into what the Federal funds rate foretells for other short-term interest rates and for long-term rates.

Many investors watch the Federal funds rate in conjunction with other short-term money market rates, such as the 90-day Treasury bill yield rate and the commercial banks' prime lending rate to corporate borrowers, to determine whether all these rates are reflecting a trend toward tightness or ease over the near- to intermediate-term. If the other short-term money market rates are acting similarly with the Federal funds rate, there is a better chance that interest rates will move in the direction suggested by the movements of these "early warning indicators." If, however, other short-term money market rates are moving in divergent directions from movements of the Federal funds rate, the investor should probe further to try to find out whether the divergence stems from *fundamental* reasons (meaning that the other short-term interest rates will begin to move in the same direction as the Federal funds rate movement) or from *technical* reasons (meaning that seasonal, weekly, or other recurring influences have caused the Federal funds rate to move in a different direction than the true underlying trend of short-term interest rates).

Other indicators to watch The weekly reserve settlement process gives us several additional sensitive indicators of the relative tightness or ease of the money market. If total borrowings of some member banks from the Federal Reserve exceed total surplus reserves of other member banks, the difference is termed *net borrowed reserves*. If, on the other hand, a net surplus occurs, it is called *net free reserves*. Also, it is useful to monitor the *absolute amount of member bank borrowings from the Federal Reserve* as a gauge of interest rate and money market pressures and as a signal of which way interest rates might be headed. Figure 5-2 shows that, in general, when net borrowed reserves are at a high level, short-term interest rates (as evidenced by the 90-day Treasury bill rate) also tend to be high.

Each Friday, the newspapers carry a listing of the changes in weekly averages of member bank reserves for the week ended that previous Wednesday. In order to compare the positions of the

FIGURE 5-2. *Federal Reserve policy—net borrowed reserves.* *(By permission of the Goldman Sachs Economics Group.)*

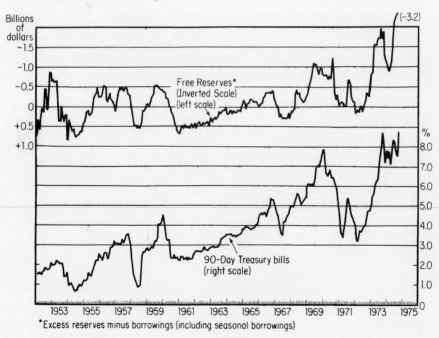

*Excess reserves minus borrowings (including seasonal borrowings)

TABLE 5-1   Sample Weekly Statement of Member Bank Reserve Changes
(in millions of dollars)

	May 8, 1974	Chg fm wk end May 1, 1974	May 9, 1973
Reserve bank credit:			
U.S. Gov't securities:			
Bought outright	79,432	+231	+4,661
Held under repurch agreemt	904	+ 37	+ 484
Federal agency issues:			
Bought outright	2,436		+1,180
Held under repurch agreemt	418	+191	+ 364
Acceptances—bought outright	88	+ 6	− 1
Held under repurch agreemt	200	+ 17	+ 132
① ► Member bank borrowings	1,535	−548	+ 69
Seasonal bank borrowings	82	+ 8	+ 64
Float	1,871	− 41	− 490
Other Federal Reserve Assets	1,342	+ 50	+ 147
Total Reserve Bank credit	88,309	− 49	+6,611
Gold stock	11,567		+1,157
SDR certificates	400		
Treasury currency outstanding	8,827	+ 5	+ 363
Total	109,103	− 44	+8,130
② ► Money in circulation	72,457	+409	+6,007
Treasury cash holdings	299	− 2	− 122
Treasury dpts with F.R. Bnks	2,959	+499	−1,538
Foreign deposits with F.R. Bnks	294	− 49	− 38
Other deposits with F.R. Banks	660	− 12	+ 12
Other F.R. liabilities & capital	2,960	−172	+ 226
Total	79,631	+676	+4,550
Member bank reserves			
③ ► With F.R. Banks	29,472	−719	+3,578
Cash allowed as res.	6,894	+303	+ 714
Total reserves held	36,424	−416	+4,178
Required reserves	36,211	−471	+3,884
Excess reserves	213	+ 55	+ 294
④ ► Free reserves	−1,322	+603	

member banks with earlier totals, changes from the previous week and from the week which ended 1 year earlier are also included. Similar to Federal funds rate levels, net reserve statistics and figures on the absolute amount of member bank borrowings from the Federal Reserve can fluctuate a good deal from one week to another. Accordingly, they should be watched regularly, particularly in comparison with the week-earlier and the year-earlier figures, to discover the underlying trend toward higher or lower interest rates. A sample version of these figures as they appeared in the newspaper on Friday, May 10, 1974, for the week ending Wednesday, May 8, 1974, has been included in Table 5-1.

Arrow 1 points to the *total* member bank borrowings figure, and arrow 4 shows the *net* reserves figure, in the example above a net borrowed reserve figure of −$1.322 billion. The week's statement shows a strong degree of restraint imposed by the Federal Reserve in its efforts to curb inflation during the first half of 1974. Whenever member bank borrowings are at a high absolute level and if they continue to show gains on a recurrent basis from week-earlier and year-earlier totals, the system is deemed to be in a tight, high-interest condition. Similarly, if reserves are in a net borrowed position (as they are here), it indicates that the Federal Reserve is not permitting member reserves to expand at a rate which meets the demands for funds, with a continued high- or perhaps even higher-interest-rate environment to come. The Federal Reserve regularly watches and actively influences on a week to week basis both the net reserve position (free reserves or borrowed reserves) and the monetary base figure (composed of total money in circulation—arrow 2 on Table 5-1—plus member bank reserves with Federal Reserve banks—arrow 3 on Table 5-1), which amounted to $72.457 billion + $29,472 billion = $101.929 billion on May 8, 1974. These statistics are thus carefully monitored by bankers, investors, and others throughout the economy to assess the Federal Reserve Board's current thinking over the appropriate availability and cost of short-term funds, which in turn influences the cost of long-term money.

To give further background to the investor in determining whether a level of member bank reserves, as well as total bank borrowings from the Federal Reserve, is one of tightness or ease,

TABLE 5-2 Money Market Indicators, 1950–1974

Year	90-day bill rates % (discount basis)	Free bank reserves (mil. of dols.)	Bank borrowings from Fed. Reserve (mil. of dols.)	Fed. Reserve dis. rates %	Prime comm. lend. rate %	Federal Reserve credit policy
1950	1⅛ to 1½	+500 to +900	50 to 200	1½ to 1¾	2¼ to 3	Active ease
1951	1½ to 1¾	+170 to +600	200 to 800	1¾	3	Ease
1952	1¾ to 2⅛	+723 to −870	300 to 1,600	1¾	2 to 2¼	Ease to restraint
1953	1⅜ to 2⅜	+360 to −650	200 to 1,200	2	3 to 3¼	Restraint to ease
1954	⅝ to 1¼	+340 to +830	200 to 400	1½ to 2	3 to 3¼	Ease
1955	1⅜ to 2⅝	+370 to −490	400 to 1,000	1½ to 2½	3 to 3½	Mild restraint
1956	2¼ to 3¼	−35 to −255	800 to 1,300	2½ to 3	3½ to 4	Mild restraint to active restraint
1957	3 to 3⅝	+120 to −510	350 to 1,250	3 to 3½	4 to 4½	Active restraint ended in November
1958	⅝ to 2¾	+570 to −35	200 to 600	1¾ to 2¾	3½ to 4	Ease to neutrality to mild restraint
1959	3 to 4½	−95 to −540	400 to 1,100	3 to 4	4 to 5	Active to severe restraint
1960	2⅛ to 4⅛	+645 to −371	100 to 1,000	3 to 4	4½ to 5	Severe restraint to ease
1961	2⅝ to 3	+340 to +960	100 to 500	3	4½	Ease
1962	2⅝ to 2⅞	+270 to +470	100 to 700	3	4½	Ease
1963	2⅞ to 3	+100 to +400	100 to 700	3 to 3½	4½	Moderate ease to neutrality
1964	3½ to 3⅞	−50 to +250	200 to 600	3½ to 4	4½	Neutrality to mild restraint
1965	3¾ to 4⅜	−2 to −200	250 to 700	4 to 4½	4½ to 5	Mild restraint to active restraint
1966	4½ to 5⅜	−44 to −583	402 to 880	4½	5 to 6	Active restraint to restraint
1967	3½ to 5	−170 to +574	46 to 585	4 to 4½	5½ to 6	Aggressive ease to mild restraint
1968	5 to 5⅝	+405 to −542	180 to 807	4½ to 5½	6 to 6½	Restraint to ease to firm restraint
1969	5.88 to 8.10	−480 to −1,269	499 to 1,634	5½ to 6	6¾ to 8½	Active restraint
1970	4.75 to 7.96	−1,485 to +68	270 to 1,680	5½ to 6	6¾ to 8½	Less restraint to moderate ease
1971	3.24 to 5.52	−986 to +191	25 to 1,179	4½ to 5½	5¼ to 6¾	Moderate to aggressive ease
1972	2.98 to 5.18	−1,015 to +292	12 to 1,221	4½	4¾ to 6	Moderately stimulative
1973	5.16 to 9.02	−2,253 to −527	600 to 2,376	4½ to 7½	6 to 10	Active to moderate restraint
1974	6.10 to 9.14	−3,418 to −240	613 to 3,754	7½ to 8	8¾ to 12	Active restraint to moderate ease

SOURCE: *The Bond Buyer.*

Table 5-2 lists the condition of several money market indicators from 1950 through 1973, together with a short summary comment on the direction of Federal Reserve credit policy during each year.

Comparing the net borrowed reserve figure of $1.322 billion for May 8, 1974, to Table 5-2, we can see just how tight a week May 8th's was—in only 2 out of the last 23 years had net borrowed reserves exceeded that total, yet Figure 5-2 shows that conditions became even more stringent as 1974 progressed.

Another barometer of recent Federal Reserve policy, and thus somewhat of a guide to its current thinking, is the *change in the level of the money supply*. It is derived from the statement of member bank reserve changes and is usually set apart from the review of member bank reserve changes in the newspaper. The money supply figure as posted in the newspaper is a 4-week daily average of the money supply in the United States, adjusted for seasonal influences. By calculating the growth rate in the money supply over a period of time, usually 6 months to a year or more, we can arrive at another glimpse of Federal Reserve policy. The money supply is customarily defined in one of two ways, and economists debate over which is the appropriate policy indicator. The "narrow definition" of the money supply, or M_1, consists of total private checking deposits plus currency in the hands of the public, exclusive of banks and the government. The "broad definition" of the money supply, or M_2, consists of everything in M_1 plus the public's time deposits (savings deposits).

When computing the growth rate in the money supply, the investor should make sure he is comparing either a current M_1 with an earlier-period M_1, or a current M_2 figure with an earlier-period M_2 figure, but he should not mix the two definitions.

The money supply growth rate is difficult to interpret correctly, because it is necessary to gauge its *actual* growth relative to the Federal Reserve's money supply growth *targets*. If the money supply has been showing rapid growth but is still below the Federal Reserve's target growth rate, it may mean that the Federal Reserve will continue to pursue a policy of monetary ease, leading to lower interest rates. On the other hand, if the Federal Reserve Board has set a certain growth rate in the money supply as a target, a more rapid growth rate in the money supply might mean that the Federal Reserve will tighten the monetary reins in the future in order to slow down the growth rate, causing interest rates to rise. Also, the investor must be careful not to take too short a time period to measure the growth rate in the money supply, or he will lose sight of the underlying trend. For instance, the money supply growth rate in the last month may have been at an 11 percent annual rate, but for the last quarter, the money supply growth rate may work out to a 7 percent annual growth rate, and going back 1 year, the growth rate over the past 12 months may have been 5.5 percent. To know what the growth rate in the money supply is, one needs first to know the period over which the rate is being measured.

For these reasons, it is best to watch the money supply growth rate *in conjunction with* the other barometers mentioned earlier (such as the Federal funds rate, the prime commercial lending rate, the 90-day Treasury bill rate, the net reserve position, and the total amount of borrowings by member banks from the Federal Reserve). In looking at all these indicators, the investor is trying to confirm or refute conclusions which may be drawn from any one individual indicator, to derive a feeling for the recent and current growth rate in the supply side of the funds' availability situation in the economy, which in turn should provide some insight into the direction and level of interest rates in the future. If the investor wants to monitor a direct indicator of the strength of commercial and industrial loan demands for funds, the weekly report of the assets and liabilities of 12 of the weekly reporting member banks in New York City is also published in the newspaper each Friday. A sample of this report is shown in Table 5-3.

Arrow 1 points to the category which many professional investors watch to gauge the strength of loan demand compared with the week-earlier and the year-earlier week. Continued strong gains in "business loans of the 12 New York reporters," as these banks are called, presage continued firmness in interest rates, while declines versus earlier periods may be a sign that interest rates will begin to turn downward.

Caveats in drawing conclusions from the indicators Although everyone has access to the regularly published indicators reviewed in the last few pages, varying conclusions are often drawn from them, by sophisticated professionals and armchair investors alike. This

TABLE 5-3   Key Assets and Liabilities of 12 Weekly Reporting Member Banks in New York City (in millions of dollars)

	May 8, 1974	May 1, 1974	May 9, 1973
ASSETS:			
Total assets	115,887	116,808	95,512
Total loans and investments	82,992	85,858	69,835
Included:			
Fed funds sold and like assets	1,468	2,869	1,053
Commercial and indust loans	34,841	34,878	29,031
U.S. Treasury securities	3,919	4,116	3,472
Municipal securities:			
Short-term	2,152	2,138	2,222
Long-term	5,709	5,378	4,767
Other key assets:			
Cash items in proc of collection	11,485	12,157	8,952
Reserves with F.R. bank	7,385	6,166	6,048
Currency and coin	504	481	473
LIABILITIES:			
Total demand deposits	45,186	48,068	38,128
Demand deposits adjusted*	20,983	23,803	19,440
Time & savings deposits	38,642	38,060	31,871
Includes negotiable CDs			
of $100,000 or more	24,007	23,452	18,873
Federal funds purchased and			
similar liabilities	11,718	10,706	8,107
Other key liabilities:			
From own foreign branches	1,960	1,789	1,672
Borrowings from F.R. bank	645	0	1,215
Reserves for loans	1,401	1,399	1,274
Total capital accounts	8,592	8,562	7,679

*All demand deposits except U.S. government and domestic commercial banks, less cash items in process of collection.

prompts us to mention a few caveats in analyzing these numbers. First of all, the Federal Reserve does not disclose its immediate thinking on monetary policy, because if it did, fixed-income securities investors would take actions which might hamper, or even cause the opposite of, the objectives which the Federal Reserve might be pursuing at any given moment in time.

Also, in addition to executing its broad monetary policies, the

Federal Reserve is responsible for stabilizing any seasonal or erratic funds flows which may occur in the economy. Seasonal patterns in credit needs, and thus the availability of money, can be affected by the Christmas and Easter shopping seasons, tax payment dates for individuals and corporations, the desire of numerous businesses and financial institutions to show certain balance sheet totals on annual or quarterly reporting dates (called "window dressing"), and even weather-related funds flows in businesses such as construction and agriculture. Unless corrected and counterbalanced by the Federal Reserve, these seasonal and erratic money flows can cause abnormal gains or declines in the cost and availability of credit, and these flows can even work counter to Federal Reserve monetary policy. Consequently, in any 1 week, specific Federal Reserve actions which are seemingly contradictory to other recent weeks' actions may have been taken to offset seasonal patterns or other extraordinary quirks in money flows. For this reason, the investor should look at the *trend of these indicators over a period of time* and not hope to arrive at a completely accurate reading of the future course of interest rates merely by looking at the indicators on a sporadic basis. Sound conclusions cannot be drawn from isolated observations of money market conditions.

Tools of the Federal Reserve Board in setting policy One major but somewhat blunt policy tool at the disposal of the Federal Reserve Board is the ability to vary member banks' *percentage reserve requirements*. For example, if the amount of required reserves backing up deposits were 10 percent, with $100 in reserves supporting $1,000 in deposits, the Federal Reserve Board could expand the money supply (to stimulate economic activity or to promote one of the other objectives mentioned earlier in this chapter) by lowering reserve requirements to 9 percent. This would mean that $100 could then support $1,111.11 in deposits rather than $1,000 ($100 *divided by* 9 percent equals $1,111.11), and the member bank could expand its loans accordingly through the deposit creation process.

Because changes in reserve requirement percentages have such an immediate and broad impact on member banks'' reserve positions, this policy tool is used infrequently. When the Federal Reserve Board does change reserve requirement percentages, it usually signals an important policy decision, very often with significant implications for interest rates. When reserve requirements are raised, a policy of tight money (higher interest rates) is normally being confirmed, since banks will have to slow, or even reverse, the money creation process by stopping new loan activities and perhaps calling in loans. With lesser amounts of money to be allocated among borrowers, the price of money, as reflected in the prevailing interest rates, is likely to rise. Conversely, when reserve requirements are lowered, the Federal Reserve is usually confirming an easier stance, as banks find it easier to make money available to borrowers, which could signal a drop in interest rates.

A policy tool of the Federal Reserve System which is used with some occasional ambiguity in meaning is the *discount rate*. The discount rate is the interest rate which is charged to member banks who borrow money from the Federal Reserve System. The ambiguity of the discount rate as a policy tool stems from the fact that the discount rate frequently follows, rather than leads, other short-term interest rate movements, merely reflecting existing conditions instead of predicting them. When the discount rate is changed upward or downward, it is usually being brought into line with market interest rates and thus is not a reliable signal of future Federal Reserve intentions.

An additional element of ambiguity enters in when discount rate changes are actually intended to encourage or discourage borrowing at the Federal Reserve "discount window," thus confirming the degree of conviction of the Federal Reserve Board's monetary stance at that moment in time. In general, therefore, it is recommended that the discount rate be used more as a broad guide to the direction of future interest rates. Indeed, it might be used more as an ancillary symptom of the current state of money market conditions and pressures, with a high discount rate indicating a good degree of monetary tightness in the credit and capital markets, while a low discount rate would indicate the opposite. Table 5-2 shows the range of the discount rate level in each year during the period 1950–1974.

The most commonly used and the most flexible tool of the Federal

Reserve System is its practice of *open-market operations,* which consists of buying and selling government securities to directly influence member bank reserve positions. The Federal Open Market Committee, acting through the manager of the System Open Market Account at the New York Federal Reserve Bank, can *increase* member bank reserves by *purchasing* a specific dollar amount of government securities (usually Treasury bills, and much less frequently, longer-term coupon bonds of the U.S. government, Federal Agency securities, and sometimes bankers' acceptances) from any one of twenty-odd bank and nonbank securities dealers authorized to trade directly with the Federal Reserve. Payment for the securities purchased by the Open Market Committee is arranged by crediting the Federal Reserve account of the bank (or the bank of the nonbank securities dealer) which sold the securities to the Federal Reserve. This expansion of the bank's reserve position at the Federal Reserve permits the bank to *expand credit* by making loans, limited of course by the reserve requirement percentage in effect at that time.

Conversely, when the Federal Reserve *sells* government securities through open-market operations, dealers pay for the securities by drawing down their reserve positions at the Federal Reserve—the money is no longer the property of the bank (or the bank of the nonbank securities dealer). Thus, Federal Reserve System *sales* of government securities reduce member banks' reserve positions and *retard their ability to expand the money supply,* which may put *upward* pressure on interest rates. The Federal Reserve can also reduce member banks' reserves by allowing some of the Treasury bills it customarily holds (for its own investment purposes) to be turned in for cash at the Treasury when they mature, rather than using the maturing bills to reinvest in 3-month or 6-month bills at the weekly Treasury bill auction held each Monday. This has the same effect as the *sale* of government securities by the Federal Reserve Open Market Account.

Another flexible and commonly used part of the Federal Reserve's open-market repertoire is a device known as a *repurchase agreement.* At its own initiative, the Federal Reserve enters into repurchase agreements with nonbank dealers in U.S. government securities, Federal Agency issues, or bankers' acceptances. In a repurchase agreement, the Federal Reserve *purchases* short-term securities from a dealer who in turn agrees to *repurchase* the security from the Federal Reserve within an agreed upon period, ranging from 1 to 15 days, at the original price with a specified rate of interest, usually the discount rate, paid to the Federal Reserve. Either the Federal Reserve or the dealer can terminate the repurchase agreement any time before its maturity, though this rarely occurs in practice. When the Federal Reserve purchases securities under a repurchase agreement, this maneuver temporarily *supplies* reserves to the banking system, and the closing out of the transaction removes these additional reserves. As might be expected, repurchase agreements are of great use in counterbalancing extraordinary seasonal or other funds flows into or out of the banking system, because their life and size can be tailored to each particular transaction.

The Federal Reserve can temporarily *absorb* member banks' reserves through a *reverse repurchase agreement,* also known as *matched sale-purchase transactions.* In this process, the Federal Reserve *sells* short-term securities of the type mentioned above for cash, simultaneously agreeing to buy the same securities back after 1 day or a longer period of time, up to 15 days.

Through the operations of the Federal Open Market Committee, the Federal Reserve can thus actively influence banks' reserve positions, thereby affecting the supply of money, which in turn affects the level and direction of interest rates. Continued outright purchases of government securities (or the continued use of repurchase agreements) by the Federal Reserve may indicate that it is pursuing an expansionary credit policy, expanding member banks' reserves and leading to lower interest rates. On the other hand, recurrent sales of government securities (or the recurrent use of reverse repurchase agreements) by the Federal Reserve may foretell a more stringent monetary stance, which through the contraction of member banks' reserve positions may lead to higher interest rates.

The Federal Reserve Board has certain other implements besides the ability to alter member banks' percentage reserve requirements, the discount rate, and open-market operations. These tools, of a more specialized and minor nature, include the power to set margin requirements on borrowing to finance the purchase or holding of listed stocks and bonds, and the authority to set interest rate ceilings which member banks can pay on time deposits, savings accounts, and certificates of deposit. In periods of high interest rates, these ceilings can have a powerful impact on banks' abilities to attract deposits. If the interest rate ceiling is set below market rates of interest on other types of fixed-income securities, investors will withdraw deposits from the member banks to invest directly in the higher-yielding securities, thus causing banks to curtail credit expansion, possibly resulting in a further general interest rate rise. When investors withdraw funds from commercial banks, savings banks, and other investing intermediaries to invest their money directly in short-term money market instruments, this process is called *disintermediation*.

Often, in tight money periods when the commercial banks are restrained by the Federal Reserve interest rate ceilings (so-called *Regulation Q* ceilings when they are in effect) from being able to attract time deposits, the commercial banks may attempt to raise funds to meet businesses' loan demands by borrowing in the Eurodollar market (through the banks' overseas branches or affiliates). Commercial banks which are part of a holding company structure can also gain access to funds by having their corporate parent issue commercial paper. These additional demands for money can serve to intensify pressures toward higher interest rates in the Eurodollar and the commercial paper markets and are mentioned as an example of how the Federal Reserve's influence can be felt throughout the full range of fixed-income securities.

As with all Federal Reserve actions, it is vitally important to try to separate *policy* moves from moves taken to offset other factors not under the direct control of the Federal Reserve (such as seasonal fluctuations) which happen to be changing member bank reserves. The Federal Reserve may be acting to offset extraordinary money flows, or it may be acting for an official foreign customer (such as an international agency or a foreign central bank), or reacting to additions or reductions in the U.S. Treasury's level of deposits at the Federal Reserve banks. For instance, when the U.S. Treasury reduces its deposits at the Federal Reserve banks, it is generally done to pay for goods and services purchased by the United States government. The vendors of the goods and services usually deposit the proceeds in their own bank accounts, thus increasing total bank deposits and adding to the ability of banks to expand the money supply. Conversely, when taxes are paid to the United States government, Treasury deposits at Federal Reserve banks *increase* while member banks' deposits *decrease* (since the banks' corporate and individual customers are withdrawing their funds to pay their tax bills).

Sometimes, one of these reserve-changing events may occur, and the Federal Reserve Board may carry out its policy objectives by doing *nothing* to offset the event. This underscores once again the need to watch all Federal Reserve Board actions, as well as the indicators reviewed earlier in the chapter, *with care and regularity.*

Limitations of Federal Reserve policy The broad range of major and minor policy tools at the disposal of the Federal Reserve System are carefully coordinated with each other at all times. This permits a high degree of flexibility in achieving desired goals, while leaving to the marketplace the ultimate decision as to how the supply of credit should be allocated among borrowers. Federal Reserve policy also has its limitations, chief among which is the fact that it influences only the *supply* side of the money and credit picture. Federal Reserve efforts to curb credit expansion, in order to reduce inflationary pressures, may not be entirely successful if member banks choose to reduce their *excess* reserves (reserves greater than the required percentage amount) or borrow more frequently from the Federal Reserve, even at a high discount rate. Similarly, the Federal Reserve may not completely succeed when it encourages credit growth in order to stimulate economic expansion, if banks decide not to lend the maximum amounts permitted by the reserve requirement, or if businesses and consumers are not seeking new loans, even at lower interest rates. A further limitation of Federal Reserve monetary policy may stem from the fact that certain areas are outside the direct control of the Federal Reserve, including (1) member bank affiliates' borrowing activity in the commercial paper and Eurodollar markets and (2) the deposits of banks which are *not* members of the Federal Reserve System.

Also, since the Federal Reserve is politically independent, it may at times find itself pursuing *monetary* policies which run counter to more politically oriented *fiscal* policies of the United States government relating to government spending and taxation. For example, the Federal Reserve Board may feel that the economy is being buffetted by inflationary pressures and thus might take actions which restrict the growth and availability of money and credit, while Congress may read the outlook differently and decide that a tax cut is needed to boost national income and stimulate production. Under such a scenario, the effectiveness of Federal Reserve moves may be diminished.

During inflationary-prone periods, limitations on the effectiveness of Federal Reserve Board policies may stem from anticipatory and psychological factors. In inflationary times, when interest rates are high, the Federal Reserve may decide to increase reserves in an attempt to lower interest rates somewhat as more credit becomes available to borrowers. However, under such conditions, borrowers may perceive an increase in the supply of credit as a sign that inflationary pressures will increase as well. Instead of borrowing the previously anticipated amounts of lower-cost money, corporate borrowers may decide to *increase* their borrowing activity to make inventory purchases and other investments before any possible future increases in price. This greater demand for money thus causes interest rates to move even higher, which may again lead to policies designed to make more credit available, resulting in another round of increased borrowing, and so on, in a vicious circle which runs completely counter to the Federal Reserve Board's original aims.

Psychological effects can sometimes hinder Federal Reserve actions when government securities dealers, operating in the short-term money market, observe that the Federal Reserve Board is moving toward a stance of greater ease through actions which are increasing member bank reserves and causing the money supply to grow. Reasoning that the Federal Reserve will have to tighten the system again at some future point by causing interest rates to rise and fixed-income securities prices to fall, dealers begin selling off their holdings of short-term securities to avoid inventory price declines. Such selling activity itself causes short-term fixed-income securities prices to decline and yields to rise, even though the Federal Reserve has just begun to take measures which are designed to reduce yields in a lower-interest-rate environment.

The investor should be aware of the limitations of Federal Reserve policy when trying to assess how its actions exert their powerful influence on interest rates and thus on fixed-income securities prices. Specifically, member banks' preferences for holding more or less than required reserve levels, United States government fiscal policies, psychological factors, and anticipatory reactions may all dampen somewhat the originally desired effects of Federal Reserve actions.

Security Dealers' Positions and the Technical State of the Market

While exploring the supply side of the money and credit equation, it might be helpful to pause for a moment and discuss the role which short-term securities dealers have in supplying funds and in influencing interest rates. While nonbank dealers finance a major portion of their securities inventories with *borrowed* funds, and thus might be considered a part of the *demand* for funds rather than the *supply* of funds, they are in fact supplying funds to the United States government for a certain length of time whenever they purchase Treasury bills, bonds, or notes, all of which are a form of governmental borrowing, just as business loans, notes, and bonds are various types of corporate borrowing. Banks which act as securities dealers technically do not borrow funds to finance their inventories, but they are assigned an internal charge by the banks' management representing the bank's own weighted average incremental cost of funds, and so inventory financing "costs" are also a consideration to bank securities traders.

In buying or selling U.S. government securities with the public and with one another, dealers can cause prices to rise or fall, resulting in an increase or decrease in yield levels, respectively. Thus dealers not only react to the Federal Reserve's open-market decisions to buy or sell government securities, but also independently and continuously assess price moves and consequently adjust their own prices and markets in secondary market trading with other dealers and with institutional and individual investors. The willingness of fixed-income security dealers to *supply* new funds (by adding to their inventories) depends on their own estimation of which way interest rates will move and the absolute level of their current inventories. The dealers' inventory configurations, termed the *technical* state of the market, might be contrasted with *fundamental* influences, such as Federal Reserve policy or the overall demand for credit and capital funds by the government, corporations, and other borrowers.

The investor should keep in mind the important influence which dealer positions can have on short-term fixed-income securities prices and yields. For instance, if a particular dealer is selling, or has sold, more securities than he owns (called *selling short*) in hopes of buying the securities back (called *covering* a short sale) at lower prices to return to the party who lent the securities to the dealer to sell, that dealer may be anticipating an interest rate *rise* and may even be contributing to the rise in yields through selling pressure on prices. On the other hand, several dealers may believe that securities prices will rise (as interest rates and yields decline), and will accumulate large securities inventories to benefit from the expected price upswing. If interest rates should move counter to earlier expectations and the hoped-for profits fail to materialize, dealers may unload their positions, further aggravating selling pressures and pushing short-term yields higher.

Suppliers of Long-Term Credit

Thus far, we have primarily concentrated on the short-term supply of money and credit, since it is in this sector of the fixed-income securities market that the overall majority of official policy measures are executed. As we saw in Chapters 3 and 4, changes in short-term securities prices and short-term yields inevitably spill over into and influence long-term yields and prices. Most of the long-term credit in the United States economy is supplied by various types of financial institutions, which in turn receive their funds from individual savers. Financial institutions encompass both *depositary* institutions, such as savings and loan associations, mutual savings banks, credit unions, and commercial bank savings accounts, and *contractual* institutions, such as life insurance companies, pension funds, and government employee retirement funds. Depositary institutions generally provide the individual with safe liquid savings outlets, while contractual institutions help protect the individual against longer-term contingencies, such as retirement.

Each type of financial institution is subject to various tax provisions and state or federal regulations which determine the type of investments it can make. These restrictions are to protect the individual who has entrusted his funds to a particular institution. For example, a life insurance company must be able to pay off its obligations to the survivors of a policyholder, and consequently, it is prohibited from making unduly speculative or risky investments which might endanger the reserves which must be set aside to cover policy claims as they occur. Obviously, savings and loan associations are not subject to the same type of periodic cash inflows or cash outflows which life insurance companies face, and so some of their regulatory guidelines might be designed to provide a degree of liquidity in case depositors decide to make withdrawals.

At certain times, the supply of long-term funds controlled by these financial intermediaries will exceed or fall short of the demand for funds by businesses, the government, and others (the demand side of the picture will be reviewed shortly). When an imbalance occurs, interest rates will tend to fall or rise on the particular securities in which an institution normally invests. For example, commercial banks, which for tax and other reasons traditionally are the major investors in tax-exempt securities, will cut back, or even sell off, their new investments in their tax-exempt holdings (and sometimes a portion of their U.S. government securities holdings), when credit availability is tightened by the Federal Reserve. They do this in order to obtain funds to lend to their regular customers, borrowers with whom they have a long-standing relationship. In order to appeal to other buyers, the prices of municipal securities must then fall (which raises yields) to a level at which individuals and other investors find the new yields attractive. Similarly, life insurance companies might have to reduce their new acquisitions of corporate bonds, or sell off bonds from their portfolios when life insurance policyholders borrow money against their policies. The selling pressures on corporate bonds will tend to cause yields to rise until new buying interest is found. When savings and loan associations are receiving very large inflows which cannot be immediately re-lent in the long-term mortgage market, they may step up their investments in U.S. government and Federal Agency securities, causing prices to rise and yields to fall in these sectors of the fixed-income securities market.

It should be apparent that buying or selling pressures arise in specific types of securities whenever a traditional class of institutional investors increase or decrease their normal patterns of investing. These shifts can be caused by heavy outflows of funds from, or heavy inflows of funds to, the institutional group involved. When interest rates on short-term securities are high enough to cause individual investors to withdraw their funds from the lower-paying financial intermediaries and invest this money themselves, as mentioned earlier, this process is called *disintermediation*.

Besides disintermediation, another reason why an institution may shift its investing patterns relates to how that institution perceives the outlook for alternative investment possibilities. Pension and retirement funds may decide that an improved outlook for corporate profits or for real estate investments dictates a shift of funds from long-term corporate, governmental, and Federal Agency bonds into the stock market or ownership of land and mortgages.

In addition, institutional investors' expectations and attitudes concerning the returns available in investments other than fixed-income securities are a significant determinant of where they will allocate the supply of long-term funds. The prospects of an increasing rate of inflation, as measured by gains in the *consumer price index,* the *wholesale price index,* and the overall inflation rate of the *gross national product,* may be seen by suppliers of long-term capital as eroding the purchasing power of fixed-income securities returns and therefore may cause long-term interest rates to rise. This may cause a psychological shift away from fixed-income securities by institutional investors. On the other hand, the fixed return of high-quality fixed-income securities may be considered very attractive in recessionary economic periods, resulting in lower yields on fixed-income securities as investors purchase them in quantity and their prices move up.

Inflationary or recessionary psychology thus plays an important role in shaping institutional investing tendencies, and this should be kept in mind by the individual investor as he evaluates various securities.

When certain institutional investors are not restricted to a particular maturity investment, their *expectations* about the future course of interest rates will influence whether they prefer to place their money in short-maturity or long-maturity investments. If current interest rates are expected to rise, the preference will be (as we saw in Chapter 3) for holding short-term securities (1) in order to minimize price risk and (2) to be able to buy securities at the new higher yields after interest rates have moved up and the short-term securities mature. On the other hand, if current interest rates are expected to fall, many investors will want to hold long-term securities (1) to lock in the higher yields and (2) to benefit from the greater upside price fluctuation possibilities on long-term as compared with short-term securities.

Flow of Funds Analysis

At this point, it is appropriate to mention a special system which has been utilized since the early 1950s for measuring the money flows from suppliers of funds to users of funds. It is called *flow of funds analysis*. Although a bit too detailed for the scope of this book, the flow of funds accounts can be very helpful in discovering trends and patterns of investment in various types of securities by the principal groups of domestic and foreign portfolio investors. Studying the flow of funds accounts may show, for instance, that foreigners were motivated to supply funds to United States borrowers through purchases of short-term fixed-income securities or other types of long-term debt and equity issues. This may have been because of the fact that interest rates were higher in the United States than abroad, or because the United States dollar was expected to rise in value relative to other currencies, or because of liquidity and safety reasons.

The flow of funds accounts are published quarterly by the Division of Research and Statistics, Board of Governors of the Federal Reserve System, Washington, D.C. 20551. Each year, the economics division of the Bankers Trust Company of New York publishes an excellent, down-to-earth *Review of the Credit and Capital Markets*. This publication is derived in part from the Federal Reserve's flow of funds statistics and other sources, and the investor can gain a good deal of perspective and insight by reading and reflecting upon the tables and commentary in the Bankers Trust *Review*.

The Demand for Money and Credit

In our review of the major influences on the level and direction of interest rates, we have analyzed the various components of the *supply* side of the money and credit picture. We have seen how they are influenced by the Federal Reserve Board and the nation's commercial banking system, dealer positions, the technical state of the market, and institutional investment patterns and expectations. We will now turn to the *demand* side of the credit and capital supply-demand relationship, with particular emphasis on how demands for funds affect the level and direction of interest rates.

Where do demands for money and credit come from, and why? The answer is not difficult—from all levels of the government, from corporations, from consumers. We all need money and credit, to satisfy short-term needs and to make long-term purchases. The level of economic activity itself has often influenced *how much* credit and capital is demanded from all sources. When economic activity is high, consumers borrow to finance the purchase of homes, automobiles, and a myriad of other products. Businesses are demanding funds for capital investment and other purposes, in order to satisfy the increased needs of consumers for their products, and depending on the level of tax revenues, governments—federal, state, and local—may also want to borrow to pay for projects and services to improve the commonweal of their citizenry.

If overall demands for funds rise faster than the supplies of money and credit from all sources, upward pressure will be exerted on interest rates. Similarly, as economic activity slows and demands for funds contract, interest rates may move downward, unless the supply of money and credit contracts even more rapidly. It is on the demand side of the equation that the maturity decision is made. A business may look at long-term interest rates and, deciding they are at too high a level, may borrow from a commercial bank or issue a 7-

year note rather than issuing a 20- or 30-year bond. All types of governmental borrowers look at the maturity decision in a similar way. If long-term interest rates are at a low level and expected to rise, the United States government may choose to issue long-term bonds and cut back on the amount of Treasury bills issued at their regular weekly and monthly auctions. A closer investigation of why governments and corporations borrow would help the investor gain a better comprehension of their influence, from a demand standpoint, on the level and direction of interest rates.

The United States government   One of the most significant factors in the total demand for funds is the U.S. Treasury. When governmental expenditures exceed income from taxes and other sources, the Treasury, like anyone else, must borrow to finance the deficit. On the other hand, when outlays are less than receipts, the government can add to its cash balances or redeem a part of the outstanding public debt.

The size of the anticipated and the actual budget surplus or deficit thus has an important influence on the degree of governmental borrowing during a given year. If a large deficit is expected, it can be assumed that the Treasury will make heavy demands on the credit and capital markets, which may very well cause interest rates to rise. Even in years of a budget surplus or a balanced budget, however, the government can decide to tap the money and capital markets for funds in order to increase its cash balances or to pay off a debt issue maturing in that year.

The amount of the federal government's surplus or deficit can also *indirectly* affect the level and direction of interest rates, although the impact of the net budget position can sometimes be misleading. As an indicator of the degree of government spending, it tends to reflect the stimulative (if a budget *deficit*) or restrictive (if a budget *surplus*) sentiments of Congress and the executive branch. If a large deficit is forecast while the economy is strong, the increase in economic activity which results from government spending at a higher rate than its receipts may (but not always) lead businesses and consumers to spend and borrow more also, thus intensifying credit demands and causing interest rates to rise, even without taking into consideration the government's *own* needs for funds. On the other hand, if a large budget deficit occurs during a *weak* economic environment (in part owing to a shortfall in tax receipts), the Treasury's borrowing demands to finance the deficit may not add excessively to (most probably) weakened corporate credit demands, and thus increased Treasury capital demands may not *always* cause interest rates to rise.

The investor should think through the implications of any measures which have a large impact on the budget, not only for their direct effects in terms of governmental borrowing needs but also for their indirect effects on economic activity. For example, a substantial income tax *increase* would tend to lower credit demands and cause interest rates to decline, in two ways. First, it would move the budget toward, or strongly into, a surplus position, thereby lessening Treasury needs for funds. Second, the tax would reduce consumers' incomes, weakening their ability to spend and thus causing corporations to postpone additional spending plans in order to increase capacity and expand output. In turn, this would generally motivate corporations to cut back their demands for funds.

The investor should also keep abreast of any announcements of major increases or decreases in government spending or income, with an eye toward how this will influence the budget or deficit. To gain a better feeling for where the government's money comes from and how it is spent, the actual budget for fiscal year 1973 (which runs from July 1, 1972 to June 30, 1973) is presented in Table 5-4. The investor should also take note of the fact that the Treasury can borrow from other sources besides the public, such as foreign central banks and other sources. In addition, the total amount of the budget deficit (or surplus) does not always *exactly* equal the amount of borrowing from the public (or reduction in debt, if a surplus is run). Rather, the actual budget deficit (or surplus) gives more an idea of the order of magnitude of United States government borrowing for a particular fiscal year.

As can be seen in Table 5-4, the excess of budget outlays over budget receipts in fiscal year 1973 of $14.3 billion necessitated that the Treasury borrow the $14.3 billion from the public, through the sale of Treasury bonds, bills, and notes. The investor should also

TABLE 5-4 The Fiscal Year 1973 Budget of the United States Government (Actual) (in billions of dollars)

Budget receipts by source		Budget outlays by function	
Individual income taxes	$103.2	National defense	$ 76.0
Corporate income taxes	36.2	Social security	73.1
Social insurance taxes	64.5	Interest	22.8
Excise taxes	16.3	Health	18.4
Estate and gift taxes	4.9	Commerce and transportation	13.1
Customs duties	3.2	Veterans' benefits	12.0
Miscellaneous receipts	3.9	Education and manpower	10.2
		General revenue sharing	6.6
		Agriculture and rural development	6.2
		General government	5.5
		Community development and housing	4.1
		Space research and technology	3.3
		International affairs	2.9
		Less: undistributed inter-government transfers	−8.3
Total budget receipts:	$232.2	Total budget outlays:	$246.5

SUMMARY:

	Total budget outlays:	$246.5 billion
	less total budget receipts:	232.2 billion
	equals budget deficit:	$ 14.3 billion

TOTAL FEDERAL BORROWING FROM THE PUBLIC IN FISCAL YEAR 1973

	Financing the budget deficit:	$ 14.3 billion
	Other borrowing:	0.8 billion
	All other items:	4.1 billion
	Total borrowing in fiscal 1973:	$ 19.3 billion

notice that the actual total of Treasury borrowing was somewhat higher than the total budget deficit—$19.3 billion total borrowing as compared with a budget deficit of $14.3 billion—but as mentioned previously, the size of the budget deficit gives the investor an idea of the rough order of magnitude of total borrowing by the United States government for that particular fiscal year.

Several other important facts about the budget should also be mentioned. First, there are several ways of presenting the budget—on a *national income accounts* basis, on a *unified budget* basis, and on a *full employment* basis. Each method differs from the others in the way receipts and expenditures are accounted for and in the inclusion or exclusion of certain government agencies' receipts and expenditures. Second, the *actual* budget deficit or surplus can differ from the *estimated* deficit or surplus (prepared 1 year or more earlier) because of variations in national income levels (which can cause tax receipts to vary from earlier estimates), additional appropriations or vetoes of planned expenditures by Congress, and by several other factors. Finally, numerous Federal Agency programs are no longer included in any of the three main methods of budget presentation, and these particular Agencies' financing needs must be considered separately in looking at total demand pressures for money and credit. At this point, we will briefly review the demands of the Federal Agencies which are not included in the demands for funds of the United States government.

Federal agencies   In recent years, more than 40 Federal Agencies have made enormous demands for funds in our money and capital markets. Yet defining exactly what a Federal Agency is has become very difficult, because of the multiplicity of new agencies, the changing budget status of many Agencies, and their varying forms of guarantee, endorsement, or quasi-guarantee by the United States government. Since we are primarily concerned with the various agencies' impact on total *credit* demands, we will postpone a discussion of the specific features of Federal Agency securities until Chapter 7.

Most Federal Agencies have been established to channel funds into sectors of the economy which have had difficulty in attracting money through conventional means. Agriculture- and housing-related activities account for a substantial majority of Federal Agencies' borrowing activities, but numerous other types of agencies have been created in recent years to assist a varied group of economic sectors.

As mentioned earlier, some agencies' income and outlays are still included in the United States government's budget, and their borrowings are contained in total national debt figures. The principal

TABLE 5-5   List of Direct U.S. Government Agencies (as of 1974)

Farmers Home Administration*	Export-Import Bank
Federal Housing Administration	Tennessee Valley Authority
Small Business Administration	Government National Mortgage Association*
U.S. Postal Service	

*Only a *part* of these agencies' operations are included in the United States government budget, but their obligations are guaranteed by the United States government.

agencies in this category (also known as *direct government agencies*) are listed in Table 5-5.

While the list of direct government agencies' income and outlays are included in the United States government budget statistics, the activities of several major agency borrowers are *not* included in the budget or in United States government debt totals. These agencies are now officially known as *government-sponsored enterprises,* or *privatized agencies,* a list of which is presented in Table 5-6.

TABLE 5-6   List of Government-Sponsored Enterprises (as of 1974)

Federal National Mortgage Association	Federal Land Banks
Banks for Cooperatives	Federal Home Loan Banks
Federal Intermediate Credit Banks	Federal Home Loan Mortgage Corp.

In order to help the investor obtain a feeling for the growth rates in borrowing and the relative amounts of securities outstanding of the United States government, as well as direct and privatized agencies, Table 5-7 presents statistics on the debt outstanding of each of these three categories as of a recent date, compared with 1965.

As can be seen in Table 5-7, while the total of U.S. government and direct agency securities outstanding grew 26 percent from June 30, 1970 to February 28, 1974, the amount of privatized agency securities outstanding has shown a much faster growth rate, 63 percent, during the same time period, resulting in increased demands for credit from this latter sector and contributing to upward pressures on interest rates.

TABLE 5-7 Total United States Government and Agency Debt Outstanding (in billions of dollars)

Date	Included in the U.S. budget and in national debt totals		Not included in the U.S. budget or national debt totals
	U.S. government securities	Direct agency securities	Privatized agency securities
June 30, 1965	$317.3	$ 9.3	$ 8.3
June 30, 1970	370.9	12.5	35.7
June 30, 1973	458.1	11.1	51.3
Feb. 28, 1974	470.7	11.6	59.2

During each of the years from 1967 through 1973, the total amount of new money (net of retirements of debt issues) raised from the public by the United States government, direct government agencies, and privatized government agencies together has ranged from a low of $1.5 billion in 1969 to a high of $23.1 billion in 1972. As might be expected with these and numerous other agencies frequently tapping the money and capital markets for funds, periodic stresses and strains in interest rates have resulted in higher-interest-rate levels when several agencies and the United States government have attempted to raise large amounts of funds within the same time period.

In order to partially alleviate these imbalances, and the investor's confusion stemming from the proliferation of agencies, in early 1974 Congress passed legislation establishing a *Federal Financing Bank,* which offers its securities to the public several times per year and turns over the proceeds to other government agencies who are seeking to raise additional funds. Use of the Federal Financing Bank by agencies is entirely voluntary, and several of the large privatized government agencies have continued to raise money on their own.

Whatever the form used by Federal Agencies to satisfy their demands for capital, the investor should be aware of their presence and appetite for funds. From time to time, the newspaper will publish a *forward calendar* of future borrowing plans by Federal Agencies, and this can be of assistance to the investor in trying to judge the general influence of agencies' credit demands on the level and direction of interest rates. All other things being equal, when total upcoming agency credit demands are large, it will tend to put upward pressure on interest rates. When agencies' announced borrowing plans (including the Federal Financing Bank) slack off, interest rates may decline somewhat.

State and local governments   The final group of *governmental* bodies which make demands for credit are state and local governments. They have accounted for about 25 percent of all new capital market securities issued during the past 5 years, and these state and local government issuers have also shown a strong rate of growth in net *new* short-term and long-term borrowing (which equals total borrowing less debt retirements), rising from $7.9 billion in 1967 to over $15 billion in 1974.

The principal reason for borrowing by state and local governments is to finance capital expenditures for education, roads and bridges, housing and recreational facilities, sports and convention centers, and to help corporations finance pollution control equipment. Interest and principal on state and local government bonds, notes, and short-term securities are paid off through property, income, and other taxes levied on the residents of the city, state, or other locality issuing the bonds, or perhaps by revenues generated from the sale of the services provided by the facility built with the funds raised, such as a water works or toll bridge.

As of the end of 1973, total state and local government debts outstanding amounted to $184.6 billion, about 10 percent of which represented short-term issues with less than 1 year to maturity. State and local governments rarely rely on short-term credit to try to finance long-term projects. Much of the short-term debt they issue is to finance government operations until major tax collection dates. Over 30,000 different state and local government units have come to the money and capital markets for funds, with about one-half of the total raised by cities, one-quarter by states, and the rest by various types of school districts and other authorities. Past experience has shown that in periods of high interest rates, the larger state and local governments have tended to scale back their borrowing demands (or even postpone them), and in lower-interest-rate environments they have increased their borrowing demands somewhat. On the other hand, smaller state and local government issuers have tended to raise funds in the marketplace regardless of changing interest rate conditions. Attracted by their tax-free interest status, commercial banks, fire and casualty insurance companies, and wealthy individuals have been the major buyers of state and local government securities, but since all these investor groups are also significant buyers of corporate, agency, and U.S. Treasury issues, the total demands made by state and local governments can have an important influence on the overall level and direction of interest rates.

Investors can monitor two indicators of the relative impact of state and local government financing plans on interest rates. The first is the so-called placement ratio, which gives the amount of state and local government securities distributed to investors as a percentage of the total newly issued state and local government securities during that particular week. A 60 percent placement ratio would mean that securities dealers had sold 60 percent of the total state and local government securities underwritten that week, meaning that 40 percent of the total issues brought to market were still in dealers' inventories. The higher the placement ratio, the more receptive investors are to new offerings. The *Bond Buyer* placement ratio, compiled weekly as of every Thursday by the *Bond Buyer* magazine, reached its highest percentage ever the week of July 19, 1951 (99.4 percent), and its lowest ratio to date was reached the week of November 23, 1960 (29.2 percent). All other things being equal, a low placement ratio indicates that difficulty is being experienced in selling new issues, and this might presage a decline in prices (higher interest rates) to attract investor interest. The other indicator is the *30-day visible supply* of announced new state and local government financings during the coming 30 days. A large amount of upcoming state and local government financings may put upward pressure on interest rates to entice investors to accept their expanded demands for credit, whereas a small 30-day visible supply (similar to the forward calendar mentioned earlier) may mean that investors desiring to buy fixed-income securities will have only a small amount of new issues to choose from and will therefore divert their buying interest to already outstanding issues, causing prices to rise and interest rates to fall.

The business sector   Corporations of all types, sizes, and industries are also major factors in the demand for funds. The amount of all businesses' appetite for funds, relative to (1) governmental demands for credit and (2) the supply of funds available, significantly influences the level and direction of interest rates. Over the 1967–1973 period, the amount of new corporate bond issues ranged between $12 billion and $20 billion, and the amount of total new borrowing from banks varied from a low of $5 billion to a high of $30 billion. At the end of 1972, total corporate long-term debt was $447 billion, and total corporate short-term debt amounted to $506 billion. Generally speaking, *the more credit business needs, the more interest rates will tend to move higher.*

What determines how much credit business needs to borrow, in the form of bank loans, commercial paper, notes, and bonds? Over the past 7 years, business has financed its new working capital and other short-term needs, as well as its spending on new plant equipment and other long-term items by obtaining funds from the sources listed in Table 5-8.

While the percentage figures presented in Table 5-8 are merely averages and have in practice fluctuated a good deal from one year to the next, it should be apparent that the level of profits, new stock issues, and depreciation allowances will largely determine how much

TABLE 5-8   Sources of Business Funds, 1967–1973

Source of funds	Percentage of total sources
Commercial paper	1
Short-term bank loans	6
Finance company loans	2
Long-term bank loans	4
Mortgages	7
New stock issues (after retirements)	5
New bond issues (after retirements)	12
Depreciation allowances	43
Profits after taxes and dividends	16
Other miscellaneous sources	4
Total sources	100

business needs to borrow from various short-term and long-term sources. Normally, the investor should be aware that business borrowing needs, and thus the possible upward or downward pressures on interest rates from the business sector, will be reduced if (1) corporations generate a high level of profits after taxes and dividends, (2) large amounts of money are raised from the sale of stock, or (3) depreciation allowances are at a high level. If total corporate profits are low, businesses may be reluctant to sell more stock because this often means that stock prices are low also. If businesses plan to increase their outlays for capital goods and for inventories, this may mean greater borrowing demands from the corporate sector.

Whether business plans to increase or decrease its investment in new facilities and working capital depends in large part on how corporate managers expect the overall economy to perform in the future. If economic growth is projected, business tends to step up its spending on plant and equipment, but if a recession is forecast, business will generally be reluctant to do so.

How can the investor get an idea of how the economy is expected to perform? No one can predict the future with certainty, but the Department of Commerce publishes a number of leading indicators of economic activity, most of which the investor can spot in the newspaper on a monthly or quarterly basis. Table 5-9 reviews the 12 most often quoted leading economic indicators (the full list of leading, coincident, and lagging indicators is given each month in *Busi-*

TABLE 5-9   Frequently Quoted Leading Economic Indicators

1. Average workweek (production workers in manufacturing industries)
2. Average weekly initial claims (state unemployment insurance)
3. Index of net business formation
4. New orders (durable goods industries)
5. Contracts and orders (plant and equipment)
6. New building permits (private housing)
7. Change in book value of manufacturing and trade inventories
8. Industrial materials prices
9. Stock prices (500 common stocks)
10. Corporate profits after taxes
11. Ratio of prices to unit labor costs (manufacturing industries)
12. Change in consumer installment debt

ness Conditions Digest, published by the U.S. Department of Commerce, Washington, D.C. 20230).

Corporations may make the decision to borrow, or not, for financial as well as operational and economic reasons. For example, a company may decide to lengthen the maturity of part of its short-term debt by issuing bonds or notes to pay off its commercial paper or short-term bank loans. Whether the corporation borrows funds from short-term or long-term sources depends on (1) the current level of short-term interest rates compared with long-term rates (if either is significantly higher or lower than the other or than normal levels, the corporation may choose the least costly source of funds); (2) the outlook for inflation (if the rate of inflation is expected to rise in the future, businesses may step up their current borrowing plans, and vice versa); and (3) the condition of the corporation's balance sheet (if, for reasons of safety, a certain type of borrowing would cause a company to deviate significantly from standard financing practices within its industry, the firm may have to employ short-term or long-term debt financing or even equity financing to maintain its balance sheets in line with industry norms).

The investor can gauge the strength of business borrowing needs by watching several indicators: (1) the level of business loans as reported by the 12 weekly reporting banks in the New York Federal Reserve District (mentioned in the *supply* section of this chapter); (2) the commercial banks' prime lending rate (the higher the rate, the greater the amount of businesses' borrowing demands relative to the available supply of short-term bank loans); (3) the leading economic indicators mentioned earlier; and (4) the corporate debt calendar. This last item is similar to the 30-day visible supply of state and local securities issues, and the forward calendar of Federal Agency financing. The corporate debt calendar reflects corporations' announced borrowing plans, and all things being equal, the larger the amount of financing on the corporate calendar, the more likely there will be upward pressure on interest rates.

On the following pages a worksheet for analyzing interest rate trends has been provided to help the investor judge whether fixed-income securities prices will rise in the future (falling interest rate levels) or fall in the future (rising interest rate levels). This worksheet should be used in conjunction with the worksheet at the end of

Chapter 4, which helps the investor evaluate specific fixed-income securities.

**WORKSHEET: ANALYZING INTEREST
RATE TRENDS**

Note: Answers to almost all the following questions can be found fairly easily by the investor in readily available sources such as the daily newspaper or widely distributed business magazines. If the investor has difficulty locating the specific information desired, he should check with his securities broker, commercial banker, or any other professional familiar with fixed-income securities.

We should reiterate that it is necessary to watch and analyze the factors influencing the level and direction of interest rates not merely at one moment in time but *over a period of time,* comparing particularly the various factors and indicators with their levels of the prior week, month, 6 months, and even a year or more earlier, in order to develop perspective and to discern underlying interest rate movements.

Finally, the investor should remember that the many sectors (short-term and long-term; taxable and tax-exempt; and several other subcategories) of the fixed-income securities markets *can each respond to various pressures which affect that sector only,* to the exclusion of other fixed-income securities. This worksheet seeks to help the investor develop a broad sense of which way interest rates are heading, much as a navigator would analyze the flow of currents in the ocean. Continuing the metaphor further, there may be many sidestreams, whirlpools, and eddies along and within the broad flow of a current, and the navigator must be aware of these as well. So, too, for the investor. Although this worksheet looks at the trend of interest rates in general, the investor must be conscious of special considerations affecting certain groups of fixed-income securities in a particular way, even as the mainstream of fixed-income securities prices are moving in another way.

POINT 1: *What is the net reserve position of the Federal Reserve System's member banks, what are their total borrowings from the Federal Reserve, and how have these been moving?* _____

COMMENT: A high level of net *borrowed* reserves over a period of weeks indicates a degree of tightness in the monetary system, with higher interest rates in the offing. On the other hand, a high level of net *free* reserves for a period of time displays ease in the monetary system, with lower interest rates possible in the near term.

POINT 2: *What is the Federal funds rate?* _____
What is the prime commercial bank corporate lending rate?
_____

COMMENT: Both of the above interest rates are sensitive indicators of possible pressures in the short-term end of the fixed-income securities markets, but each must be observed with caution and on a regular basis to spot true trends. A high Federal funds rate and a high prime rate may mean that interest rates will remain high or move higher, while a low figure for these two rates, or a downward trend, may presage lower interest rates in general. Both rates should be watched in conjunction with the 90-day Treasury-bill rate.

POINT 3: *What has been the annualized growth rate for the following measures over the past 3 months, 6 months, and 1 year?* _____

Measure	Definition	Growth rates
Monetary base	Total money in circulation plus member bank reserves with Federal Reserve banks	_____
Narrow money supply (M_1)	Private demand (checking) deposits plus currency in the hands of the public	_____
Broad money supply (M_2)	Private demand (checking) deposits plus currency in the hands of the public plus time (savings) deposits	_____

COMMENT: Because of the varying components of each of the four measures above, their growth rates during the prior 3, 6, and 12 months may differ from one another. However, these growth rates when taken together give a good overview of the supply of funds which has become available to borrowers recently. These statistics must be interpreted with care, since high growth rates *may* mean declining interest rates, but not if the *demands* for funds are expanding even faster (funds demands will be covered momentarily). Also, many analysts feel that if the above measures have been growing at *too* fast a rate, the Federal Reserve will adopt a more restrictive stance, causing interest rates to rise.

POINT 4: *What type of open-market operations (if any) has the Federal Reserve taken recently, and of what size and frequency?* _____

COMMENT: The investor must take care to separate Federal Reserve open-market operations which are of an *active* policy nature from those more isolated operations which are taken to counterbalance seasonal and erratic funds flows. If the Federal Reserve continues to *inject* sizable amounts of funds into the system through *purchases* of government securities, or through *repurchase agreements,* it can be interpreted as a sign that interest rates may move lower. On the other hand, if the Federal Reserve continues to *withdraw* sizable amounts of funds from the system through *sales* of government securities, or through *reverse repurchase agreements,* it can be interpreted as a sign that interest rates may move higher.

POINT 5: *Are any events (such as disintermediation) causing long-term suppliers of capital to increase or decrease their normal patterns of investing in a particular sector of the fixed-income securities markets?*
_____

COMMENT: The investor should think through the implications of economic and other events and what impact they will have on the particular fixed-income security he holds or is thinking of buying. For instance, as mentioned earlier, a tight-money high-interest-rate situation might cause commercial banks to sell tax-exempt (and possibly U.S. government) securities from their portfolios to satisfy businesses' loan demands, putting downward pressure on the prices (and upward pressure on yields) of tax-exempt and U.S. government securities.

POINT 6: *What is the outlook for inflation or recession?* _____

COMMENT: Investors' expectations about the possibility of inflation or recession can significantly influence the yields of both short-term and long-term fixed-income securities. If investors expect inflation, they will generally assume that interest rates will rise, and thus they may shift out of long-term securities (subject to wider price fluctuations) into short-term securities and *increase* yields on long-term issues and *decrease* yields on short-term issues. If recessionary developments are expected, investors will assume that credit demands will drop off and interest rates will fall. Accordingly, investors will tend to buy long-term securities (to take advantage of the expected price rise) on which yields will fall relative to short-term securities whose yields may rise to reflect the selling pressure of investors who are switching into longer-term issues.

POINT 7: *What is the outlook for economic growth?* _____

COMMENT: The degree of economic activity has a strong influence on interest rates. When consumers and businesses are experiencing strong economic growth, their demands for funds increase and so does the upward pressure on interest rates. An economic slowdown tends to reduce demands for funds, causing interest levels to decline. The investor should also keep aware of how leading indicators of economic activity are trending (a list of leading economic indicators is included in Table 5-9) in order to spot possible changes in the economy's real growth rate.

POINT 8: *What is the expected size of the United States government budget surplus or deficit?* _____

COMMENT: A large deficit implies that the Treasury will have to make sizable offerings of securities in the marketplace. Depending on the degree of strength or weakness in the economy, a deficit *may* cause upward pressure on interest rates for government and other fixed-income securities, whereas a surplus *may* mean that the Treasury will not be seeking funds, and perhaps it will even retire an amount of outstanding issues, possibly causing moderate downward pressure on interest rates.

POINT 9: *Are any fiscal measures (such as a tax increase) expected to affect the government's income picture, or are any large government securities offerings expected in the near future?* _____

COMMENT: If a fiscal measure which would decrease the government's income level or a large government securities offering is expected in the future, upward pressure would be put on government securities yields, and vice versa.

POINT 10: *What is the total dollar amount of new offerings expected during the next month (and longer, if known) for the following securities:*

_____

Type of security	Dollar amount of new offerings expected during next 30 days
Federal Agency issues	_____
State and local government issues	_____
Corporate issues	_____
Total	_____

COMMENT: Large amounts of new securities coming to the market for any of the above types of issues may tend to cause interest rates on that particular type of security to move higher, and if the total for any particular category is large enough, it may draw buying interest away from other types of securities and lead to a general upward movement in interest rates for all fixed-income securities of that maturity. An absence of new offerings, by decreasing the available supply of issues, may cause prices to move up and yields on those securities to fall, if there is sufficient buying interest.

POINT 11: *What is the total amount of industrial and commercial loans of the 12 weekly reporting member banks in the New York Federal Reserve District?* _____

COMMENT: These figures should be monitored over a period of time and are a useful guide to the strength of corporate demand for short-term funds. If large gains are posted in these figures over a period of weeks, this means that the money demands of businesses are increasing, with likely upward pressure on interest rates. If, on the other hand, these totals show declines over a period of time, businesses' demands for short-term funds may be declining, with downward movements in interest rates expected to come.

SIX

U.S. Government Securities

Securities of the United States government, issued by the U.S. Treasury, are undoubtedly the most familiar, and perhaps the most popular, type of fixed-income security for individual investors and many other types of investors as well. Their popularity stems from several features. First, everyone comes into contact with the federal government in one form or another, making virtually all investors aware, at least to some degree, of the sizable money-raising and financing activities of the government. Second, U.S. government securities carry the highest possible credit rating, since they are backed by the full faith and credit, including the ability to tax, of the United States. They are thus the safest type of investment available for a guaranteed payment of principal and interest. Third, with few exceptions, publicly traded U.S. government securities are more liquid and marketable than any other type of portfolio investment. Billions of dollars worth of short- and long-term Treasury securities are bought and sold on a normal trading day, many times the total daily trading volume in other types of securities. Finally, it should be mentioned that the income from U.S. government securities, while subject to federal income taxes, is *exempt* from state and local income taxes. This increases their attractiveness to investors in areas of high state and local income taxation.

Yet even with all these advantages and investors' familiarity with the government, many individuals are not clearly aware of the broad range of ways to invest in U.S. government securities, nor do they realize the degree of differences in yield between Treasury issues as compared with Federal Agency, corporate, or tax-exempt obligations. Because government securities are so safe and liquid, they sell at a higher price (thus providing a lower yield) than other investments. (Figure 6-1 shows historical yields on the various types of U.S. government securities.) During the last 10 years, 3-month Treasury bills have had an average yield 35 basis points *less* than short-term Federal Agency securities, over 65 basis points *less* than bankers' acceptances, over 75 basis points *less* than certificates of deposit, and over 85 basis points *less* than commercial paper.

Over the same time period, long-term U.S. government bonds have ranged anywhere from 20 to over 180 basis points less in yield than Moody's corporate bond index for comparable-maturity securities (see Chapter 10, Figure 10-1, Bond Yields). U.S. government securities tend to sell at a relatively higher price and consequently yield less than other similar short- and long-term investments to an even greater degree whenever one or more of certain conditions occur.

First, when investors are concerned about the credit safety of other fixed-income security investments, they generally seek refuge by buying U.S. government securities, causing their yields to drop and the differential between government and other securities to widen. For example, in mid-1974, bank certificates of deposit yielded as much as 300 basis points more than Treasury bills of similar maturity, as compared with a normal difference of 75 basis points for certificates of deposit versus Treasury bills. In many cases, such periods can provide selected bargains in the form of higher-than-normal-yielding investments, but the venturesome investor must exercise caution and analysis when investing in nongovernment securities under such conditions. However, the average investor generally does not have the time or resources needed to separate *real* credit risks from *apparent* ones, and if in doubt, he would be wise

FIGURE 6-1. *Yields on U.S. government securities. (By permission of the Board of Governors of the Federal Reserve System.)*

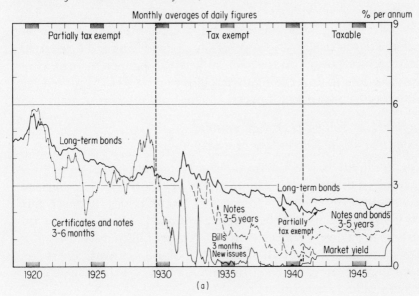

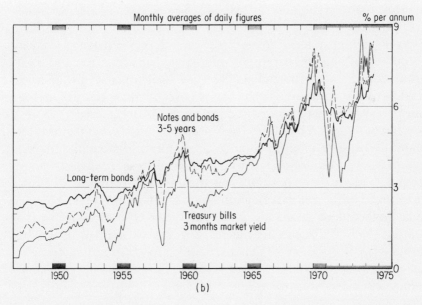

to play it safe until any concerns over widespread (or even specific) credit risks have been allayed.

Second, if corporations, municipalities, or Federal Agencies happen to be raising large amounts of new capital relative to their own and the United States government's normal supply of securities, prices on corporate, municipal, or Federal Agency securities may have to weaken, thus raising their yields relative to U.S. government securities, to attract new buyers.

Buying and Selling U.S. Government Securities in the Secondary Market

As mentioned earlier, the overall marketability of U.S. government securities is unparalleled. However, the investor should be conscious of how dealers' positions and attitudes can influence the marketability of specific sectors of the government market. For example, on a particular day, very-short-maturity Treasury bills may be quite difficult to buy in size, or the market in a very-long-maturity government bond may be thin and good for only the bid or offered side of the dealer's price quotation.

While many of the publicly traded U.S. government security issues are listed on the New York Stock Exchange, almost all secondary-market trading is done in the over-the-counter market, primarily composed of approximately 25 commercial bank and nonbank dealers who trade with the public and with each other. A list of these dealers is contained in Table 6-1. These primary dealers are the only firms allowed to trade directly with the Federal Reserve System when it is acting on behalf of the Federal Open Market Committee. In addition, several large commercial banks and securities brokerage firms who do not report to the Federal Reserve are also active in government securities. Odd-lot trades in government securities can also be done on the American Stock Exchange. When dealing in U.S. government securities, or in any other type of issue for that matter, the investor should select a brokerage firm or bank which is accustomed to trading in that particular type of security. Government securities dealers rely on short-term borrowings to finance their securities inventories. This high ratio of loans and repurchase agreements to capital for nonbank dealers is possible because vir-

TABLE 6-1   List of the Government Securities Dealers Reporting to the Market Statistics Division of the Federal Reserve Bank of New York

Bank of America NT & SA	First National Bank of Chicago
Bankers Trust Company	First National City Bank
A. G. Becker & Co.,	First Pennco Securities, Inc.
Incorporated	Goldman, Sachs & Co.
Briggs, Schaedle & Co., Inc.	Harris Trust and Savings Bank
The Chase Manhattan Bank,	Aubrey G. Lanston & Co., Inc.
N.A.	Merrill Lynch Government Securities Inc.
Chemical Bank	Morgan Guaranty Trust Company of New York
Continental Illinois National	New York Hanseatic Corporation
Bank and Trust Company of	The Northern Trust Company
Chicago	John Nuveen & Co., Incorporated
Discount Corporation of New	Wm. E. Pollock & Co., Inc.
York	Chas. E. Quincey & Co.
Donaldson Lufkin & Jenrette	Salomon Brothers
Securities Corporation	Second District Securities Co., Inc.
The First Boston Corporation	United California Bank

Note: This list has been compiled and made available for statistical purposes only and has no significance with respect to other relationships between dealers and the Federal Reserve Bank of New York. Qualification for the reporting list is based on the achievement and maintenance of reasonable standards of activity.

Market Statistics Division
Federal Reserve Bank of New York

tually all borrowing utilizes the government securities as collateral, thereby lessening the chances of loss for the lender.

Dealers' borrowing practices to finance their positions can give rise to profits or losses resulting from the difference between the interest *earned* from their inventories and the interest *paid* on loans to carry these inventories. A "positive carry" occurs when interest rates earned from the dealer's position exceeds the interest paid to finance that position, and a "negative carry" happens when the interest paid to finance the inventory exceeds the interest earned from holding the securities.

Government securities dealers usually do not charge a commission for buy or sell orders on round lots (lots of securities having a par value of $100,000 or multiples of $100,000). On trades under

$100,000 in size, certain odd-lot charges may be levied which have the effect of reducing the investor's overall rate of return earned from holding the security (for example, $20 for up to $20,000 in Treasury bills). Regardless of the size of the trade, if the investor keeps his government securities at a bank or securities brokerage firm, a custody fee or a transaction charge may be assessed. The larger the par value involved in the trade, the lower the reductive effect on the total return earned by the investor. It should be remembered that on small trades, custody fees and odd-lot charges can significantly influence the overall investment yield. For example, if a $10,000 par value 91-day Treasury bill were purchased in the secondary market at a price of $9,800 (resulting in an annualized interest rate of 8 percent), a $20 odd-lot (less than $100,000 par value) charge plus a $30 custody charge per investment will effectively reduce the return by $50, or one-quarter of the $200 discount—lowering the annualized interest rate to the 6 percent level.

Settlement on odd-lot transactions in government securities generally takes 5 business days. Round-lot transactions usually settle on the next business day following the day of the trade. In special cases, arrangements can be made for settlement on the same day as the trade (called a "cash" settlement), or on a delayed basis, such as "skip day" settlement, which takes place 2 business days following trade date. In buying and selling securities, the investor should be aware of the applicable settlement period, so that sales and purchases can be timed to settle on the same date. Otherwise, the investor may come up short when payment has to be made for securities purchased, or his funds may remain idle when they should be earning a return after a particular investment has been liquidated. The investor should also be cognizant of his obligation to effect timely delivery of securities he has sold. Most government securities are delivered to the buyer (or to the buyer's agent) (1) by messenger or in person, (2) with a draft attached which must be paid when the securities are received, or (3) through the Federal Reserve System's telegraphic transfer network. Each of these methods may entail certain costs, and the investor should check with his securities broker or commercial bank to find out the means of delivering securities with the greatest efficiency and least possible cost.

The Various Types of U.S. Government Securities

As of early 1975, the United States government had about $377 billion outstanding in publicly issued securities. This total is divided into two categories: (1) nonmarketable, or non-freely tradable, issues, which, among other issues, include $64 billion in the form of Series E and Series H savings bonds and (2) marketable, or freely tradable, issues, which comprise $121 billion in Treasury bills, $132 billion in Treasury notes, and $33 billion in Treasury bonds.

The wide variety of securities the government can issue gives the Treasury flexibility in structuring the maturity pattern of its debt. At the same time, however, constraints exist on the type of securities which can be brought to market in a given interest rate environment. One example stems from Congressionally imposed interest rate ceilings on government bonds. When market yields are above the specific ceiling, it becomes very difficult, if not impossible, to issue government bonds. For this reason, during the past 10 years, the Treasury has had to issue large amounts of shorter-maturity securities not subject to the interest ceilings, such as bills and notes, when it needed additional capital. This has effectively reduced the average maturity of marketable government debt from 5 years and 4 months in 1965 to 3 years as of early 1975. Of $286 billion in public marketable debt outstanding at that time, $149 billion was due within 1 year, $87 billion was due between 1 and 5 years, $28 billion in 5 to 10 years, $15 billion in 10 to 20 years, and $7 billion in over 20 years. In view of the constraints under which it operates, the Treasury Department has done an admirable job of designing imaginative ways of financing the operations of the United States government. Some of these new techniques, as well as the conventional forms of raising money, will be reviewed in the following paragraphs.

Savings bonds As of May 1975, the Treasury was offering two types of savings bonds. The first type, Series E, provides an effective yield of 6 percent through a steady gain in the cash value of the bond as it approaches a 5-year maturity. The initial purchase price for any denomination of Series E bond is 75 percent of its final maturity value, and the price the Treasury will pay if it is turned in for cash by the investor goes up in increments every 6 months. Series E bonds cannot be turned in for cash until 2 months after they were originally purchased, and if the investor turns in a Series E bond for cash prior to maturity, his effective return works out to *less* than the 6 percent received if held until maturity.

The second type of savings bond, called Series H, has a 10-year maturity and pays interest semiannually—5.6 percent per year for the first 5 years and 6.5 percent per year for the last 5 years. Series H bonds can be turned in at the investor's option for the full cash amount of their face value any time after 6 months from the date of original purchase. If redeemed prior to maturity, Series H bonds return somewhat less than their stated interest rate.

Savings bonds of the United States government have several advantages. They can be purchased in very small amounts—in as small as $25 denominations for Series E issues and with a $500 minimum for Series H issues. No commission is paid to purchase a savings bond, and the Series E and H bonds are available at any Federal Reserve bank or branch, as well as directly from the U.S. Treasury. Series E savings bonds can also be bought at some post offices and at commercial banks. They provide an attractive yield with protection against interest rate fluctuations which cause price changes in other types of fixed-income securities—since the redemption value is fixed, no capital loss is incurred even if interest rates rise. Savings bonds are noncallable. If market yields drop during the life of the savings bonds, the Treasury cannot redeem them before maturity, even though the Treasury can, as it has done several times in the past to reflect current interest rate levels, alter the rate of interest earned on *newly purchased* savings bonds.

Series E and H savings bonds are available in registered form only and cannot be bought by commercial banks acting for their own account. All other investors can buy a maximum of only $10,000 worth of each series in each year. Interest on both types of savings bonds is exempt from state and local income taxes, and if Series E bonds are held for their entire 5-year life, investors can elect to postpone federal income taxes on the gain in principal amount until final maturity.

Series E bonds can be exchanged into Series H issues (but not vice versa) at any time during their life, and Series E bonds also offer the investor an option of automatically extending the maturity for up to 10, 20, or 30 years after their original maturity, with interest rates set in accordance with prevailing interest rate levels prior to the start of each 10-year period.

Treasury bills Treasury bills are U.S. government obligations with an initial maturity of 1 year or less. Each week, $2.5 billion worth of Treasury bills (also known as "T bills") are currently offered with a maturity of 91 days (also called the 13-week, or 3-month, bill), and $1.8 billion worth of T bills are currently offered with a maturity of 182 days (also called the 26-week, or 6-month, bill). Once a month, $1.8 billion worth of Treasury bills are currently offered with a 52-week (also called the 1-year bill) maturity. At its discretion, the Treasury can introduce new maturities of bills or its can vary the frequency and size of specific bill offerings. For example, the Treasury has conducted regular offerings of 9-month bills at certain times in the past, and it currently issues specialized types of bills, called "strip offerings" and "tax anticipation bills," on a periodic basis.

Investors can thus have a choice of bills for a wide variety of maturity dates, either by purchasing already outstanding bills (which move a week closer to maturity each week) in the secondary market—this will be discussed later on in this chapter—or by buying newly issued bills in one of the regular Treasury offerings. If an investor decides to purchase newly issued bills, an order can be placed through a commercial bank, which normally charges a fee for placing the investor's order, effectively reducing the rate of return earned on the investment. One way of purchasing newly offered T bills which saves commission charges or fees is to buy them directly from a main office or branch office of the Federal Reserve Bank, which serves as the Treasury's agent in bill offerings. Only new bills can be purchased at the Federal Reserve. Bills which have been issued previously have to be purchased in the secondary securities markets.

The following paragraphs describe the general procedures for investors to follow in buying Treasury bills, as of early 1975. These guidelines may vary from one Federal Reserve district to another, and they may be changed from time to time by the Treasury or the Federal Reserve bank or branch in the investor's district of residence. If the investor has questions on the practices to follow in buying, redeeming, or exchanging Treasury bills (as well as U.S. government bonds or notes), he should call or write the Public Information Department or the Government Bond Division of the nearest Federal Reserve bank or branch.

Since early 1970, the minimum purchase requirement for Treasury bills has been $10,000, and purchases over that amount have to be in multiples of $5,000. T bills come in six denominations, ranging from $10,000 to $1 million, and they are issued in bearer form only. This means that Treasury bills must be as carefully protected as cash, since the Treasury is not responsible if an investor's bills are lost or stolen. New T bills are sold on an auction basis conducted every week through the Federal Reserve banks (a list of the addresses of the 12 district Federal Reserve banks is contained in Chapter 15; by contacting the nearest district bank, the investor should be able to find out the nearest Federal Reserve bank or branch nearest his own home). Since T bills are non-interest-bearing securities, to earn a return, investors bid prices lower than the bills' face value, which is paid in full at maturity. The investor's interest return is the difference between the purchase price for the bills and (1) the face value of the bills paid off at maturity or (2) the sale price of the bills if they are sold before maturity. When held to maturity, a quick way to calculate the approximate return on the bills is to divide the amount of the discount by the purchase price and then divide it by the fraction of a year represented by the bill's maturity. For example, if the discount on a $10,000 6-month bill is $400, the purchase price is $10,000 minus $400, or $9,600, and $400 divided by $9,600 equals 0.0417 (4.17 percent). This number is then *divided by* $6/12$ (which is the same as multiplying it by $12/6$, or 2) to produce an approximate *annualized* discount rate return during the 6-month period of 0.0834 (or 8.34 percent).

The weekly auctions for new 3-month and 6-month bills are held each Monday (or on the Friday before if Monday is a bank holiday). The monthly auction date for new 12-month bills is announced in the business section of the newspaper several days prior to the auction. Bids can be submitted by mail or in person between 9 A.M. and 3 P.M. at a Federal Reserve bank or branch during the week preceding the auction. All bids must be in by 1:30 P.M. Eastern time on the day of the auction (Mondays for the 3-month and 6-month bills). If the bid arrives too late for the regular weekly auction, it is held for the next week's auction unless the bidder indicates he wants his money returned. Late bids for the monthly auctions of 52-week bills are automatically returned to the bidder.

Bill auction results are reported in the newspapers on the day after the auction. On Tuesday following the Monday auction, investors can begin trading in the newly offered bills, on a *when-issued* basis, even though the bills are dated and become available on Thursday of the same week. The Treasury announces the lowest bid price accepted (which is the highest discount from par value), and if the investor bid *competitively,* he will know from his own bid whether it was accepted or not. If the investor bid *noncompetitively,* the amount of his discount is the *average* discount rate accepted in that auction. The newspaper also lists the *coupon-equivalent* rate of the average bids' discount rate. As we saw in Chapter 4, the coupon-equivalent rate represents the investor's true rate of return and is higher than the average discount rate.

What determines whether an investor's bid (also called a *tender*) is accepted at the Treasury's auction? Just as at any other type of auction, if someone's bid is too low relative to all the other competing bids, it will not be accepted by the Treasury. Remember that many other banks, securities firms, and investors are also bidding for the T bills, and their bidding competition actually determines the yield on the bills, in a true free-market process. If bidders think T bill yields should be a shade higher this week than last week, they will bid at lower prices. But some investors may have different thoughts and bid higher prices, thus edging the lower price bidder out of acquiring any bills on that week's auction. Bid prices are expressed as percentages of par to three decimal places, e.g., 98.500. A sample *competitive* tender form for 91-day Treasury bills is shown in Figure 6-2.

Instead of submitting a competitive tender, the individual can

FIGURE 6-2. *Sample of a specific competitive tender form for 91-day Treasury bill.**
(By permission of the Federal Reserve Bank of New York.)

(Closing date for receipt of this tender is Monday, January 6, 1975)

TENDER FOR 91-DAY TREASURY BILLS

Additional Amount, Series Dated October 10, 1974, Maturing April 10, 1975

(To Be Issued January 9, 1975)

To FEDERAL RESERVE BANK OF NEW YORK,   Dated at ....
Fiscal Agent of the United States.
...., 1974

Pursuant to the provisions of Treasury Department Circular No. 418 (current revision) and to the provisions of the public notice issued by the Treasury Department inviting tenders for the above-described Treasury bills, the undersigned hereby offers to purchase such Treasury bills in the amount indicated below, and agrees to make payment therefor at your Bank on or before the issue date at the price indicated-below:

COMPETITIVE TENDER | *Do not fill in both Competitive and Noncompetitive tenders on one form* | **NONCOMPETITIVE TENDER**

$..................................... (maturity value), $..................................... (maturity value)
or any lesser amount that may be awarded.   *(Not to exceed $200,000 for the bidder through all sources)*

Price: ....per 100.
(Price must be expressed with not more than three decimal places, for example, 99.925)
At the average price of accepted competitive bids.

Subject to allotment, please issue, deliver, and accept payment for the bills as indicated below:

Pieces	Denomination	Maturity value			
	$ 10,000		☐ 1. Deliver over the counter to the undersigned	Payment will be made as follows: ☐ By charge to our reserve account	
	15,000		☐ 2. Ship to the undersigned	☐ By cash or check in *immediately available funds* on delivery	
	50,000		☐ 3. Hold in safekeeping (for member bank only) in—	*(Payment cannot be made through Treasury Tax and Loan Account)*	
	100,000		☐ Investment Account	☐ 5. Special instructions:	
	500,000		☐ General Account		
	1,000,000		☐ Trust Account		
	Totals		☐ 4. Allotment transfer (see list attached)		
			(No changes in delivery instructions will be accepted)		

The undersigned (member bank) hereby certifies that the Treasury bills which you are hereby instructed to dispose of in the manner indicated in item 3 above are owned solely by the undersigned.

┌─────────────┐
│ *Insert tender* │   ....
│ *in special envelope* │   (Name of subscriber—please print or type)
│ *marked "Tender for* │   ....
│ *Treasury Bills"* │   (Address—please print or type)
└─────────────┘
     (Tel. No.)   (Signature of subscriber or authorized signature)
     ....
     (Title of authorized signer)

(Banking institutions submitting tenders for customer account must list customers' names on lines below or on an attached rider)

....
(Name of Customer)   (Name of Customer)

INSTRUCTIONS:
1. No tender for less than $10,000 will be considered, and each tender must be for an even multiple of $5,000 (maturity value).

2. Only banking institutions, and dealers who make primary markets in Government securities and report daily to this Bank their positions with respect to Government securities and borrowings thereon, may submit tenders for customer account; in doing so, they may consolidate competitive tenders *at the same price* and may consolidate noncompetitive tenders, provided a list is attached showing the name of each bidder and the amount bid for his account. Others will not be permitted to submit tenders except for their own account.

3. If the person making the tender is a corporation, the tender should be signed by an officer of the corporation authorized to make the tender, and the signing of the tender by an officer of the corporation will be construed as a representation by him that he has been so authorized. If the tender is made by a partnership, it should be signed by a member of the firm, who should sign in the form "..................................., a copartnership, by ...., a member of the firm."

4. Tenders will be received without deposit from incorporated banks and trust companies and from responsible and recognized dealers in investment securities. Tenders from others must be accompanied by payment of 2 percent of the face amount of Treasury bills applied for, unless the tenders are accompanied by an express guaranty of payment by an incorporated bank or trust company. All checks must be drawn to the order of the Federal Reserve Bank of New York; checks endorsed to this Bank will not be accepted.

5. If the language of this tender is changed in any respect. which, in the opinion of the Secretary of the Treasury, is material, the tender may be disregarded.

*When reviewing the above form, the investor should keep in mind that (1) it is solely for illustrative purposes and should not be used in lieu of the actual forms; (2) the specific layout of the form can be and is changed from time to time; (3) tender forms for Treasury bills of different maturities are slightly different from the 91-day Treasury bill form; (4) the form above is used by the New York Federal Reserve Bank—other Federal Reserve district banks print their own forms, and often they differ considerably from the ones used by the New York Federal Reserve; and (5) in some cases, additional forms may have to be filled out for a particular bid.

avoid the risk of not getting any bills if his bid is too low by submitting a noncompetitive tender. While there is no limit on the amount of bills which can be bought by competitive tender, noncompetitive tenders in any one name are limited to $200,000 for each new bill auction. The Treasury totals all noncompetitive bids and subtracts this amount from the total offering size. The Treasury then allocates the remainder to competitive bidders at their bid prices in descending sequence, with the highest bids accepted first. The lowest bid accepted is called the *stop-out price*. The Treasury determines the price charged to noncompetitive bidders by using an average price of all the tenders accepted at each bid price. A sample *noncompetitive* tender form for 3-month Treasury bills is shown in Figure 6-3. New 3- and 6-month bills are issued on the Thursday following the regular weekly auction (or on Friday if Thursday is a bank holiday). New 12-month bills are issued on the Tuesday following the specific auction date announced by the Treasury, or on Wednesday if that Tuesday is a bank holiday.

Bills can be paid for by submitting payment for the full face value of the bills with the tender in cash, certified personal check, or official bank check, or in Treasury bills maturing *on or before* the issue date of the new bills. When this last method is used, the Treasury mails the investor a discount check for the difference between the purchase price and the face value of the bills on the day the T bills are issued. For example, the investor would receive a check for $160 if the purchase price turned out to be $9,840 for a $10,000 face value bill.

Another way to pay for bills involves making a down payment of 2 percent of the face value of the bill ($200 on a $10,000 bill) together with the investor's tender, with the remaining payment of the purchase price (another $9,200 if the bills were bought at a price of $9,400) made on issue date. However, this remaining payment can be made on the issue date only if the funds are immediately collectible by the Treasury, that is, in the form of cash, Federal funds check, or in Treasury bills maturing on the issue date. If the investor chooses to make this remainder payment by certified personal check or by official bank check, it must be made at least 2 business days before the issue date so that the check can be cleared by the date of issue of the bills. If the final payment is not made in an acceptable

FIGURE 6-3. *Sample of a general noncompetitive tender form for 3-month Treasury bills.* *(By permission of the Federal Reserve Bank of New York.)*

GB 631 6/74

A-07915

NONCOMPETITIVE TENDER FOR 3 MONTH TREASURY BILLS

Date _____

Securities Department
Federal Reserve Bank of New York
33 Liberty Street
New York, N. Y. 10045

Gentlemen:

This noncompetive tender is submitted in the amount of $_____
                                                    $10,000 Minimum

for the next auction of 3 month Treasury bills.

Payment for the full face amount of the bills is enclosed in the form of:

☐   a certified personal check or a bank (cashier's) check payable to the Federal Reserve Bank of New York;

☐   cash;

☐   Treasury bills maturing on or before the issue date.

On issuance, the bills.

☐   should be mailed to the bidder;

☐   will be picked up by the bidder (See item #7 (Delivery of New Bills) in the Brochure "Basic Information on Treasury Bills".)

Where appropriate, all discount checks will be mailed to the bidder and no changes in delivery instructions will be accepted.

The bidder's name and complete address is:

_____
Name of Subscriber (Print)

_____

_____
Street

_____
City   State   Zip

_____
Telephone Number

_____
Bidder's Signature

FOR FEDERAL, RESERVE USE ONLY

Series dated   _____
Date issued   _____
Maturity date _____

Checks
_____

Cash
_____

Other
_____

_____

_____

GOVERNMENT BOND DIVISION

Teller _____

*See the footnote to Figure 6-2.

form by the issue date, the investor's tender will be cancelled and his partial payment subject to possible forfeiture to the Treasury.

Once purchased, bills cannot be left at a Federal Reserve bank or branch. If payment is made in *cash,* maturing Treasury bills, or Federal funds check, they can be picked up in person only by the buyer (or an agent with written authorization from the buyer, including a sample of the agent's signature in the buyer's authorization letter) between 11 A.M. and 3 P.M. on the next business day after the issue date or from 9 A.M. to 3 P.M. during any of the next 5 business days. If payment is made by *official bank check or certified personal check,* bills can be picked up in person (or by an agent, under the conditions mentioned above) from 9 A.M. to 3 P.M. on the *third through eighth* business day after issue date. If the investor does not choose to pick up his bills in person or through an authorized agent, they can be sent to the investor by registered, insured, first class mail, and they become the investor's responsibility once delivery is accepted. Delivery time can take anywhere from 2 to 4 weeks. However the investor indicates he wants his bills when he submits his tender form to the Securities Department of the Federal Reserve bank or branch, these instructions cannot be changed once they have been made.

Bills cannot be cashed at the Federal Reserve or the Treasury Department prior to maturity. If the investor wishes to convert his bills to cash, he would normally sell them in the secondary trading market through a securities broker or commercial bank. As mentioned earlier, when bills mature, they can be used to pay for new bills. A new discount check will be mailed from the Treasury to the investor on the issue date of the new bills, which can be picked up in the same manner as newly purchased bills are obtained. If the investor decides he needs his funds back when the Treasury bills mature, they should be presented at a Federal Reserve bank or branch (not at the Treasury) at least 2 days before maturity date and a Treasury check (not cash) will be issued, to be picked up by, or mailed to, the investor on the maturity date.

Income from Treasury bills is considered earned in the year the bills are redeemed or sold. Unlike other government securities, if bills are sold prior to maturity, any gain or loss is considered an ordinary gain or loss, regardless of whether they were held for a period greater than 6 months.

Treasury bill strips In the early 1960s the Treasury developed another method of auctioning bills which involves equal additions to each of several outstanding bill series. Tenders for a strip offering must be submitted for the entire series. For example, in May of 1974 the Treasury auctioned an $800 million strip of bills, consisting of $100 million additions to each of eight outstanding weekly series of T bills maturing from September 19 through November 7. Since the minimum purchase of a Treasury bill is $10,000, a minimum tender for the strip in this example would consist of $80,000, with larger tenders in multiples of $40,000. One-eighth of the total amount tendered by each investor was applied equally to each of the maturing bills. Since a strip comprises more than one maturity, it is somewhat more difficult to price a tender in a strip offering than in a regular T bill offering.

Tax anticipation bills Tax anticipation bills, generally referred to as TABs, were designed to help the Treasury smooth out its uneven flow of funds and to attract the funds which corporations set aside for their income tax payments. These bills are issued irregularly, and they generally mature 7 days after corporate quarterly income tax payment dates. They can be turned in at face value when taxes are paid, thus giving the holder an extra week's interest. If not used for paying taxes, TABs are redeemable at face value upon maturity, just like any other T bills. For example, if a 6.0 percent *discount* TAB with 130 days to final maturity were used at face value in the payment of taxes 1 week prior to maturity, the investor's actual effective *coupon equivalent yield* would jump from 6.21 to 6.56 percent.

The principal bidders in the auctions for TABs are the commercial banks, since they can thus obtain the U.S. Treasury as a depositor at their bank. This happens because the banks can pay for the TABs they purchase at auction merely by crediting all or a part of the price to a special Treasury account at the bank, called a *Treasury tax and loan account*. These accounts were set up to leave a portion of tax collections on deposit at Federal Reserve member banks in a particular region of the country, rather than transferring the funds to the Treasury's account at the Federal Reserve Bank in Washington. The latter action would abnormally contract the money supply since tax payments are generally drawn out of corporations' and individuals' bank accounts. This would tend to cause interest rates to rise abnormally around tax payment dates. Corporations and other nonbank investors who wish to buy TABs can purchase them at a better price by purchasing them in the secondary trading market rather than bidding against the banks in the TAB auctions.

Treasury bill price quotations   In both initial offerings and in secondary-market trading of all types of Treasury bills, bill prices are quoted in terms of their annualized discount rate, rather than in terms of their dollar price. Thus, the investor might see a T bill quotation among a series of bill price quotes in the newspaper such as the following:

Nov. 19. . . . . 8.16   7.94   +2   8.35

The above quotation was taken from the newspaper of Tuesday, June 11, 1974, and contained prices as of 3:30 P.M. on Monday, June 10, 1974. The daily government securities prices published in the newspaper reflect the average closing quotations of five major dealer firms as submitted to the Federal Reserve Board at 3:30 P.M. each business day. The date, November 19, indicates the maturity of the bills, and the 8.16 indicates the discount rate which results from the *bid* prices which dealers will pay to *buy* the November 19 bills from investors. The 7.94 indicates the discount rate resulting from the *offered* price at which dealers will *sell* the bills to investors (any odd-lot charges are not included in the newspaper price quotes, which are for round-lot transactions). What would the actual dollar buying and selling prices for the November 19 bills be?

Dollar prices for bills, when the discount rate is known. can be worked out according to the following formula:

$$\text{Dollar price per \$10,000 bill} = \$10,000 - \left(\begin{array}{c} \text{discount rate} \\ \text{in basis points} \end{array} \times \begin{array}{c} \text{days to} \\ \text{maturity} \end{array} \times \$0.00277778 \right)$$

The \$0.00277778 number is the value of 1 basis point in cents per day for a $10,000 Treasury bill. In general, when computing the number of days between two dates, the first day should be *excluded* and the last day *included*. This method gives 162 days remaining from June 10 (the day of the quotation) until November 19 (the day of final maturity for the T bill issue quoted). The formula for the *bid* price then becomes:

$10,000 − (816 basis points × $0.00277778 × 162 days) = $9,632.80

Thus, $9,632.80 is the price the investor would receive if he sold the November 19 bills to a dealer at an 8.16 percent discount on June 10, 1974.

Using the same formula, the offered price (per $10,000 face value) at which the dealer would sell the November 19 T bills to an investor works out to $9,642.70. As we learned in Chapter 3, the dealer's compensation comes from the difference between the prices at which the dealer firm *buys* securities *from* the investor and *sells* them *to* other dealers or investors. In this case, the dealer's compensation, or spread, works out to $9,642.70 − $9,632.80, or $9.90 per $10,000 Treasury bill.

The +2 in the newspaper price quotation means that the bid price of the November 19 T bills changed by 2 basis points, or from an 8.14 percent bid discount rate to an 8.16 percent bid discount rate, from the previous business day to the day of the quotation. Since prices decline when yields rise, this means that these T bills dropped slightly in the price which dealers would buy them from investors. Exactly how much in dollar terms did these November 19 bills change in price? The investor could laboriously perform the calculations outlined above, using 8.14 percent (814 basis points) as the bid rate and then subtracting the price at an 8.16 percent rate to find the price change, but there is a quicker way. If the investor knows the number of days remaining to maturity of the bill, by referring to Table 6-2 he can find out the dollar value of *any* particular basis-point change. In our example, with a bill having 162 days remaining to maturity, a 1-basis-point change in price results in a dollar price change of $0.45. Thus, a 2-basis-point *increase* in the discount interest rate results in a 2 × $0.45 = $0.90 price *decrease* in the price of a $10,000 November 19 T bill. If the newspaper had instead showed a basis-point change of −15 from the previous day's quotation for the

TABLE 6-2 Dollar Value of 1-Basis-Point Discount (for a $10,000 principal value Treasury bill)

Days to mat.	Dollar value of 1 basis pt	Days to mat.	Dollar value of 1 basis pt	Days to mat.	Dollar value of 1 basis pt	Days to mat.	Dollar value of 1 basis pt	Days to mat.	Dollar value of 1 basis pt	Days to mat.	Dollar value of 1 basis pt
1	$.0028	62	$.1722	123	$.3417	184	$.5111	245	$.6806	306	$.8500
2	.0056	63	.1750	124	.3444	185	.5139	246	.6833	307	.8528
3	.0083	64	.1778	125	.3472	186	.5167	247	.6861	308	.8556
4	.0111	65	.1806	126	.3500	187	.5194	248	.6889	309	.8583
5	.0139	66	.1833	127	.3528	188	.5222	249	.6917	310	.8611
6	.0167	67	.1861	128	.3556	189	.5250	250	.6944	311	.8639
7	.0194	68	.1889	129	.3583	190	.5278	251	.6972	312	.8667
8	.0222	69	.1917	130	.3611	191	.5306	252	.7000	313	.8694
9	.0250	70	.1944	131	.3639	192	.5333	253	.7028	314	.8722
10	.0278	71	.1972	132	.3667	193	.5361	254	.7056	315	.8750
11	.0306	72	.2000	133	.3694	194	.5389	255	.7083	316	.8778
12	.0333	73	.2028	134	.3722	195	.5417	256	.7111	317	.8806
13	.0361	74	.2056	135	.3750	196	.5444	257	.7139	318	.8833
14	.0389	75	.2083	136	.3778	197	.5472	258	.7167	319	.8861
15	.0417	76	.2111	137	.3806	198	.5500	259	.7194	320	.8889
16	.0444	77	.2139	138	.3833	199	.5528	260	.7222	321	.8917
17	.0472	78	.2167	139	.3861	200	.5556	261	.7250	322	.8944
18	.0500	79	.2194	140	.3889	201	.5583	262	.7278	323	.8972
19	.0528	80	.2222	141	.3917	202	.5611	263	.7306	324	.9000
20	.0556	81	.2250	142	.3944	203	.5639	264	.7333	325	.9028
21	.0583	82	.2278	143	.3972	204	.5667	265	.7361	326	.9056
22	.0611	83	.2306	144	.4000	205	.5694	266	.7389	327	.9083
23	.0639	84	.2333	145	.4028	206	.5722	267	.7417	328	.9111
24	.0667	85	.2361	146	.4056	207	.5750	268	.7444	329	.9139
25	.0694	86	.2389	147	.4083	208	.5778	269	.7472	330	.9167
26	.0722	87	.2417	148	.4111	209	.5806	270	.7500	331	.9194
27	.0750	88	.2444	149	.4139	210	.5833	271	.7528	332	.9222
28	.0778	89	.2472	150	.4167	211	.5861	272	.7556	333	.9250
29	.0806	90	.2500	151	.4194	212	.5889	273	.7583	334	.9278
30	.0833	91	.2528	152	.4222	213	.5917	274	.7611	335	.9306
31	.0861	92	.2556	153	.4250	214	.5944	275	.7639	336	.9333
32	.0889	93	.2583	154	.4278	215	.5972	276	.7667	337	.9361
33	.0917	94	.2611	155	.4306	216	.6000	277	.7694	338	.9389
34	.0944	95	.2639	156	.4333	217	.6028	278	.7722	339	.9417
35	.0972	96	.2667	157	.4361	218	.6056	279	.7750	340	.9444
36	.1000	97	.2694	158	.4389	219	.6083	280	.7778	341	.9472
37	.1028	98	.2722	159	.4417	220	.6111	281	.7806	342	.9500
38	.1056	99	.2750	160	.4444	221	.6139	282	.7833	343	.9528
39	.1083	100	.2778	161	.4472	222	.6167	283	.7861	344	.9556
40	.1111	101	.2806	162	.4500	223	.6194	284	.7889	345	.9583
41	.1139	102	.2833	163	.4528	224	.6222	285	.7917	346	.9611
42	.1167	103	.2861	164	.4556	225	.6250	286	.7944	347	.9639
43	.1194	104	.2889	165	.4583	226	.6278	287	.7972	348	.9667
44	.1222	105	.2917	166	.4611	227	.6306	288	.8000	349	.9694
45	.1250	106	.2944	167	.4639	228	.6333	289	.8028	350	.9722
46	.1278	107	.2972	168	.4667	229	.6361	290	.8056	351	.9750
47	.1306	108	.3000	169	.4694	230	.6389	291	.8083	352	.9778
48	.1333	109	.3028	170	.4722	231	.6417	292	.8111	353	.9806
49	.1361	→110	.3056	171	.4750	232	.6444	293	.8139	354	.9833
50	.1389	111	.3083	172	.4778	233	.6472	294	.8167	355	.9861
51	.1417	112	.3111	173	.4806	234	.6500	295	.8194	356	.9889
52	.1444	113	.3139	174	.4833	235	.6528	296	.8222	357	.9917
53	.1472	114	.3167	175	.4861	236	.6556	297	.8250	358	.9944
54	.1500	115	.3194	176	.4889	237	.6583	298	.8278	359	.9972
55	.1528	116	.3222	177	.4917	238	.6611	299	.8306	360	1.0000
56	.1556	117	.3250	178	.4944	239	.6639	300	.8333	361	1.0028
57	.1583	118	.3278	179	.4972	240	.6667	301	.8361	362	1.0056
58	.1611	119	.3306	180	.5000	241	.6694	302	.8389	363	1.0083
59	.1639	120	.3333	181	.5028	242	.6722	303	.8417	364	1.0111
60	.1667	121	.3361	182	.5056	243	.6750	304	.8444	365	1.0139
61	.1694	122	.3389	183	.5083	244	.6778	305	.8472	366	1.0167

EXAMPLE: If a $10,000 T bill with 110 days remaining to maturity *rises* 10 basis points in yield, the dollar price will *decline* by $3.06 (10 basis points × $0.3056 = $3.056). To use this table for T bill investments over $10,000, merely multiply the result by the number of times $10,000 goes into your investment. In the above example, $40,000 worth of T bills would *decline* in price by 4 × $3.056 = $12.22 for a 10-basis-point rise in yield.

November 19 bill, this would have meant that the November 19 bill price *rose* by 15 × $0.45 = $6.75 per $10,000 bill. The investor should remember that, with each passing day, T bills move closer to maturity. Accordingly, when using the table on the preceding page to calculate price changes on T bills, the investor must always compute the number of days remaining to maturity before multiplying the basis-point change by a factor to obtain the dollar price change.

The final number in the sample newspaper quotation is 8.35, which gives the true bond equivalent yield (annualized to a 365-day yearly basis rather than the 360 days used in T bill discount quotations). If the investor had paid a discount rate of 7.94 percent for the November 19 bills, his bond equivalent yield works out to be 8.35 percent, and it is this rate which should be used in comparing Treasury bill yields to bonds, savings account interest rates, or any other type of security paying a semiannual coupon interest rate. When the discount rate is known, the true bond equivalent yield can be computed according to the following formula:

$$\text{True bond equivalent yield} = \frac{365 \times \text{the discount yield rate}}{360 - (\text{discount yield rate} \times \text{days to maturity})}$$

As an example of how this formula works, assume that the discount yield rate on a 91-day newly offered T bill is 5.00 percent, What is the true bond equivalent yield? The following formula gives the answer:

$$\text{True bond equivalent yield} = \frac{365 \times 0.05}{360 - (0.05 \times 91)} = \frac{18.25}{360 - 4.5} = \frac{18.25}{355.5} = 5.13 \text{ percent}$$

The true bond equivalent yield is higher than the discount yield, 5.13 percent versus 5 percent. This will be true in all cases. Table 6-2 relates various discount yields to their bond equivalent yields.

It can be seen from Table 6-3 that the higher the discount yield rate is, the greater the effective addition to the discount yield to arrive at the bond equivalent yield. For example, at a 2.00 percent discount yield, the difference between it and the bond equivalent yield on a T bill with 91 days remaining to maturity is 4 basis points

TABLE 6-3 Discount Yields Converted into Bond Equivalent Yields

Discount yield, %	Bond equivalent yields for maturity, %			
	30 days	91 days	182 days	364 days
2.00	2.03	2.04	2.05	2.07
2.50	2.54	2.55	2.57	2.60
3.00	3.05	3.07	3.09	3.11
3.50	3.56	3.58	3.61	3.65
4.00	4.07	4.10	4.14	4.18
4.50	4.58	4.61	4.67	4.73
5.00	5.09	5.13	5.20	5.27
5.50	5.60	5.65	5.74	5.82
6.00	6.11	6.18	6.27	6.38
6.50	6.63	6.70	6.81	6.94
7.00	7.14	7.22	7.36	7.50
7.50	7.65	7.75	7.90	8.07
8.00	8.17	8.28	8.45	8.82
8.50	8.68	8.81	9.01	9.43
9.00	9.19	9.34	9.56	10.04

(2.04 percent minus 2.00 percent), but at a 9.00 percent discount yield, the difference between it and the bond equivalent yield has grown to 34 basis points (9.34 percent minus 9.00 percent).

Also, the greater the amount of time remaining to maturity, the larger the difference between the bond equivalent yield and the discount yield. For instance, with 30 days remaining to maturity on a T bill, the difference between the discount yield rate and the bond equivalent yield rate is 11 basis points for a Treasury bill quoted at a 6.00 percent yield (6.11 percent minus 6.00 percent), whereas with 364 days remaining to maturity at the same 6.00 percent discount yield level, the difference has widened to 38 basis points (6.38 percent minus 6.00 percent).

The practical effect of the foregoing discussion is that the higher the general level of interest rates and the longer the T bill has to run until maturity, the greater the difference between the bond equivalent yield and the discount yield. The investor can get a rough idea of the bond equivalent yield for discount yield levels and remaining maturity periods not contained in Table 6-3 by approximating the differences between the actual quotation and the ones in the table, or by using the formula mentioned earlier to find the true bond equivalent yield.

In the secondary market for Treasury bill trading, most of the activity is concentrated in the most recently offered 13-week bills and 26-week bills. As a result, price quotation spreads are generally narrowest on T bills of these two maturities each week. On the other non-13 or 26-week bills, and on bills with between a 52-week and a 26-week maturity, price quotation spreads between the bid and offered side of the dealers' markets are wider and trading is much less active. Investors who can purchase T bills in sufficient quantity (so that transactions charges do not greatly affect the overall yield returns offered by the bills) and who can devote time to following and participating in the weekly Treasury auctions will find that the *new* 13- and 26-week bills are *generally priced slightly lower* than the already outstanding 13- and 26-week bills. It is thus possible to gain a few extra basis points in yield by continually switching into the newly offered bills, although this type of transaction generally has to be done in amounts well over $100,000 in size to cover transactions charges and to receive a decent bid on the bills being sold. For these reasons, smaller investors in most cases will not be able to invest in this manner, commonly referred to as the "bill roll."

As mentioned in Chapter 3, the investor should remember that it is best to invest in short-maturity securities when interest rates are expected to rise, and to lengthen the maturity of his investments when interest rates are expected to drop. This maneuver permits the investor to protect his capital from substantial price declines and then, if interest rates rise, to reinvest the proceeds of shorter-maturity securities at the higher interest rates once they mature. This principle not only implies that the investor will want to switch from longer-term bonds and notes into T bills or other short-term securities when interest rates are about to go up, but it also holds true for investments within the T bill market. From Table 6-2 it can be seen that if interest rates *rise* by 100 basis points, 90-day Treasury bills will *fall* in price by $25 per $10,000 par value, while a bill with 365 days to maturity will *fall* $101.39 per $10,000 par value— roughly four times as much as the 90-day bill for the same rise in interest rates. For the same reasons, when selecting a T bill, the investor should choose the longer-maturity bill if he feels confident that interest rates are going to fall in the T bill market.

Treasury coupon issues The Treasury issues publicly three types of securities which pay interest by the coupon method: (1) *Treasury certificates* (with a maturity up to 1 year), (2) *Treasury notes* (with a maturity between 1 and 7 years), and (3) *Treasury bonds* (generally with a maturity of over 5 years). Treasury notes and bonds are among the most broadly held and actively traded longer-term securities. Because of their absolute safety as to payment of interest and principal, yields on Treasury coupon issues run below yields on other taxable fixed-income securities of similar maturity. The amount of the yield spread depends on investors' preferences for safety and quality at a given point in time, changes in the supply of Treasury coupon securities versus changes in the supply of corporate, Federal Agency, and other bonds, and other factors. For instance, yields on government bonds have ranged from 20 basis points *lower* to over 180 basis points *lower* (meaning that prices have been higher) than yields on Aaa corporate bonds during the past 15 years.

Treasury *certificates* have not been offered to the public since 1967, when total certificates outstanding amounted to slightly over $5 billion. Since certificates cannot be used to pay taxes, their attractiveness to investors declined after TABs became more widely used. Also, the more frequent offerings of 52-week T bills since late 1963 contributed to the lessened use of certificates. Certificates are issued in bearer form only and come in six denominations ranging from $1,000 to $500,000. Income from Treasury certificates is exempt from state and local income taxes but not from federal income taxes. Generally, the marketing procedures for certificates are similar to those described below for Treasury notes and bonds.

As with Treasury bills, investors can purchase Treasury *notes* and *bonds* either on the initial offering (directly from the Federal Reserve or with a government securities dealer bidding on their behalf), or in the secondary trading market. New issues of Treasury notes and bonds are announced 1 to 3 weeks before their offering date. When the Treasury has decided on the exact size and maturity of the issues to be offered, an announcement is made on Wednesday afternoon and subscriptions for the securities are usually accepted beginning the following Monday and normally ending at 1:30 P.M. 2 days later.

Treasury bonds and notes are available in bearer or registered form. Interest payments, which are taxable for federal income tax purposes, but not for state and local tax returns, are made semiannually either by mailing a check to registered security holders, or by paying cash in return for coupons clipped and returned to any Federal Reserve bank or branch, or to any commercial bank. The minimum purchase for most Treasury bonds and notes is $1,000, and the bonds and notes come in denominations of $1,000, $5,000, $10,000, $100,000, and $1 million (the notes are also available in denominations of $100,000 and $500,000).

New issues of Treasury bonds and notes are brought to market in a variety of ways. Most frequently, the Treasury offers new securities in exchange for securities which are about to mature. Under this method, called *exchange refunding,* the investor can either turn in the maturing issue for cash or exchange the old securities for the same face amount of the new securities. The investor also has the option of selling his subscription rights for the new issue to others who wish to purchase the new issue, and if he has decided not to purchase the new issue, he should sell these rights in the marketplace rather than let them expire. These subscription rights are actively traded by the major government securities dealers from the Friday after the final terms of the offering are announced until the close of the offering on the following Wednesday.

The amount of the maturing issue which is turned in by investors for cash (called *attrition*) is of concern to the Treasury, since it is a gauge of the relative success of the exchange refunding. When interest rates are expected to rise, a high attrition rate may occur as investors wait for rates to rise (prices to fall) in order to purchase the new securities at a lower price sometime after the offering. To keep attrition to a low level, an intermediate-term note is generally offered with the new longer-maturity bond, so that investors will have a shorter-term investment alternative if they prefer not to invest in the new long-term issue.

The Treasury can also issue new securities in exchange for outstanding Treasury bonds and/or notes which are not immediately due to mature. This financing method, called *advance refunding,* has been frequently employed and gives the Treasury much latitude in timing new offerings of long-term debt, for periods when investor interest in such securities is favorable. Advance refundings sometimes allow the investor to exchange any one of up to ten outstanding bond or note issues (with anywhere from 1 to 10 years remaining to maturity) into several new issues which have ranged from 5 up to 40 years in maturity.

A variation of the exchange refunding involves the sale of a stated amount of securities directly for new cash, with the proceeds used to refund a maturing issue (called *cash refunding*). Of course, Treasury bonds and notes can also be sold directly for cash and the proceeds not used by the Treasury to refund any maturing issue. These two methods do not involve the use of subscription rights, and the Treasury normally sets a limit on the amount of bonds which can be purchased by any one investor.

As with Treasury bill auctions, in buying new issues of Treasury bonds or notes the investor can submit either a competitive or a noncompetitive tender, in multiples of $1,000, by mail or in person at the Federal Reserve no later than the end of the subscription period. Late subscriptions will not be accepted. Government securities dealers who submit tenders on behalf of others offer a convenient means of placing bids but generally charge individual investors a fee for this service, which effectively reduces the yield earned on the Treasury notes or bonds bought through a commercial bank. If the investor decides to save this commission fee and bid on his own, he can bid competitively by submitting a tender expressed to two decimal places on the basis of 100, for example, 100.00, or 99.50, or 100.50. Fractions may not be used, and often, a minimum tender price is stated. A sample of a specific tender form for a recent issue of U.S. Treasury notes has been included in Figure 6-4, and a sample of a general form for noncompetitive tenders for U.S. Treasury notes has been included in Figure 6-5. Forms used for U.S. Treasury bonds are similar to the ones used for U.S. Treasury notes.

Generally, the total amount of noncompetitive bonds or notes which can be tendered for by any one bidder is limited. Competitive tenders are selected by the Treasury at the close of the offering

FIGURE 6-4. *(a) Sample of a specific tender form for U.S. Treasury notes; (b) reverse side of sample of a specific tender form for U.S. Treasury notes.* * *(By permission of the Federal Reserve Bank of New York.)*

FORM NA-1

IMPORTANT — Closing time for receipt of this tender is 1:30 p.m., Thursday, January 2, 1975.

TENDER FOR 8 PERCENT TREASURY NOTES OF SERIES H-1976
ADDITIONAL AMOUNT
Dated April 9, 1974, With Interest From January 9, 1975, Due March 31, 1976

FEDERAL RESERVE BANK OF NEW YORK,
Fiscal Agent of the United States,
New York, N. Y. 10045

Dated at ....
............................, 19 . .

Pursuant to the provisions of Treasury Department Circular No. 17-74, Public Debt Series, dated December 23, 1974, the undersigned hereby offers to purchase United States of America 8 percent Treasury Notes of Series H-1976 in the amount indicated below, and agrees to make payment therefor at your Bank on or before the issue date at the price indicated below (plus accrued interest of $22.19780 per $1,000).

COMPETITIVE TENDER	*Do not fill in both Competitive and Noncompetitive tenders on one form*	NONCOMPETITIVE TENDER
$ _____ (maturity value), or any lesser amount that may be awarded.		$ _____ (maturity value) *(Not to exceed $500,000 for one bidder through all sources)*
Price: ___ per 100 (minimum of 99.76) *(Price must be expressed with not more than two decimal places, for example, 100.00)*		at the average price of accepted competitive bids.

Subject to allotment, please issue, deliver, and accept payment for the notes as indicated below and on the reverse side (if *registered notes are* desired, please also complete schedule on reverse side):

Pieces	Denomination	Maturity value			
	$ 1,000		☐ 1. Deliver over the counter to the undersigned		Payment will be made as follows:
	5,000		☐ 2. Ship to the undersigned ☐ 3. Hold in safekeeping (for member bank only) in —		☐ By charge to our reserve account ☐ By cash or check in *immediately available funds* on delivery
	10,000		☐ Investment Account		
	100,000		☐ General Account ☐ Trust Account		☐ 5. Special instructions:
	1,000,000		☐ 4. Hold as collateral for Treasury Tax and Loan Account*		
	Totals		*(No changes in delivery instructions will be accepted)*		

* The undersigned certifies that the allotted notes will be owned solely by the undersigned.

We hereby agree not to buy or to sell, or to make agreements with respect to the purchase or sale or other disposition of any notes of this issue at a specific rate or price, until after one-thirty p.m., Eastern Standard time, Thursday, January 2, 1975.

(If a commercial bank is subscribing for its own account or for account of customers, the following certifications are made a part of this tender.)

WE HEREBY CERTIFY that we have received tenders from our customers in the amounts set opposite the customers' names on the list which is made a part of this tender; that there has been paid to us by each such customer as required by the official offering circular, not subject to withdrawal until after allotment, not less than 5 percent of the amount bid for; that we have not made unsecured loans, or loans collateralized in whole or in part by the notes bid for, to supply the amounts of such payments to any of such customers; that we have no beneficial interest in the tenders of such customers; and that none of our customers has any beneficial interest in the amount bid for our own account.

WE FURTHER CERTIFY that tenders received by us, if any, from other commercial banks for their own account or for the account of their customers have been entered with us under the same conditions, agreements, and certifications as set forth in this form.

```
Insert this tender in
special envelope marked
"Tender for Treasury
Notes"
```

....
(Name of subscriber — please print or type)

....
(Address — incl. City and State)   (Tel. No.)

....
(Signature of subscriber or authorized signature)

....
(Title of authorized signer)

(Banking institutions submitting tenders for customer account must list customers' names on lines below or on an attached rider)

....
(Name of Customer)   (Name of Customer)

INSTRUCTIONS:

1. No tender for less than $5,000 will be considered; and each tender must be for a multiple of $1,000 (maturity value).

2. Only banking institutions, and dealers who make primary markets in Government securities and report daily to this Bank their positions with respect to Government securities and borrowings thereon, may submit tenders for customer account; in doing so, they may consolidate competitive tenders *at the same price* and may consolidate noncompetitive tenders, provided a list is attached showing the name of each bidder and the amount bid for his account. Others will not be permitted to submit tenders except for their own account.

3. If the person making the tender is a corporation, the tender should be signed by an officer of the corporation authorized to make the tender, and the signing of the tender by an officer of the corporation will be construed as a representation by him that he has been so authorized. If the tender is made by a partnership, it should be signed by a member of the firm, who should sign in the form "......................, a member of the firm."......................, a copartnership, by

4. Tenders will be received without deposit from commercial and other banks for their own account, Federally-insured savings and loan associations, States, political subdivisions or instrumentalities thereof, public pension and retirement and other public funds, international organizations in which the United States holds membership, foreign central banks and foreign States, dealers who make primary markets in Government securities and report daily to the Federal Reserve Bank of New York their positions with respect to Government securities and borrowings thereon, and Government accounts. Tenders from others must be accompanied by payment of 5 percent of the face amount of securities applied for. All checks must be drawn to the order of the Federal Reserve Bank of New York; checks endorsed to this Bank will not be accepted.

5. If the language of this tender is changed in any respect, which, in the opinion of the Secretary of the Treasury is material, the tender may be disregarded.

128

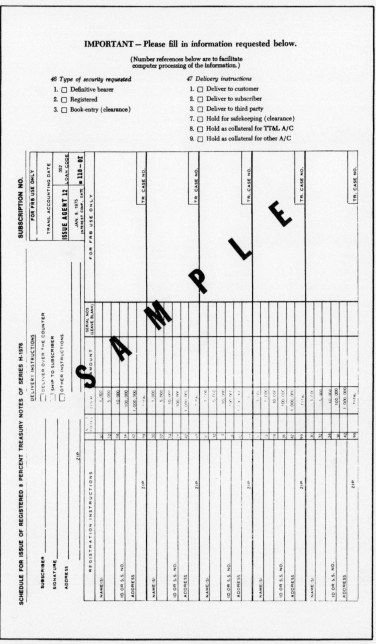

*When reviewing the above form, the investor should keep in mind that (1) it is solely for illustrative purposes and should not be used in lieu of the actual forms; (2) the specific layout of the form can be and is changed from time to time; (3) tender forms for U.S. Treasury bonds are slightly different from the forms used for U.S. Treasury notes; (4) the form above is used by the New York Federal Reserve Bank—other Federal Reserve district banks print their own forms, and often they differ considerably from the ones used by the New York Federal Reserve; and (5) in some cases, additional forms may have to be filled out for a particular bid.

FIGURE 6-5. *Sample of a general form for noncompetitive tenders for U.S. Treasury notes.* *(By permission of the Federal Reserve Bank of New York.)*

GB 635 9/74

NONCOMPETITIVE TENDER FOR SHORT-TERM TREASURY NOTES

DATE ◄

SUBSCRIPTION NO.

IMPORTANT
IF THIS SECURITY IS SOLD AT AUCTION THE INVESTOR MAY PAY **MORE OR LESS** THAN FACE VALUE. THIS TENDER WILL BE ACCEPTED SUBJECT TO THE TERMS AND CONDITIONS STATED IN THE OFFICIAL OFFERING CIRCULAR. THE INVESTOR AGREES NOT TO BUY OR SELL, OR TO MAKE ANY AGREEMENTS WITH RESPECT TO THE PURCHASE OR SALE OR OTHER DISPOSITION OF ANY NOTES OF THIS ISSUE AT A SPECIFIC RATE OR PRICE, UNTIL AFTER THE TIME SPECIFIED IN THE OFFICIAL OFFERING CIRCULAR.

TO: FEDERAL RESERVE BANK OF NEW YORK,
Fiscal Agent of the United States

I HEREBY SUBMIT THIS NONCOMPETITIVE TENDER FOR CURRENTLY OFFERED SHORT-TERM TREASURY NOTES IN THE FACE AMOUNT OF

(in multiples of $1,000) ➤ $

TYPE OF SECURITIES TO BE ISSUED (CHECK ONE)
☐ BEARER   ☐ REGISTERED (Complete Registration Instructions)

DELIVERY INSTRUCTIONS (CHECK ONE)
☐ By Mail   ☐ Over the counter to the undersigned

SPECIAL INSTRUCTIONS

Complete Denominations for Bearer Securities Only

Pieces	Denomination	Maturity Value		
	$ 1,000			
	$ 5,000			
	$ 10,000			
	$100,000			
	Total			

FOR FRB USE ONLY

TYPE OF PAYMENT SUBMITTED WITH TENDER | AMOUNT
☐ Check Payable to the Fed. Res. Bk. of N.Y. .... $
☐ Cash .... $
☐ Eligible Maturing Securities .... $

Rate	Descript.	Date	Due

Teller's Signature

PLEASE *PRINT* ALL INFORMATION, EXCEPT YOUR SIGNATURE

Name of Subscriber
Street Address
City — State — Zip
Home Phone — Business Phone
Signature of Person Completing this Form

REGISTRATION INSTRUCTIONS

COMPLETE FOR REGISTERED SECURITIES ONLY

Name(s) Print Only

ID or S.S. No.

Street Address

City — State — Zip

No. of Pieces	Denomination	Amount	Serial Nos. (Leave Blank)
30	$ 1,000		
32	$ 5,000		
34	$ 10,000		
38	$ 100,000		
99	TOTAL		

FOR FRB USE ONLY

TR. CASE NO.

TO BE USED FOR SECOND REGISTRATION

Name(s) Print Only

ID or S.S. No.

Street Address

City — State — Zip

No. of Pieces	Denomination	Amount	Serial Nos. (Leave Blank)
30	$ 1,000		
32	$ 5,000		
34	$ 10,000		
38	$ 100,000		
99	TOTAL		

FOR FRB USE ONLY

TR. CASE NO.

TRANS. ACCOUNTING DATE	ISSUE AGENT 12	LOAN CODE	INTEREST COMP. DATE	110 — 0I

TENDER COPY 1

*See the footnote to Figure 6-4.

period, and noncompetitive buyers pay a weighted average price which may be below, equal to, or above 100.00. In the conventional auctioned. Instead of bidding *percentage-of-par prices* for notes with others (as in regular T bill offerings), although the Treasury also utilizes the uniform price method, sometimes called the "Dutch auction" method, in which all accepted tenders (both competitive and noncompetitive) are awarded at the price of the lowest accepted bid.

In mid-1974, the Treasury introduced the yield-basis auction for note and bond issues, which is similar to the way Treasury bills are auctioned. Instead of bidding *percentage-of-par prices* for notes with an established coupon (as has traditionally been done in the past), investors' tenders in this type of auction are submitted in terms of *yields* carried out to two decimal places. After the auction, the coupon is set at a level which produces an issue price at or below par for the average accepted yield tender. Successful bidders pay a price equivalent to their yield bid, and noncompetitive tenders pay the average accepted price.

Investors can pay for their notes or bonds by including full payment in cash, cashier's check, a certified personal check, or certain maturing government securities (as specified in the details of the particular offering) with their subscription. When payment is made with securities, an amount of cash may be returned to the buyer, or additional cash may be required from the buyer, if there is a difference between the face amount of securities submitted and the amount due on the new bonds or notes. As with T bills, the investor can also submit a partial payment of the face value of the securities subscribed to (usually 10 percent of the total subscription), with the remainder due to the Federal Reserve on or before the issue date. Only cash or a Federal funds check will be accepted by the Federal Reserve on the issue date. If the individual fails to make final payment on the issue date, his order will be cancelled and the partial payment becomes subject to possible forfeiture to the U.S. Treasury. On the payment and delivery date, usually 2 weeks after the subscription books were opened, the notes or bonds can be picked up at the Federal Reserve bank or branch where purchased, or the investor can request (at the time of tender) that the securities be sent to him by registered mail at the Treasury's expense, which generally takes several weeks.

Treasury bond and note price quotations   In the secondary trading market, Treasury bond and note prices are quoted in percentages of $1,000 par value, with changes expressed in thirty-seconds of a point. (The reader should note that these prices are expressed in terms directly convertible into dollar prices, whereas the T bills encountered earlier are expressed in discount yield terms, which makes translation into dollar prices a bit more complicated.) The newspapers carry the average 3:30 P.M. quotations of five large government securities dealers from the previous day. As an example, one of the 52 U.S. government bond and note issues outstanding as of mid-1974 carried the following price in the newspaper:

June '76, 8¾s . . . . . .   101.5   101.9   +.1   8.05

The first part of the price quotation describes the issue, a Treasury note with an 8¾ percent coupon, maturing in June of 1976. As with Treasury bills, the dealers' *bid* quotation (the price at which the investor could *sell* the notes) was 101.5, or 101⁵⁄₃₂, equal to $1,011.56 per $1,000 par value, and the *offered* side of the quote (the price at which the investor could *buy* the notes) was 101⁹⁄₃₂, or $1,012.81 per $1,000 par value. The newspaper quotations do not include any odd-lot charges for amounts less than $100,000. The +.1 indicates that the *bid* price of the bonds rose by one thirty-second of a point from the previous day's quotation. Sometimes, price changes are even more finely subdivided than thirty-seconds of a point, with changes of sixty-fourths of a point noted by a + sign after the decimal part of the quotation. Thus, when a quote of 101.9+ is seen, it would equal 101¹⁹⁄₆₄ (⁹⁄₃₂ plus ¹⁄₆₄).

The last column of the newspaper price quotation represents the yield to maturity of the notes, based on the *offered* side of the quotation (the price the investor would have to pay). In the example above, the yield to maturity is 8.05 percent. The yield to maturity is lower than the coupon rate of 8.75 percent because the investor has paid a price greater than par for the notes, and the notes will be paid off at par when they mature in June of 1976.

The spreads between dealers' bid and offered prices tend to widen on bonds of longer maturity. Whereas the spread was only ¹⁄₃₂ of a point in the example above (on a 2-years-to-maturity issue at the time it was quoted), spreads on longer-term government bonds range up to a full point or more. Some issues show two maturities in the newspaper, such as the May '98-'93 7s. This means that the final maturity of this 7 percent bond issue is in 1998, but the bonds may be called for redemption by the Treasury any time after 1993.

Settlement and delivery for government bonds and notes is effected according to the same procedure as that for Treasury bills, with payment normally due the next business day after the transaction, unless same-day ("cash") or delayed delivery is prearranged. On odd-lot trades of under $100,000 par value, settlement usually takes place 5 business days after the transaction. When an investor buys or sells Treasury bills or notes between their semiannual interest payment dates, the *accrued interest* since the last payment date is taken into account. Thus, the buyer will have to pay the seller the accrued interest on the bonds or notes, and if the investor sells the bonds or notes before the next interest payment date, the person buying the securities will have to pay the accrued interest to the investor.

Special Tax Features of U.S. Government Securities

As with Treasury bills, the interest income from Treasury bonds and notes is subject to federal income taxes but is exempt from state and local income taxes. In states and cities where the top incremental income tax rate is sizable, this exemption feature can be of significant value. For example, a married couple living in New York City with total taxable income of $35,000 per year would fall into the 42 percent incremental federal tax bracket, the 15 percent tax bracket on incremental income at the New York State level, and the 3.5 percent tax bracket on incremental income at the New York City level. If the investor purchased $10,000 worth of a U.S. bill, note, or bond with a current yield of 6.0 percent, the annualized income before all taxes would be $600, subject only to the incremental federal tax rate of 42 percent, giving a federal tax due of $252 and

TABLE 6-4   Married Couple Living in New York City Earning $35,000 Annually

	U.S. government security	Any other fully taxable security
Interest income	$600.00	$727.00
State & local taxes (18.5%)	. . .	127.00
Income after state and local tax	600.00	600.00
Federal tax (42%)	252.00	252.00
Income after all taxes	$348.00	$348.00

$348 after federal taxes. Since no state or local taxes are due on the income, the investor retains the full $348. What would $10,000 worth of a security which *is* subject to New York City and State income taxes have to yield for the investor to be able to keep $348 after *all* taxes? If we assume that the $600 income were *after* New York City and State taxes at a combined rate of 18.5 percent, the *pretax* income would have to have been $727, or 7.27 percent on $10,000 worth of a fully taxable security such as a corporate bond or a bankers' acceptance. Thus, a 6.00 percent yield from a U.S. government security gives the same yield as a 7.27 percent yielding security which is fully taxable at the state and local level, and at the same time the government security is safer, more liquid, and more easily marketable. Table 6-4 summarizes the situation.

From this type of analysis, a formula has been derived which can be applied to *any* state and local tax environment to compare U.S. government securities' yields after all taxes with the yields generated after all taxes by any other fully taxable security:

$$\text{Fully taxable security yield equivalent} = \frac{\text{U.S. government security yield}}{1 - (\text{incremental state} + \text{local tax rate})}$$

Whenever judging an investment's yield attractiveness, the investor should subject the fully taxable security yield and the yield on a U.S. government security of similar maturity to the above formula. Thus, for an investor living in a locality where the sum of the incremental state and local tax rates is 10 percent, a Series E savings bond is in fact equal in its yield after all taxes to:

$$\frac{6 \text{ percent}}{1 - 10 \text{ percent}} = \frac{6 \text{ percent}}{0.90} = 6.67 \text{ percent yield generated on a fully taxable security}$$

Certain Treasury bonds, nicknamed "flower bonds," can provide another type of tax break to the investor when they are selling below par value. Flower bonds get their nickname from their frequent use in the settlement of estate taxes after death. Flower bonds save estate taxes since they are appraised by the Internal Revenue Service at market value in computing the total value of the estate, while for estate *tax* purposes they are accepted at their full face value. A list of currently outstanding flower bonds is set forth in Table 6-5.

Flower bonds are most useful for investors who are well on in years and who plan to bequeath a moderately large estate. Their advantages over conventional fixed-income investments diminish (1) if the estate is of small size and thus not subject to substantial estate taxes; (2) if market interest rates for government bonds drop to the 4 percent level or below (which would cause many of the bonds to sell around or above par, decreasing the difference between their market value and their face value); or (3) if the bonds are held for a long period of time, since the total amount of bond discount is prorated over its life, and the discount is deemed by the IRS to decrease by a certain amount each year. Flower bonds purchased by an estate after a person's death are of no extra benefit, since under these conditions they are included in tax payments only at market value and not at face value.

TABLE 6-5   U.S. Government "Flower Bonds"

Issue	Amount outstanding (in $ millions) (As of December 31, 1974)
4s due February 15, 1980	$ 2,570
3½s due November 15, 1980	1,894
3¼s due June 15, 1983/78	1,459
3¼s due May 15, 1985	915
4¼s due May 15, 1985/75	1,197
3½s due February 15, 1990	3,750
4¼s due August 15, 1992/87	3,605
4s due February 15, 1993/88	224
4⅛s due May 15, 1994/89	1,384
3s due February 15, 1995	757
3½s due November 15, 1998	2,901
Total flower bonds outstanding	$20,656

Buying U.S. Government Securities on Margin

Because of the high credit standing of the U.S. government, Treasury securities can be purchased on a much smaller margin than corporate stocks and bonds. T bills, because of their short-term maturity and reduced price volatility, can be purchased on as little as a 5 percent margin—meaning that the investor puts up cash totalling 5 percent of the total investment and borrows the rest from his securities broker at the prevailing margin interest rate. On longer-term Treasury bonds and notes, the initial margin requirement is generally somewhat higher, usually 10 percent or more, because of the greater price fluctuations which long-term securities undergo when interest rates change.

It should be emphasized that margin purchases of U.S. government securities should only be made under two conditions. First, all margin transactions of any type are speculative and involve greater than average risk. The investor should buy securities on margin with only that portion of his capital which is earmarked for high-risk investments and in which a total loss could be sustained if the investor proved wrong in his purchase. Second, the investor should feel very strongly that interest rates will fall (and prices rise) in the sector of the government securities market in which the margin investments are being made. If interest rates move up, the total funds put up by the investor could be lost altogether, and if interest rates remain at roughly the same level during the period of investment, the net interest return to the investor can be zero or even negative, which is less than what would have been earned by making a conventional nonmargin investment in government securities.

For discussion purposes, suppose that the investor has set aside a certain portion of his portfolio for speculative investments. We will also assume that the investor feels interest rates on long-term Treasury bonds will fall sometime within the next 6 months. If the investor invests $100,000, paying $10,000 in cash and borrowing $90,000 on margin at an annual interest rate of 9 percent, in long-term U.S. government bonds yielding 7 percent, over a 6-month holding period the investor would *receive* ½ of 7 percent of $100,-

000, or $3,500, and would *pay* ½ of 9 percent of $90,000, or $4,050. Thus the net interest cost of the investment ($4,050 − $3,500 = $650) is deductible from the investor's pretax income. If interest rates did in fact decline during the period of investment, the investor might be able to refinance his loan at a lower interest rate, but in our example we assume that the margin interest rate falls more slowly than long-term interest rates.

The primary purpose of the investment was to benefit from any fall in interest rates, and Table 6-6 shows what happens to the price of a 7 percent Treasury bond bought on margin with 20 years remaining to maturity under varying interest rate changes.

From Table 6-6 we can see that if interest rates decline to 6.5 percent, the investor can realize a pretax return of 55.4 percent on his investment, and for greater interest rate declines the returns are even more lucrative, with a 180.3 percent return on investment if interest rates reach the 5.5 percent level. However, the investor should also take heed of what can happen if interest rates rise, contrary to expectations. The leverage permitted by investing on margin can work two ways. As seen in the Table 6-6, the investor's original equity of $10,000 can be reduced by over 50 percent if interest rates rise from 7 to 7.5 percent, and the investment can be practically wiped out altogether if long-term U.S. government bond rates rise by 100 basis points. This underscores the need for extreme caution when investing on margin. It may also be of value to think about at what interest rate level the investor would sell out his

TABLE 6-6   Price Changes of a 7% 20-Year Treasury Bond Bought on Margin

If long-term government bond interest rates move from 7% to	$100,000 worth of 7% Treasury bonds due in 20 years are worth	Principal left after repayment of $90,000	Dollar return before taxes on $10,000 investment	% return
6.5%	$105,541	$15,541	$ 5,541	55.4
6.0%	111,538	21,538	11,538	115.4
5.5%	118,032	28,032	18,032	180.3
7.5%	94,862	4,862	−5,138	−51.4
8.0%	90,107	107	−9,893	−98.9

investment if rates begin to move upward. Often, if a ceiling interest rate level has been picked in the investor's mind *beforehand,* losses can be limited and a portion of the investment can be salvaged.

In our original example, the net loss of $650 on the interest payments and receipts can be deducted from the investor's taxable income. Under IRS regulations, the maximum *total* amount of interest which an investor can deduct for the purpose of investing in securities is $25,000. In certain interest rate environments, the investor may have a "positive carry" situation, in which the interest earned on the Treasury securities exceeds the interest paid on the margin loan to carry the securities. If Treasury bonds or notes are held for over 6 months, any gain in principal amount would be taxed at capital gains rates, which are lower than taxation rates on ordinary income. However, if Treasury bills are purchased, any gain is taxed at ordinary income tax rates, regardless of the length of the holding period.

The type of margin buying described above can be done with Federal Agency bonds, corporate bonds, and other types of securities. The investor will recall that for a given interest rate change, bond prices will change faster (1) the lower the coupon and (2) the longer the time remaining to maturity. Thus, investing in T bills on margin will generally produce a smaller absolute dollar return on investment for a given decline in interest rates. Since T bills are of much shorter maturity than Treasury bonds and notes, however, the lower margin requirements on T bills sometimes make bills equally attractive as a speculation from a percentage return point of view.

What if the investor believes that fixed-income securities prices will fall in response to rising interest rates? In theory, it is possible to borrow U.S. government securities and sell them short, in hopes of buying them back later at a lower price to return them to the lender. In practice, borrowing Treasury securities is extremely hard for the investor to accomplish and is best left to government securities dealers and other very large institutional investors who can more easily borrow securities to sell short and who have the capital and mental attitude necessary to withstand losses if securities sold short move up rather than down in price.

Mutual Funds Which Invest in Government Securities

For those investors who want to invest in government securities but who do not wish to spend time trying to forecast interest rate swings or worrying about minimum denominations and the details of submitting tenders to the Federal Reserve on time for the Treasury security auctions, a small number of mutual funds exist to invest exclusively in the debt instruments of the Treasury and various U.S. government agencies. These funds are slightly different from (1) the corporate and municipal bond funds described in Chapters 9 and 10, and (2) the cash management funds described in Chapter 8. Funds which invest in government securities permit the investor to own a diversified, professionally managed portfolio of Treasuries and agencies by making an initial investment from $100 to $1,000, depending on the specific fund (a securities brokerage firm can supply a list of these and other funds).

While funds such as these have much merit for those investors of very small size and for those who place convenience high on their list of considerations in making an investment, nevertheless, funds such as these have some drawbacks: (1) even though there is no charge for redemptions, new purchases of the fund are subject to a 1½ percent sales charge (or more, in some cases); (2) the investor may not agree with the mix of short-term, long-term, Treasury, and Federal Agency securities in the fund's portfolio; and (3) if the fund invests a large portion of its assets in long-term securities and interest rates rise, fund shareholders may incur a loss on their investment when they withdraw from the fund. With the help of this book and a bit of experience, the average investor should be able to select and profitably invest in government securities on his own.

SEVEN

Securities of U.S. Government Agencies and Related Institutions

At first glance, the securities of the various agencies of the United States government seem to present a bewildering and complicated group of fixed-income securities, with numerous names, purposes, security terms, and degrees of guarantee, quasi-guarantee, or non-guarantee by the United States government itself. One factor which has inhibited easy comprehension of the area has also been the interchangeable use of an agency's official title, its initials, an acronym, or even a nickname to describe one single entity. Yet upon closer analysis, we will find that, much like the many hard-to-keep-track-of cousins and relatives at a large family reunion, once we have organized the more than 40 agencies into broad groups and identified distinguishing characteristics, we will be able to make sense out of apparent confusion. Fixed-income securities investors should know about agency securities, not only because of their benefits but also because of agencies' burgeoning share of the total amount of short-term and long-term debt being brought to market each year.

The growth of U.S. government securities outstanding in recent years has been nothing short of enormous. By the middle of 1974, total agency debt amounted to $91.6 billion, up 80 percent from the

$50.7 billion outstanding just 4 years earlier in 1970, and up 940 percent from the $8.8 billion outstanding in 1960. The wide differences between all the agency "cousins" are notable. Several agencies trace their origins back 40, 50 years, or more, while numerous others, such as the Student Loan Marketing Association and the U.S. Railway Reorganization Corporation, have been created within the last few years. As seen in Chapter 5, many agencies are not included in the United States budget totals, while quite a few others are included. Most, but not all, of the securities issued by agencies are considered legal investments for federally supervised investment institutions. With some exceptions, agency issues can be purchased and held without limit by national banks and are eligible as security for the bank deposits of public monies of the United States government, such as Treasury tax and loan accounts. Also, a number of agency securities can be utilized as collateral by member banks for discounts and advances from the Federal Reserve System.

Even with all these and many other differentiating features, agency issues possess many homogeneous aspects as well. For example, all agency securities are exempt from registration with the U.S. Securities and Exchange Commission (as are issues of the United States government and those of state and local borrowers). Agencies share common investors, including both the contractual and depositary types of institution. Almost all short- and long-term agency issues trade in very similar yield patterns, with interest rates normally somewhat higher than U.S. government securities and somewhat lower than top-grade corporate debt. In the past 10 years for instance, short-term agency securities have averaged 15 to 20 basis points (0.15 to 0.20 percent) *more* in yield than 3-month Treasury bills, and short-term agency securities have yielded an average of 30 to 40 basis points (0.30 to 0.40 percent) *less* than the short-term commercial paper of finance companies. Yields on newly offered longer-term agency issues have generally been 25 to 100 basis points (0.25 to 1.00 percent) *above* the yields on new long-term Treasury securities, and 25 to 100 basis points (0.25 to 1.00 percent) *below* yields on new high-quality corporate utility bonds of comparable maturity.

Investors have thus been attracted to agency issues by their yields relative to governmental issues and because of their high quality, ranking second only to direct obligations of the United States government. In addition, a great number of agency issues are noncallable throughout their entire lifetime, providing protection against redemption should interest rates decline prior to maturity. Several agency issues offer other unique features, such as monthly interest payments, very small minimum purchase requirements, exemption from state and local income taxes, or the opportunity to choose any desired maturity on certain short-term securities.

The remainder of this chapter contains brief summaries of the principal characteristics of each of the most widely known and most actively borrowing agencies, including the recently formed Federal Financing Bank, which was established to combine the borrowings of over 20 agencies under a single issuer, thereby reducing interest costs and increasing marketability. We will also survey three international assistance organizations which issue securities similar in many ways to agency obligations. This will be followed by a review of trading and settlement procedures for agency securities, both on initial offerings and in the secondary market. Many of these details are summarized in the information charts contained in Chapter 12.

Characteristics of the Principal Agencies of the U.S. Government

Up to this point in the book, we have only briefly distinguished between two major categories of agencies of the United States government. The first group, called *government-sponsored enterprises,* comprises six agencies whose capital stock was originally owned by the U.S. Treasury, which has since transferred ownership to the general public and to organizations served by these six agencies. Government-sponsored enterprises are not guaranteed by the United States government, although they raise money under the Treasury's supervision. Almost all the work of these six agencies is concentrated in areas related to farm credit and housing, and government-sponsored enterprises, with outstanding securities amounting to over $76 billion as of early 1975, account for over 75 percent of the total debt issued by all types of agencies.

The second group, called *Federal Agencies,* includes a larger number of agencies which are entirely owned by the United States government. They have been authorized by the Treasury to issue debt securities on their own behalf, and most, but not all, of their issues carry the guarantee of the United States government. Federal Agencies' activities, some of which overlap the activities of government-sponsored enterprises, cover a wide spectrum, ranging from assistance to export-import financing and small businesses, to real estate and housing loan assistance programs for farmers and other rural citizens. The investor should understand and appreciate the differences between Federal Agencies and government-sponsored enterprises, in order to know exactly what form of government guarantee or other features are associated with each type of security. When we wish to refer to *both* groups of securities at once, we will simply call them "agencies," or "U.S. government agencies," and the investor should remember *not* to confuse these two terms with "Federal Agencies," one of the principal groups of agencies. While all "Federal Agencies" are "agencies," or "U.S. government agencies," the reverse is not true, since government-sponsored enterprises are included in the latter two terms and are *not* "Federal Agencies." If this seemingly confusing point can be kept in mind, the investor will have achieved a major step toward fuller comprehension of agency issues.

In the following summaries of the principal agencies, we will briefly review (1) the purpose of each agency; (2) its form of guarantee, if any, from the United States government; (3) the security denominations, minimum purchase requirements, and maturities available; the form (bearer, registered, or both) of the security; (4) its income tax status; and (5) the total amounts outstanding as of a recent date. If the investor desires more detailed information on a particular security, he should refer to the readings and sources suggested in Chapter 15 or contact a securities broker, commercial bank, the nearest Federal Reserve System office, or the agency involved. Comments on buying and selling procedures for agency securities are contained later on in this Chapter.

Government-Sponsored Enterprises

As the investor reads this section and the following section on Federal Agency securities, he should try to get a feeling for what the agency is designed to do, and look for agencies whose securities match his own investment situation and objectives as outlined in Chapter 2. An example would be if the investor desires to commit only a small amount of capital to agency securities, he may be most interested in the small minimum purchase requirement on Federal Land Bank securities or Federal Housing Authority bonds. It is also important to review carefully the details and available maturities for *all* the securities issued by *a specific agency,* as well as in comparison with *other agencies'* securities, before making an investment in the agency sector of fixed-income securities. By doing so, the investor may discover a more attractive security for his needs, such as an agency security which has a longer or shorter maturity or which is available in registered or bearer form.

Banks for Cooperatives (Co-ops)   The 13 Banks for Cooperatives (also known as Co-ops) borrow money to make loans to farmers' cooperative associations. While their securities are not guaranteed by the United States government, they are backed by all the Co-op banks and collateral, such as the notes of the cooperatives to whom money has been lent. The securities of the Banks for Cooperatives are issued in bearer form only, usually on a monthly or bimonthly basis, most often with a 6-month maturity, and are based on a 360-day year. The minimum initial purchase requirement is $5,000 and security denominations are $5,000, $10,000, $50,000, and $100,00. One interesting feature about all Co-op issues, even the longer-term securities, is that they are noncallable. They are subject to federal income taxes but exempt from state and local income taxes. As of early 1975, eight issues totalling $3.6 billion were outstanding.

Federal Intermediate Credit Banks (FICBs)   The 12 Federal Intermediate Credit Banks provide money to the various specialized banks and financing institutions which make loans to the agricultural sector. FICB securities are not guaranteed by the United States government, but they are secured by the 12 banks as a group, as well as by specific types of collateral. Federal Intermediate Credit Bank securities are issued in bearer form, usually for 9 months' maturity, and with a maximum of 5 years' maturity. The minimum purchase requirement is $5,000, and they come in denominations of $5,000, $10,000, $50,000, $100,000, and $500,000. Like Co-ops, FICB securities are not redeemable prior to maturity, and they are exempt from state and local taxes but subject to federal income taxes. Fifteen issues of FICBs, amounting to $8.6 billion, were outstanding as of January 1975.

In early 1975, the Farm Credit System, consisting of the Banks for Cooperatives, the Federal Intermediate Credit Banks, and the Federal Land Banks, began offering short-term discount notes ranging from 5 to 150 days in maturity, according to the investor's choice. These securities, called Farm Credit Bank discount notes, carry the guarantee of the total of 37 banks which make up the Farm Credit System. They serve as a complement to the other securities issues of the Banks for Cooperatives, the Federal Intermediate Credit Banks, and the Federal Land Banks by providing interim funds between the bond or note sales of each of these three agencies. The minimum-purchase requirement for the Farm Credit Bank discount notes is $50,000, and $100,000 and $1 million denominations are also available. Interest income on these discount notes is subject to federal income taxes but exempt from state and local income taxes. The three securities firms who have been designated as primary distributors and secondary market makers in Farm Credit Bank discount notes are listed in the charts in Chapter 12.

Federal Home Loan Banks (FHLBs) The 12 Federal Home Loan Banks advance funds to the nearly 5,000 savings-related institutions throughout the country when groups such as the savings and loan associations face large deposit outflows because of disintermediation or other seasonal factors. FHLB issues, backed by the 12 Federal Home Loan Banks, are not guaranteed by the United States government, but the Secretary of the Treasury is authorized to purchase up to $4 billion worth of these securities, and they are collateralized by guaranteed mortgages, cash, U.S. government securities, or other assets of the banks. Most of their issues are short-term, with securities of less than 12 months' original maturity called *notes* and those with greater than 12 months' maturity called *bonds* (the investor will note that this terminology for notes and bonds is different than that used in describing U.S. government securities). The FHLBs issue three types of securities, all of which are noncallable and in bearer form: (1) short-term discount notes of 30 to 270 days' maturity (distributed through the four securities firms listed in Chapter 12), on which interest rates for newly purchased securities are posted to reflect existing money market conditions; (2) interest-bearing notes of under 1 year's maturity; and (3) bonds of over 1 year's maturity. The minimum purchase requirement is $10,000 (for the discount notes, $100,000) and denominations include $10,000, $50,000, $100,000, and $1 million. FHLB securities are subject to federal income taxes but are exempt from state and local taxes, and the total outstanding as of early 1975 was $22.3 billion, representing 48 different issues.

Federal Home Loan Mortgage Corporation (FHLMC) The Federal Home Loan Mortgage Corporation, also known as "Freddie Mac," raises money in order to buy residential mortgages from federally insured savings institutions, such as savings and loan associations, when they need additional funds to finance new housing in periods of tight money. The FHLMC issues three different types of securities: mortgage-backed bonds, participation certificates, and guaranteed mortgage certificates, all of whose interest payments are subject to federal, state, and local income taxes. The *mortgage-backed bonds* range in maturity from 12 to 25 years and are not directly guaranteed by the United States government, but instead are guaranteed by the Government National Mortgage Association (discussed in the Federal Agencies section which follows), which is in turn backed by the full faith and credit of the United States government. FHLMC mortgage-backed bonds are issued in either bearer or registered form and are intended for larger investors, with a minimum purchase requirement of $25,000 and denominations of $25,000, $100,000, $500,000, and $1 million. As of January 1975, total mortgage-backed bonds of FHLMC amounted to 1.6 billion in six issues, three of which were callable 10 years or more after their original issue date.

The FHLMC *participation certificates* also have a $100,000 minimum purchase requirement, and they are backed by pools of conventional (non-FHA- or VA-approved) mortgages, as well as the guarantee of the FHLMC itself. Payments of interest and principal behind the certificates are passed on directly to the investor each month. Because of mortgage prepayments and other factors, the maturity on FHLMC participation certificates is generally a considerable amount shorter than the conventional mortgages underlying these securities. As of January 1975, over $1 billion worth of FHLMC participation certificates were outstanding.

Early in 1975, the FHLMC began offering *guaranteed mortgage certificates* through a group of around 30 securities brokerage firms and commercial banks. Unlike the FHLMC participation certificates, the guaranteed mortgage certificates pay interest on a semiannual basis, with a portion of the principal being repaid each year as well. These certificates do not carry the guarantee of the United States government, but they do carry the backing of the FHLMC. In addition, the FHLMC stipulates that it will buy back its guaranteed mortgage certificates at par after 15 years (if not already matured) if the investor elects to sell his securities to the FHLMC. The minimum denomination of the certificates is $100,000, and they are obtainable in registered form only.

Federal Land Banks (FLBs) The 12 Federal Land Banks borrow money to provide local Federal Land Bank associations with funds for making long-term real estate loans and other loans to farmers. FLB issues are not guaranteed by the United States government, but they are backed by the 12 Federal Land Banks and certain security in the form of farmers' mortagages and other assets. They are issued in bearer or registered form, with denominations of $1,000, $5,000, $10,000, $50,000, $100,000, and $500,000. It should be noted that Federal Land Banks have the *lowest minimum purchase requirement ($1,000) of any of the government-sponsored enterprises*, followed by the Federal Intermediate Credit Banks ($5,000). Thirty-eight issues of Federal Land Bank securities, ranging in maturity from 1 to 15 years and all but one of which were noncallable, aggregated $12.7 billion outstanding as of early 1975. Interest paid on FLB securities is exempt from state and local income taxes but subject to federal income taxes.

Federal National Mortgage Association (FNMA) The Federal National Mortgage Association, also known as "Fannie Mae," raises funds to purchase residential mortgages (primarily those which are insured or guaranteed by the Federal Housing Administration, the Veterans' Administration, or the Farmers Home Administration) from savings and loan institutions, banks and insurance companies, in order to provide additional liquidity to the mortgage market in periods of tight credit when normal capital flows to this sector diminish. Although not guaranteed by the United States government, FNMA securities are supported by the authority to borrow up to $2.25 billion from the Treasury Department. The Federal National Mortgage Association issues several types of securities of varying forms and maturities, all of which *are subject to federal, state,* and *local income taxes.* FNMA *discount notes* with a maturity between 30 and 270 days are issued through four securities dealers (listed in the information charts in Chapter 12) who maintain a secondary trading market in the notes. Discount rates of interest on the newly issued notes are set periodically and are similar to, but above, the prevailing Treasury bill rates. One interesting facet of the discount notes is that their maturity can be tailored to the specific desires of the investor. The discount notes are beyond the reach of the very small investor, however, since they have a minimum purchase requirement of $50,000. Denominations include $5,000, $10,000, $25,000, $100,000, $500,000, and $1 million. As of early 1975, $3.5 billion of the discount notes were outstanding.

FNMA also issues so-called *secondary-market notes* and *debentures* (debentures are bonds backed by the general credit of the issuer, rather than specified assets or groups of assets of the issuer), which are available only in bearer form and range in original maturity from 3 to 25 years. All but one of these issues are noncallable, and they come in denominations of $10,000, $25,000, $50,000, $100,000, and $500,000. The minimum purchase requirement is

$10,000. As of early 1975, 61 issues of these notes and debentures were outstanding, in the amount of $23.1 billion.

Another type of security issued by FNMA includes their mortgage-backed bonds, which are secured by mortgages and by the Government National Mortgage Association and thus have the backing of the United States government. Two public issues totalling $450 million were outstanding as of May 1975. These FNMA-GNMA mortgage-backed bonds have a $25,000 minimum purchase requirement and are issued in both bearer and registered form. Finally, three issues of FNMA capital debentures are also available to investors. The total amount outstanding as of May 1975 was $698 million, of which $248 million represented debentures which are convertible into FNMA common stock, listed on the New York Stock Exchange. The minimum purchase requirement for the capital debentures is $10,000, and the bonds are available in bearer and registered form.

Federal Agencies

Although Federal Agency securities account for roughly one-quarter of total agency debts outstanding, many new agencies and programs have been started up in this category in recent years. Our analysis focuses on the six Federal Agencies which are responsible for a substantial proportion of all Federal Agency borrowing. In addition, the Federal Financing Bank is discussed in this section, since this new entity will in time carry out most of the borrowing for the smaller and lesser-known Federal Agencies, as well as a large amount of the borrowing for the larger members of this group.

Export-Import Bank (Exim Bank) The Export-Import Bank raises money to provide loans, credit insurance, and other types of guarantees in order to facilitate trade between the United States and other countries. The Exim Bank's securities are backed by the full faith and credit of the United States government, and the bank can borrow up to $6 billion from the Treasury Department. Three types of debt are issued by the Exim Bank, all of which are *subject to federal, state, and local* income taxes on interest payments. The *short-term discount notes* are sold in bearer form, with a minimum purchase requirement of $100,000, which makes them more suitable for larger individual investors and institutions. The Exim Bank discount notes are not traded in the secondary market, but the investor can gain a measure of liquidity through the privilege of selecting the specific number of days until maturity (any number between 30 and 360 days) at the time the notes are purchased. In the past, the Export-Import Bank has also offered *participation certificates,* which are certificates issued against a pool of loans made by the bank. These securities are available in both bearer and registered form, with a $5,000 minimum-purchase requirement, and are denominated in amounts of $5,000, $10,000, $25,000, $100,000, $500,000, and $1 million. The participation certificates are not callable prior to maturity, and as of early 1975, one public issue totalling $250 million was outstanding. The third type of Exim Bank security consists of *debentures,* generally of 3-to-7-years' maturity. Eight issues, totalling $2.5 billion, were outstanding as of June 1974. The debentures have a minimum purchase requirement of $5,000 and are issued in either bearer or registered form.

Farmers Home Administration (FHDA)   The Farmers Home Administration uses its funds to extend real estate and housing loans to farmers and certain other rural citizens. Securities of the FHDA are guaranteed by the United States government, and maturities range from 4 to 15 years. As of early 1975, two types of Farmers Home Administration issues were outstanding: (1) *insured notes* (19 issues amounting to $5.1 billion) and (2) *certificates of beneficial ownership* (3 issues totalling $700 million), both of which are fully taxable at the federal, state, and local income level. The insured notes consist of direct offerings of large blocks of the loan notes which have been made to farmers, with the endorsement of the Farmers Home Administration (and thus the backing of the United States government) attached to the notes. No established minimum purchase sizes or denominations are currently used, though the large block offerings of the insured note are generally sold in lots of between $100,000 and $500,000 per investment, in registered form. Recently, certificates of beneficial ownership (CBOs), which are not the loans themselves but certificates representing ownership of a portion of the loan pool by the investor, have been utilized more than the insured notes. The certificates have a $25,000 minimum purchase requirement and come in both bearer and registered form. An important thing to remember about Farmers Home Administration securities is that they pay interest *annually* rather than through the usual semiannual method for agency and other interest-bearing securities.

Federal Housing Administration (FHA) The Federal Housing Administration issues somewhat unusual long-term securities which are generally not traded very frequently in the secondary market. Since these securities come into being as payment to holders of FHA-insured mortgages which have gone into default, they generally conform to the yield, maturity, and principal value of the specific defaulted mortgage, thus possessing very few features in common with all the other Federal Housing Administration securities issued in the same way. FHA securities are fully and unconditionally guaranteed by the United States government and come in registered form only, with the *smallest minimum purchase requirement and denominations of any type of agency security.* Although rarely found in such small amounts, the theoretical minimum purchase is $50, with denominations of $50, $100, $500, $1,000, $5,000, and $10,-000. In view of the transactions costs involved in trading very small amounts of these securities, and the difficulty of locating attractive bids for very small amounts of FHA issues, the investor must be willing to hold onto this type of security either until maturity or until interest rates have experienced a substantial decline (and prices have risen), in order to achieve an attractive overall return. Nevertheless, the fact that they are available in small quantities and denominations, with a government guarantee, make the FHA issues worth investing in on occasion. Interest income from these securities is fully taxable at the federal level, but exempt from state and local taxes. Two drawbacks which must also be weighed before buying FHA securities relate to (1) the small total amount of these securities outstanding relative to other agency issues—$440 million worth as of early 1975—and (2) the fact that they are callable, in full or in part, at par, on any interest date with 30 days' prior notice.

Government National Mortgage Association (GNMA) The Government National Mortgage Association, also known as "Ginnie Mae," is part of the Department of Housing and Urban Development, and GNMA provides money for financing residential housing programs where established home-financing facilities are inadequate. GNMA's credit is backed by the full faith and credit of the United States government, and it is authorized to borrow from the Treasury to ensure timely payments of principal and interest on securities which GNMA guarantees. Three types of Government National Mortgage Association securities are available, all of whose interest payments are *fully taxable* at the federal, state, and local levels.

GNMA *mortgage-backed securities* are backed by a pool of FHA- or VA-insured mortgages which have been issued by either the Federal Home Loan Mortgage Corporation or the Federal National Mortgage Association and in turn have been guaranteed by GNMA. Eight of these issues, totalling $1.8 billion, were outstanding as of early 1975 and are available in bearer or registered form, in denominations of $25,000, $100,000, $500,000, and $1 million, with $25,-000 the minimum purchase requirement.

GNMA *participation certificates* are issued primarily against the assembled loan assets of several governmental agencies whose mortgage management and liquidation functions were taken over by GNMA from FNMA in 1968. In early 1975, $4.3 billion of these certificates were outstanding, represented by nine issues, all of which are in bearer or registered form. The minimum purchase requirement is $5,000, and the securities come in denominations of $5,000, $10,000, $25,000, $100,000, $500,000, and $1 million.

The third type of GNMA issue, officially called GNMA *modified pass-through securities,* has several unusual features. The securities are created when a mortgage banker assembles a pool of at least $2 million worth of FHA- or VA-guaranteed mortgages of the same coupon and maturity and deposits them at a custodian bank. GNMA then issues securities against these mortgages, with interest and principal payments made *monthly* to the investor on a *modified* pass-through basis, which means that interest and principal are paid to the investor by GNMA regardless of whether it has been collected on time from the mortgagee (if the payments are made only as collected, this would be called a *straight* pass-through type of security). Since GNMA modified pass-through securities pay interest and principal monthly, their semiannual equivalent yield is usually 10 to 20 basis points (0.10 to 0.20 percent) higher than their stated yield, depending on the actual level of interest rates. Also, although the *original* life of the mortgages behind these modified pass-through securities is 25 to 30 years, the *average* life of a pool of mortgages behind the securities works out to about 12 to 14 years because of prepayments of principal by borrowers and mortgage refinancings. In the first half of 1974, GNMA modified pass-through yields rose *above* comparable corporate bond yields (the investor will recall that agency yields are normally *below* corporate bond yields), due in part to the fact that yields on this type of security are closely tied to *mortgage* interest rates, which rose more rapidly than corporate bond yields during the first 6 months of 1974.

The minimum purchase requirement on GNMA modified pass-through securities is $25,000, with denominations of $25,000, $30,-000, and $10,000 increments above $30,000. Over $9.5 billion of these securities were outstanding as of June 1974. While this type of security provides a liquid United States government–guaranteed way of investing in the mortgage market without the administrative burden and legal expenses of conventional mortgage investing, the investor should carefully weigh these advantages against the possibility that (1) substantial portions of his investment might be prepaid by a number of the borrowers in the pool behind his securities, thus substantially reducing the maturity of his investment, and (2) in a period of high or rising interest rates, mortgage yields might rise faster than conventional fixed-income securities yields, potentially

154 / The Complete Bond Book

causing greater loss of principal than conventional fixed-income securities, if the investor should decide to sell his investment.

Tennessee Valley Authority (TVA) The Tennessee Valley Authority raises money in order to help develop the agricultural and industrial resources of the Tennessee River valley and nearby areas, primarily through the provision of electric power and other programs. Although TVA securities are not guaranteed by the United States government, the Tennessee Valley Authority can borrow up to $150 million from the Treasury Department. In addition, TVA securities are backed by a first claim on all net power income, before depreciation and interest payments. Two types of debt are presently issued by the TVA, both of which are subject to federal income taxes, but exempt from state and local income taxes. The first type includes *short-term notes,* usually of 4-month maturity, issued monthly in discount form on an auction basis. The average investor is not eligible to bid on these discount notes, on which there is a very high minimum tender requirement ($1 million), and noncompetitive bids are not allowed. The discount notes are issued in bearer form only, in denominations of $5,000, $10,000, $100,-000, and $1 million. As of June 1974, $421 million of these short-term discount notes were outstanding.

Tennessee Valley Authority *bonds* come in either bearer or registered form and have a very small minimum purchase requirement of $1,000, with denominations of $1,000, $5,000, $10,000, $100,-000, and $1 million. The bonds are initially sold to an underwriting syndicate on a competitive bid basis, comparable to the procedures used in many corporate utility bond offerings. Further details on offering procedures are given later on in this chapter. As of early 1975, 21 TVA bond issues were outstanding, aggregating $2.1 billion.

U.S. Postal Service The U.S. Postal Service seeks funds to upgrade the national mail system. The Postal Service may borrow up to $2 billion from the Treasury Department, and although the one outstanding bond issue of the Postal Service does not carry the guarantee of the United States government, the Postal Service may request the Secretary of the Treasury to give future debt issues the guarantee of the United States government; it is up to the Treasury Secretary whether or not to provide such a guarantee. The minimum purchase requirement of the Postal Service bonds is $10,000; denominations include $10,000, $25,000, $100,000, and $500,000, in both registered and bearer form. In June 1974, the single issue of Postal Service bonds outstanding amounted to $250 million, with a final maturity in 1997 and callable after 1982.

Other Federal Agency securities The previous six Federal Agency securities, as mentioned earlier, represent about $25 billion in outstanding securities, and thus account for by far the lion's share of total borrowing by Federal Agencies as a group. In most cases, the bulk of secondary-market trading activity for Federal Agency securities is also concentrated in these issues, and investors most often select a particular Federal Agency security from among these issues because of their greater size, marketability, and liquidity. Nevertheless, the investor might encounter or hear about other Federal Agency securities, and he should at least be able to recognize the following agencies as Federal Agencies with relatively smaller amounts of bonds outstanding, all of which are guaranteed by the United States government. *District of Columbia Armory Board* bonds are the only Federal Agency securities guaranteed by the United States government which can be bought and traded in amounts as low as $1,000; FHA bonds also have this feature, in amounts all the way down to $50 (on an infrequent basis), but the investor will remember that FHA bonds come in odd amounts, maturities, and coupons, and are difficult to trade into and out of. *Washington Metropolitan Transit Authority* bonds ($5,000 minimum purchase, bearer and registered form available) and so-called *Merchant Marine* bonds (bearer form, minimum purchase varies from issue to issue) are also encountered from time to time.

In addition, the following Federal Agency securities carry either a complete or partial guarantee by the United States government and differ from one another in the minimum purchase requirement, normal maturities, denominations, taxability, and other features: the *Small Business Administration* and the *Student Loan Marketing Associa-*

tion, also known as "Sallie Mae." Several other Federal Agency securities have been issued and endorsed by the secretaries of several U.S. government departments, such as Transportation, Housing and Urban Development, and Agriculture.

Federal Financing Bank   By now, the investor should be able to appreciate the confusion, as well as the large and often competing funds demands on the securities markets, created by such a proliferation of Federal Agencies, many of which have securities terms, degrees of government guarantee, and characteristics which are unique to that agency. Another aspect of this situation is the fact that many Federal Agencies' securities have poor marketability and often sell at higher initial interest costs (lower prices) because of the small size of their issues. In early 1974, legislation was passed to rectify these weaknesses, and a Federal Financing Bank was created to borrow funds more efficiently and permit investors to trade in its larger-sized issues of securities more easily. While the entire group of Federal Agencies are eligible to use the facilities of the Federal Financing Bank on a voluntary basis, the six government-sponsored enterprises, whose securities are issued in large volume and are better known by investors, will not be permitted to use the Federal Financing Bank.

The Federal Financing Bank sells its securities several times each year in the public markets, and in turn provides money to those Federal Agencies which request funds from it. The Federal Financing Bank can also buy existing securities of any of the Federal Agencies with the money it raises. This process effectively replaces a large number of separate borrowers with a single borrower, thus enhancing the marketability of the securities of the Federal Financing Bank compared with the diverse group of Federal Agencies. The Federal Financing Bank is authorized to borrow up to $15 billion from the Treasury Department, and its securities are considered general obligations of the United States government, backed by its full faith and credit. They are tax-exempt at the state and local tax level only. The Federal Financing Bank's first public issue was $1.5 billion worth of discount bills, brought to market in July of 1974, and over the next several years the bank is expected to be a very active borrower, since it is expected to eventually shoulder a great part of the borrowing responsibility of both existing and newly established Federal Agencies. Federal Financing Bank securities have a $10,000 minimum purchase requirement on the discount bills and are available in denominations of $10,000, $15,000, $50,-000, $100,000, $500,000, and $1 million. Federal Financing Bank bills are sold by competitive auction procedures very similar to those employed in the sale of Treasury bills, as described in the previous chapter. Investors' tenders are due at the Federal Reserve Bank or branches by 1:30 P.M. Eastern time on the offering date. Noncompetitive bids are permitted up to a maximum of $300,000, with the discount rate set on noncompetitive tenders at the average of accepted competitive bids.

World Bank Securities and Related Issues

The securities of three international development organizations—the International Bank for Reconstruction and Development (commonly known as the World Bank), the Inter-American Development Bank, and the Asian Development Bank—are usually mentioned in any discussion of agency- or government-related securities, even though strictly speaking none of them is a part of the United States government. All three of these international institutions borrow money in order to make loans in certain areas of the world, and their securities have certain unique features compared with government and agency securities.

Several securities issues of these three organizations are available in foreign currencies, such as Canadian dollars, German marks, Dutch guilders, Japanese yen, Kuwaiti dinars, British pounds, and Swiss francs, among others. As mentioned in Chapter 4, the investor should keep in mind that the non-dollar-denominated securities usually respond to interest rate movements in the currency's home country, as well as investors' opinions as to whether that currency might be revalued up or devalued vis-à-vis other currencies. In addition, although none of the securities of these three international institutions carries a direct guarantee of the United States or any other government, each of the banks has the right to call on its member governments to meet its debt obligations.

World Bank   The World Bank has 125 member nations. As of January 1975, the World Bank had $10.8 billion worth of securi-. ties outstanding, of which $4.7 billion were denominated in U.S. dollars, and $6.1 billion denominated in other currencies. The amount of the subscription by the United States which can be called upon by the World Bank to pay off debt obligations, if necessary, totals $7 billion, with no additional authorization by Congress required for payment of these funds to the bank. If one or more member countries cannot pay its share of the World Bank's obliga- tions, the bank may call on its other members to raise the additional money. The dollar-denominated bonds and notes of the World Bank have a minimum purchase requirement of $1,000 and are available in both bearer and registered form in several larger denominations. World Bank securities issued in other currencies also have minimum purchase requirements and denomination sizes. Interest income on World Bank bonds is taxable for federal, state, and local income tax purposes.

Inter-American Development Bank   The Inter-American Develop- ment Bank has 24 countries of North and South America as members. As of April 1975, it had $1.6 billion in securities out- standing, of which $774 million were issued in dollars and over $797 million in other currencies. The United States subscription to the bank which can be called in by the Inter-American Develop- ment Bank amounts to over $2 billion. The minimum purchase requirement for dollar-denominated securities of the bank is $1,000, and their bonds and notes are available in registered form only. Income is fully taxable at the federal, state, and local levels.

Asian Development Bank   The Asian Development Bank has 41 member governments from North America, Europe, Australia, and Asia. As of April 1975, it had $358 million in securities out- standing, of which $156 million was in dollars and $202 million in other currencies. The Asian Development Bank can call on the Secretary of the Treasury at any time for up to $120 million, to satisfy the unpaid portion of the United States subscription to the bank's capital, in the event that it is needed to satisfy debt obligations of the Asian Development Bank. The minimum purchase requirement for the dollar-denominated securities of the bank is $1,000, and their bonds and notes are available in registered form only. Interest income on Asian Development Bank bonds is taxable in full at the federal, state, and local taxation levels.

Buying and Selling Agency Securities and Related Issues in the Primary and Secondary Markets

Many of the procedures for buying and selling securities of the agencies of the United States government and related institutions are the same as those for buying Treasury bills, notes, and bonds, as described in the previous chapter. In this section, we will focus on those methods which particularly apply to the various types of agency issues. We will review how new offerings are brought to market, secondary-market trading practices, and settlement procedures.

How new offerings are brought to market Agency issues are generally offered to investors in one of three ways. The first method involves the use of a *fiscal agent* employed by the agency. The fiscal agent is an individual who is employed on a full-time basis by the agency to monitor developments in the money and capital markets, and to recommend a total size, coupon, and maturity for upcoming offerings planned by the agency. In addition, the fiscal agent assembles a *selling group*, comprising securities dealers and commercial banks, which distributes initial offerings to the public.

About 1 week before an initial offering, the fiscal agent places in the newspapers an offering notice announcing the upcoming issue, and investors who wish to buy the security submit their subscriptions for the issue to members of the selling group. Late in the afternoon on the day before the offering date, the fiscal agent informs the selling group of the specific offering terms and coupon rate for the security, and selling group participants then indicate to the fiscal agent the total amount of their subscription. Usually, the total subscriptions submitted by the selling group firms exceed the total size of the offering by a substantial amount, and the fiscal agent has to allocate the issue among the members of the selling group, generally on the basis of how well that particular firm has sold the agency's securities in the past. A very large majority of the securities of government-sponsored enterprises are initially marketed to the public through the fiscal agent method.

The second method of offering agency securities involves the formation of an *underwriting syndicate* comprising dealer banks and securities brokerage firms which is headed by one or more managers who organize the selling group and set allocations of securities among the selling group members. The specific terms of the issue may be *negotiated* in advance of the offering between the underwriting group and the government agency, or the terms may be arrived at very near to (or on) the offering date through a *competitive* bidding procedure whereby two or more syndicates will compete with one another to provide the agency with the lowest interest cost. A large number of the Federal Agencies, such as the Tennessee Valley Authority and the Export-Import Bank, have brought securities to market through the underwriting syndicate method. It might be mentioned again that several government agencies offer their short-term discount notes through a permanent group of dealer firms who also maintain a secondary trading market in the notes.

The third way in which agency securities are brought to market entails the *auction technique,* similar to the way Treasury bills are offered to investors. In this type of offering, bids are submitted directly to the agency (or in some cases, to the Federal Reserve System) for a specified amount of the issue, and the agency selects the highest bids (lowest interest rates). The auction procedure is used by the Tennessee Valley Authority on its short-term discount notes and by the Federal Financing Bank on its bill offerings.

Many, but not all, agency securities are issued, registered, exchanged, and redeemed at the Federal Reserve Bank of New

York or at other Federal Reserve banks or branches. The investor should consult his securities broker, a commercial bank, a nearby Federal Reserve bank or branch, or the agency itself *in advance of the offering* to find out exactly how, when, where, and in what form (Federal funds or clearinghouse funds) payment is to be made for newly issued agency securities.

Secondary-market trading practices Virtually all of the secondary market in government agency and related securities is done in the same dealer over-the-counter market in which U.S. government securities are traded, since most of the securities firms who deal in governments deal also in trade agencies. In the 5 years from 1968 through 1973, dealers' trading activity rose along with the large increase in total agency debt outstanding, as average daily trading volume increased 140 percent, from $270 million per day in 1968 to $650 million per day at the end of 1973. The Federal Open Market Committee also has demonstrated that secondary trading markets in agency securities have deepened and matured somewhat in recent years by conducting open-market operations in agency securities from time to time. However, as has been mentioned earlier, not all agency issues can be traded with equal ease, with minimum impact on the price at which a transaction is accomplished. For example, larger agency issues are generally more easily traded in the secondary market than smaller issues.

Also, the most recently issued agency securities are usually the most actively traded, and price quotation spreads are comparatively narrow on these securities versus securities which have been outstanding a long while. In a high-interest-rate environment, low-coupon agency securities which were issued when interest rates were lower are often difficult to buy because the holders are reluctant to take a loss on the investment, preferring to retain the security until it is paid off at par upon maturity or until interest rates decline substantially. The price quotations for agency securities which appear in most newspapers can be of value in helping the investor choose an agency issue which is of large size. For example, the morning newspaper for July 11, 1974, showed the following quotation for one of the securities listed under the Federal Land Bank category:

550   July, '77   7.50   95.12   95.28   9.09

The first item, 550, represents the total amount outstanding, $550 million, which is a large amount for one issue of an agency security. This particular issue of Federal Land Bank notes is due to mature in July 1977, and the 7.50 represents the coupon rate, 7.50 percent. Since agency securities are quoted just like government notes and bonds, in thirty-seconds-of-a-point fractions, the 95.12 stands for a *bid price* of $95^{12}/_{32}$, or $953.75 per $1,000 bond, at which the five dealers who submit quotes to the Federal Reserve each day were willing to *buy* these Federal Land Bank securities *from* an investor at 3:30 P.M. on July 10. The 95.28 means $95^{28}/_{32}$, or $958.75 per $1,000 bond, is the *ask* (also known as the *offer*) part of the price quotation, or the price at which the dealer was willing to *sell* these securities *to* an investor. The difference, amounting to $5 per $1,000 bond, represents the dealer's *spread,* or compensation for inventorying the bonds and maintaining a market in the issue. The 9.09 at the end of the quotation line gives the yield to maturity if these securities, with a 7.50 percent coupon, were bought for a price of 95.28 and held until the issue matures in July of 1977.

The quotation spreads between the bid and ask prices on agency securities of all maturities are usually wider than the spreads on U.S. government securities because the latter are more actively traded and more marketable and because dealer inventories of agencies are generally a good deal smaller than their government positions. Also, longer-maturity agency issues have wider price quotation spreads than short-maturity agency issues, reaching up to $10 (and more in certain thinly traded issues) per $1,000 bond. Where possible, the investor should select agency issues for which the total amount outstanding is of large size to avoid wide price quotation spreads and to enhance liquidity. On some occasions, if a large buyer or a large seller of agency securities comes into the marketplace, the price level on a particular agency security might be suddenly shifted upward or downward by that investor's trading activity. Many times, as we will see in Chapter 14 on portfolio improvements, these sudden price shifts may enable the small investor to take advantage of temporary bargain prices for that particular security, compared with other agencies or other types of securities.

Settlement procedures Settlement on agency securities is very similar to procedures followed on U.S. government securities. In most new offerings, settlement is due in Federal funds form on the issue date at the Federal Reserve Bank (or in some cases, at the offices of the agency) or at the securities brokerage firm or commercial bank through which the securities were purchased, in accordance with the specific settlement practices of each particular firm. If payment for newly issued securities arrives after the settlement date, the investor's order may be cancelled and his funds returned. If not, an additional amount representing the accrued interest on the bonds since the issue date will be charged to the investor. In order to have the certificates printed and delivered, new agency securities are often issued and dated 5 to 10 business days after the offering date. When this is done, if the investor wishes to buy or sell the securities before they are available, transactions are effected on a *when-issued* basis. This is noted in the newspaper price quotations by putting "W.I." in the column where the issue size is usually printed, until the agency certificates are ready for normal trading, at which time the amount of the issue in millions of dollars is printed.

In secondary-market trading, payment for and delivery of agency securities transacted in round lots ($100,000 principal amount and multiples of $100,000 principal amount) is scheduled for the next full business day after the trade is executed. Transactions involving less than $100,000 principal amount are settled 5 business days after the trade and may involve additional odd-lot charges or fees. The investor should determine the amount of these charges beforehand. Payment is usually in Federal funds, and whenever coupon-type interest-bearing securities are purchased, the buyer must pay the seller the accrued interest since the last interest payment date (when the securities are sold, the investor will receive the amount of the accrued interest since the last interest payment date from the buyer). As with government securities, the investor can also arrange to have settlement take place either on a *cash* basis, with payment or delivery due the same day as the trade, or on a *delayed* delivery basis, with payment or delivery due on some prearranged date in the future. The investor should always coordinate the settlement dates when simultaneously buying and selling agencies, or any type of security for that matter. Otherwise, he may be short of funds or his money may sit idle in the form of cash, while waiting for settlement to be made.

Concluding comments   It is worthwhile to point out again that interest income on many (but not all) agency issues is *exempt* from state and local income taxes, yet *subject* to federal income taxes. Thus, when comparing yields after taxes on agencies with other securities which are subject to federal, state, and local income taxation, the investor should perform the calculation exercise described in the second to last section of the previous chapter on U.S. government securities. To keep track of the many features of various agencies as compared with each other and with other securities, the investor is referred to Chapter 12, which contains summary information charts on virtually all types of fixed-income securities.

EIGHT

Short-Term
Money Market Instruments

Most of the broad groups of fixed-income securities reviewed in this book offer a wide variety of maturities for the investor to choose from, ranging from a few months to 30 years or more. In this chapter we will focus primarily on three types of fixed-income securities which are classified as *short-term* in that they virtually always have an original maturity of less than 1 year: bankers' acceptances, negotiable certificates of deposit, and commercial paper. Since investors buy these three investments with temporarily idle cash balances, they are generally considered to function as a near substitute for money and thus form a part of the *money market*. Repurchase agreements, which were described in Chapter 5, are also included here, as are cash management funds, variable rate notes, and other miscellaneous short-term securities.

Although many of these short-term investments are officially called *instruments*, to distinguish them slightly from the term "security," which connotes a longer-term issue, in practice the terms "instrument" and "security" are often used interchangeably. Short-term government, agency, corporate, tax-exempt, and international securities are discussed within their respective chapters, while Chapter 12 offers a comparison of these short-term issues with bankers' acceptances, certificates of deposit, and commercial paper by displaying the entire array of short- and long-term fixed-income securities investment possibilities, grouped according to the maturities most commonly available.

The overall amount of all types of short-term securities has increased dramatically during the 1960s and early 1970s. This phenomenon has been particularly evident in the case of bankers' acceptances, certificates of deposit, and commercial paper, whose total outstandings have risen over 680 percent, from more than $20 billion in 1963 to $157 billion at the end of 1974. This rapid increase has been spurred from the *demand* side as businesses of all types looked to the short-term money markets to raise funds for their higher levels of inventories, receivables, and other working-capital items. On the *supply* side, institutional, corporate, and numerous individual investors have been attracted to short-term money market instruments by the upward trend in short-term interest rates, with some deviations during the sixties and seventies, accompanied by greater sophistication and knowledge about investing idle cash balances. Higher interest rates in general have also positively affected investors' preferences for short-term investments, which, as shown in Chapter 3, decline less in price than long-term securities as interest levels rise. Short-term instruments also permit the investor, in a period of rising interest rates, to reinvest the proceeds of his investment at maturity in higher-yielding securities.

The growth in volume of short-term instruments outstanding has also led to a gain in average daily trading volume for short-term money market instruments which have been in use for 100 years or more, as well as more recently developed securities. Commercial paper has been issued in the United States since before 1800, bankers' acceptances as we know them appeared in 1914, and negotiable certificates of deposit were developed in their present form in 1961. These three money market instruments have traditionally been dominated by large investors, with $500,000 or more of short-term funds to invest. However, in recent years, individual investors have become buyers of these securities because they are occasionally available in amounts as small as $5,000 and because of their higher yields relative to Treasury bills and short-term U.S. government agency issues.

Yields on 90-day maturity bankers' acceptances, certificates of deposit, and directly issued commercial paper have usually tended to be around 40 to 60 basis points (0.40 to 0.60 percent) *higher* than yields on 91-day Treasury bills. However, these yield spreads are subject to frequent variation. (See Figure 8-1.) In some market environments, these instruments yield almost *the same as* Treasury bills, while at certain points in 1970, 1974, and other years, when investors were very concerned about safety and the credit quality of many issues, they rushed to purchase Treasury bills relative to these other short-term investments, causing yields on bankers' acceptances, certificates of deposit, and commercial paper to *exceed* 3-month Treasury bills by as much as 300 to 400 basis points (3.00 to 4.00 percent) or more, the widest spreads witnessed in a generation.

The wide yield spreads which have occasionally occurred in the past point up the fact that short-term yields generally tend to move up and down much more rapidly than long-term interest rates, primarily because an equivalent *point* change (a change in the dollar amount of a security) affects a short-term instrument's yield much more than the yield on a long-term security. For example, a 1-point price decline (from 100 to 99) on a 7 percent coupon security with a 182-day life (½ year) causes its yield to maturity to rise 209 basis points, from 7.00 to 9.09 percent whereas the same price decline causes the yield to maturity on a 7 percent 5-year note to change by only 24 basis points, from 7.00 to 7.24 percent, and a 1-point price decline on a 7 percent 25-year bond results in a yield to maturity increase of 9 basis points, from 7.00 to 7.09 percent. Of course, these wider swings in yields on short-term rather than long-term securities also hold true for a given point change upward in price (decline in yields).

In the following sections, we will review the mechanics, marketing channels, and other features of bankers' acceptances, certificates of deposit, and commercial paper, followed by a section on other ways the individual can invest his funds for a short period of time, including cash management funds and the variable rate "dual maturity" notes first offered to investors in 1974.

FIGURE 8-1. *Short-term interest rates.* *(By permission of the Board of Governors of the Federal Reserve System.)*

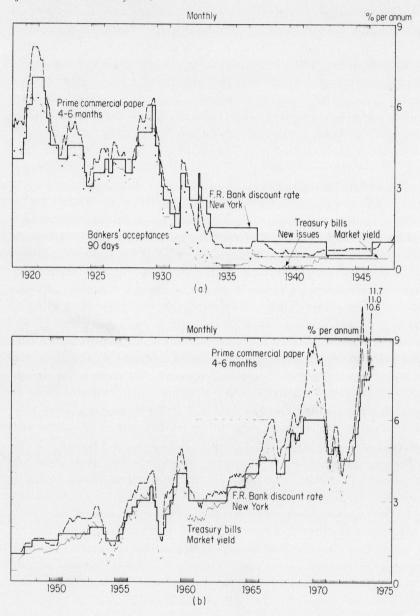

Bankers' Acceptances

Many investors have difficulty understanding exactly what a bankers' acceptance is. Almost all bankers' acceptances are created from transactions involving foreign trade. In its simplest and most traditional form, a bankers' acceptance is merely a check, drawn on a bank by a importer or exporter of goods. The payment date of the check is not immediate; rather, it corresponds to the date the goods which are being financed by the check will be delivered. Because the check underlying the bankers' acceptance is payable in the *future* (such checks are usually called *drafts*), if the recipient of the check presents it for payment at a bank before the payment date on the check, he will receive *less* than the face amount of the check— another form of discounting. Once the check has been presented to the bank for early payment, the bank has the option of (1) holding the check until maturity or (2) guaranteeing to pay off the check at maturity and then selling it at a slightly higher price (a lower discount from the check's face value) to an investor who wishes to earn the discount between the purchase price and the face value of the check.

If the latter route is followed, the bank stamps the word "accepted" (meaning "guaranteed") on the face of the check and it is free to be traded in the secondary market for bankers' acceptances. Occasionally, a domestic shipment of goods or a conventional loan which has no connection with foreign trade is converted into an acceptance and traded the same as a bankers' acceptance which arose from an international transaction.

As of early 1975, there were $16.5 billion in bankers' acceptances outstanding, up 510 percent from $2.7 billion in 1962. Of this $16.5 billion total, $3.8 billion was created to finance exports, $3.7 billion was created to finance imports, over $9 billion was issued to finance trade between two foreign countries, and a relatively small amount was issued to finance shipment or warehouse storage of goods in the United States. Not included in these totals are acceptances created out of standard short-term loans made to corporations, also known as "marketable time drafts," which totalled over $500 million as of early 1975. Another name for this last type of acceptance is an "ineligible" acceptance, because unlike other types of bankers' acceptances, marketable time drafts are not eligible for purchase (discounting) by the Federal Reserve System. Acceptances which can be discounted with (sold to) the Federal Reserve System are termed "prime" bankers' acceptances.

The popularity of prime bankers' acceptances as an investment for short-term funds stems from several factors. First is their strong credit backing, derived not only from the guarantee of the draft by the accepting bank, but also from the implicit backing of the firm drawing the check and the underlying merchandise involved in the transaction. Second, bankers' acceptance yields are usually 50 basis points or more higher than Treasury bill yields of comparable maturity. Another benefit to investors in bankers' acceptances stems from their availability in a broad spectrum of maturity dates, ranging from 1 to 270 days, with most bankers' acceptance activity concentrated in the 180-day-or-less maturities. Foreign investors, who hold a substantial percentage of the total amount of bankers' acceptances outstanding, are attracted to acceptances because the income from an acceptance—which is subject to federal, state, and local income taxes for United States investors—is free from federal income taxes imposed on foreigners and because numerous acceptances are accepted, or endorsed, by two banks rather than one, thus providing additional safety. Third, and particularly important to the small investor, bankers' acceptances come in a wide variety of principal amount sizes, with acceptances varying in face value from $5,000 up to $1 million or more. Finally, almost all bankers' acceptance dealers trade these instruments at relatively stable posted interest rates, in contrast with the more rapidly fluctuating yields found on most other short-term securities.

Because of the small amount of bankers' acceptances outstanding relative to Treasury bills ($16.5 billion in bankers' acceptances, versus over $75 billion in Treasury bills held by the public), the average daily trading activity in bankers' acceptances is somewhat limited, amounting to $100 million worth per day, compared with $2.5 billion for Treasury bills. Because of this fact, bankers' acceptances in the exact amount and maturity desired by the investor are sometimes difficult to find. An investor can purchase bankers' acceptances through his bank or securities broker. Primary trading markets in acceptances are maintained by the major money-center banks and by six dealer firms, all of which also trade government securities. Like Treasury bills, bankers' acceptances trade on a yield basis, with prices quoted not in percentage-of-par terms but in terms of a bid and offered discount yield (the term "offered" is the same as the term "ask" as used in the previous discussions on dealers' price quotations). The following line was excerpted from a newspaper summary of short-term money market instrument yields:

Bankers' Acceptances Quoted by One Dealer:
   60–90 days, 8% bid; $7^3/_4$% offered

This excerpt means that the investor could *buy* the bankers' acceptance *from* the dealer making the price quotation at a price to yield 7¾ percent (on an annualized basis) for acceptances between 60 and 90 days' maturity and that it could be *sold to* the dealer at a lower price (to yield 8 percent).

This sample quotation points up several slight differences in the way bankers' acceptances are quoted compared with quotations on government securities. First, bankers' acceptance quotations are given in discount rate terms, but the actual bond equivalent yield is not given, as is sometimes done in each line of the newspaper price quotations on Treasury bills. To convert the discount yields on bankers' acceptances to true bond equivalent yields, the investor must use Table 6-3 or the special formula given in Chapter 6 for making these conversions. Following the formula, the investor will see that a 7.75 percent discount yield on a *90*-day bankers' acceptance is comparable to a bond equivalent yield of 8.0 percent. The investor should keep in mind that the maturity of the instrument influences the size of the adjustment between a discount yield and a bond equivalent yield—for a *60*-day acceptance, the bond equivalent yield of a 7.75 percent discount yield is 7.85 percent.

Second, bankers' acceptance discount yields are usually not finely divided into hundredths of a percent, as are Treasury bill discount yields, although some acceptance dealers have recently begun to change from the traditional system of posted rates. Instead, bankers' acceptance yields are quoted in fractions and multiples of ⅛ percent, e.g., 7⅛, 7¼, 7⅜, and so forth. Third, depending on interest rate patterns, bankers' acceptance discount yields are quoted in 30-day intervals from 1 to 270 days, sometimes with a ⅛ percent rate differential between each maturity category. On other occasions, there may be only a single interest rate quoted for all bankers' acceptances maturing between 1 and 270 days, on both newly issued acceptances and acceptances bought in the secondary trading market. Fourth, the spread between the bid and offered yields is usually fixed at ¼ percent, not variable as in the case of Treasury bills. At very high short-term interest rate levels, the spread between the bid and offered yields on bankers' acceptances has occasionally widened to ½, ¾, or even a full 1 percent.

As with other short-term fixed-income securities, transactions fees and custody charges can significantly affect the total yield derived from an investment in a bankers' acceptance. The shorter the maturity and the smaller the face value of the acceptance, the greater the reductive effect on the actual yield of the bankers' acceptance. Most banks and securities brokerage firms charge a $20 fee per transaction in bankers' acceptances, which can have a sizable impact on the investor's overall return if much in-and-out trading is done on bankers' acceptances in the $20,000 to $50,000 range. To calculate the dollar price of a bankers' acceptance when the discount rate is known, a method similar to the formula for finding the dollar price of a Treasury bill is used:

$$\text{Discount per \$1,000 in face value of bankers' acceptance} = \text{discount rate in basis points} \times \text{days to maturity} \times 0.000277778$$

Numerically minded readers will recognize the factor used at the end of the above formula as the same number used in the Treasury bill discount rate-to-dollar price formula, only with the decimal point on the number moved one place to the left, since we are concerned here with the amount of discount per *$1,000* on bankers' acceptances, rather than the discount per *$10,000* which is used in Treasury bill calculations.

To find the discount to be subtracted in order to compute the purchase price of a $19,000 face value bankers' acceptance with 90 days to maturity, purchased at a 7.75 percent yield, the formula works out as follows:

Discount per $1,000 = 775 basis points × 90 days to maturity × 0.000277778
in face value   = $19.30 per $1,000 face value

The discount for the bill then becomes $19.30 × 19 (the number of times $1,000 divides into $19,000), or $366.70. Subtracting the discount from the face value to obtain the purchase price, we arrive at:

Purchase price = $19,000 face value − $366.70 = *$18,633.30*

The investor can see how a $20 service charge will effectively raise the purchase price to $18,653.30, thereby reducing the discount and lowering the effective yield from 7.75 to 7.32 percent, providing, of course, that the bankers' acceptance is not sold prior to maturity. If the acceptance is sold prior to maturity and an additional $20 transaction charge is levied on the trade, the investor's yield will be lowered below 7.0 percent, assuming no change upward or downward in the overall level of interest rates has taken place.

Certificates of Deposit

A short-term money market instrument which has shown substantial growth in usage during recent years is the negotiable certificate of deposit (also known as CDs). A certificate of deposit is a receipt from a bank for a deposit of money at a specified rate of interest for a specified period of time. Principal and interest is paid back at maturity, which is generally from 1 to 12 months, occasionally ranging up to 18 months. Most certificates of deposit are appropriate investments for large corporate, institutional, or wealthy individual investors, with a $25,000 certificate of deposit virtually the smallest size available (and these are not frequently encountered).

Most certificates of deposit are issued in amounts of $100,000 to $1 million and up.

Because certificates of deposit are *negotiable,* they can be bought and sold in secondary-market trading before their maturity. The resulting marketability of negotiable certificates of deposit distinguishes this instrument from the wide variety of special time deposit programs, some of which have the word "certificate" in their name, offered by savings institutions to depositors of $1,000 to $100,000 and above. In mid-1974, the Federal Home Loan Bank Board allowed savings institutions, which had previously been prohibited from issuing negotiable certificates of deposit, to offer negotiable certificates of deposits in amounts of $100,000 or more, thus permitting large depositors to trade into or out of a certificate of deposit investment without forfeiting interest, as described below on the smaller time deposit programs.

To earn an attractive rate of interest on the smaller special program time deposits, the investor usually has to agree to keep a certain minimum amount on deposit for a specified length of time. Since this type of time deposit is *nonnegotiable,* it cannot be sold in the open market, and in almost all cases, if the investor decides to withdraw his money from this special high-interest savings account before the maturity date, 90 days' interest is forfeited and the yield on the investment is reduced to the interest rate on ordinary passbook savings accounts. Thus, even though very small certificates of deposit are difficult to buy in the secondary trading market, with the investor having to accept much lower yields and less advantageous price quotations than on large-denomination certificates of deposit, they do have a least *some* marketability and opportunity for price gain should interest rates decline.

Before purchasing a certificate of deposit, the investor should find out exactly how much of a yield sacrifice he might have to accept by buying a smaller, less marketable certificate of deposit. If a substantially smaller return will be earned on a very small certificate of deposit, the investor should consider investing in other types of short-term instruments in which small trades are more commonplace, such as Treasury bills, certain government agency securities, bankers' acceptances, or short-term tax-exempt notes, which are described further in the next chapter.*

As of the end of January 1975, total certificates of deposit outstanding amounted to $88.5 billion, up 265 percent from the $24.3 billion outstanding at the end of 1968. During 1973, the average daily trading volume in certificates of deposit amounted to $1.2 billion, or roughly half of the average daily trading volume in Treasury bills. This large trading activity in certificates of deposit underscores the popularity of this instrument with many corporate, institutional, and individual investors of large size. This is because of the relative simplicity and high quality of certificates of deposit, which are backed by the bank which issued the instrument. The yields offered by certificates of deposit are above those available on Treasury bills and short-term government agency securities and usually approximate the yields available on bankers' acceptances and commercial paper. Interest income earned on certificates of deposit is fully taxable at the federal, state, and local levels.

The investor should remember, however, that unlike bankers' acceptances and commercial paper, interest yields on newly issued certificates of deposit are governed by Regulation Q of the Federal Reserve System, which sets a ceiling on the maximum interest rate which banks can pay on time deposits. When market rates of interest on other money market instruments rise above Regulation Q ceilings, investors prefer to buy these other investments instead of certificates of deposit, forcing the banks to look to the Eurodollar

---

*A new type of "quasi-CD" in smaller amounts was issued in late 1974, when commercial banks and savings and loan institutions were allowed to issue so-called investment certificates, in denominations of $1,000 or more but less than $100,000, with a minimum maturity of at least 6 years. Investment certificates can be issued in either negotiable form or nonnegotiable form. The negotiable certificates are not redeemable by the issuer under any conditions, but they can be sold on the open market or used as collateral for loans by the owner (with the loan carrying an interest rate at least 2 percentage points higher than the interest rate on the investment certificate). The nonnegotiable certificates may be redeemed prior to maturity under existing rules for early withdrawal of time deposits, thus involving an effective interest rate penalty to the owner of the certificate. Banks are not permitted to purchase investment certificates for their own account.

market and other sources for funds to lend. The Regulation Q ceilings can be raised, lowered, or even suspended (as they have been for certain periods of time). When Regulation Q ceilings have been suspended on negotiable certificates of deposit, interest rates on new issues of this instrument move upward and downward along with market interest rates. The Regulation Q ceiling does not apply to the yields at which certificates of deposit are traded in the secondary market.

Another point the investor should keep in mind is that not all certificates of deposit are of equal marketability. While the vast majority of issuance and trading is done in the very marketable certificates of deposit of major New York and Chicago money-center banks, the certificates of deposit of smaller regional banks are somewhat less marketable than the major banks' CDs. Consequently, yields on the smaller banks' certificates of deposit are usually several basis points higher than yields on the certificates of deposit of large, well-known money-center banks. In periods of tight credit (high interest rates) or investor concern over quality, the difference in yield between the certificates of deposit of large banks as compared with those of small banks can become even greater. In evaluating certificates of deposit, the investor should carefully scrutinize the financial strength of the bank backing the certificate of deposit, particularly since the Federal Deposit Insurance Corporation insures only the first $40,000 worth of an FDIC-covered bank's CDs held by any one investor, not the entire amount of the CD.

This $40,000 FDIC insurance coverage limitation brings up a practice which the investor should approach with extreme caution, if at all. This practice consists of money brokerage firms pooling the funds of a large number of small investors throughout the United States in order to purchase at least a $100,000-denominated certificate of deposit with these aggregated funds. Not all the money collected goes into the CD—the money broker keeps part of the money as a commission for his services. The "shared" certificate of deposit is held in a custodial bank account and the investor receives an assignment form, which shows exactly how much of the certificate he owns. The liquidity benefits of owning a negotiated certificate of deposit are forgone when buying a certificate of deposit under this pooling method, since the plan usually entails holding onto the instrument until it matures. If the investor needs his funds beforehand, it may be extremely difficult, if not impossible, to obtain them. In the event that the bank which issued the certificate fails, the investor would not receive the $40,000 FDIC insurance protection unless the bank had been informed of the pooling arrangement at the time the CD was purchased. The investor should *check thoroughly* to see whether his share of the CD is registered with the bank, and he might also make sure that the bank itself is protected by the FDIC. In addition, many money brokers offering these plans advertise that they are members of the Securities Investor Protection Corporation (SIPC), which provides protection of up to $50,000 per account, of which $20,000 may be in cash. The investor should *verify* whether the money broker is in fact a SIPC member in good standing. For SIPC coverage to apply, the CD or the customer's funds must be in the *broker's possession* when a problem develops with the *brokerage firm*. Generally, the money brokerage firm should *not* have the customer's funds *or* the CD in its possession (except when the certificate of deposit is being paid for), since the CD is supposed to be held in a custody account at an authorized *bank*. Because of the numerous doubtful characteristics inherent in these pooling programs, and in view of the many other simpler and safer ways of earning an attractive yield on short-term investments, the investor is advised to *avoid* this method of investment. If the investor decides to participate in this type of program, he should do so *only* if he is *certain* that (1) his funds will not be needed prior to the maturity of the instrument; (2) the money brokerage firm is of unquestionable integrity and in sound financial condition, protected by the SIPC; (3) the bank *issuing* the CD is in very strong financial shape and shows the investors' names *individually* on its records as co-owners of the certificate of deposit; and (4) the bank *holding* the CD in a custody account is in very strong financial condition and shows the investors' names individually on its records as co-owners of the certificate of deposit.

When a certificate of deposit is originally issued, the bank usually posts a set of base interest rates for various maturities, with the actual interest rate on the CD negotiated between the issuing bank and the purchaser. The rate which is arrived at depends on the size and reputation of the issuing bank (the larger and better known the bank, the lower the interest rate), the total size of their money needs, the size of the CD being purchased, and the maturity of the CD. Certificate of deposit rates published in the newspaper usually quote the rates paid by major banks in the newly issued market (rather than yields prevailing in the secondary market), for maturities of 1, 2, 3, and 6 months, as well as 1 year. Although many other maturities are available, these are the most commonly issued maturities. Except under unusual circumstances, issuing banks are not permitted to *redeem* their own CDs prior to the certificate's scheduled maturity.

Investors try to avoid CDs with maturity dates falling on a holiday or on a weekend, since interest income would be sacrificed while the funds sit idle a day or two before being reinvested after the CD matures. CDs purchased in the secondary market usually yield a few basis points more than originally issued CDs, since the maturity was chosen by the original investor, not by the secondary-market investor, who has to accommodate his maturity choice to what is available in the secondary market, in addition to the fact that an intermediary dealer earns a small margin on the trade.

Most secondary-market trading comes about as a result of (1) a decision on the part of a holder of a CD to *sell* because of cash needs or to realize a profit if interest rates have fallen since the instrument was originally purchased or (2) a decision on the part of an investor to *buy* a certificate of deposit because of attractive yields or in order to find a CD with a certain maturity more cheaply than the newly issued CDs with similar maturity dates. Secondary trading activities are conducted on a net basis by banks and securities dealers, many of whom are among the group of leading government and agency securities trading firms. Banks are not allowed to *purchase* their own CDs.

Unlike bankers' acceptances, commercial paper, Treasury bills, and many other short-term instruments, certificates of deposit trade on an *interest-bearing* basis rather than on a discount basis. The certificate of deposit is usually bought at par, and principal plus interest is repaid when the CD matures. Prices of CDs with a certain original interest rate are computed at various yields in a manner similar to the method (using yield tables) for calculating corporate bond prices if the coupon rate, maturity, and yield are known. As with other interest-bearing securities, the purchaser of a CD in the secondary market must pay to the seller the total amount of accrued interest on the instrument since the original issue date. If the CD is sold before maturity, the investor will receive the total accrued interest from the original issue date to the sale date from the new buyer, with the investor's actual interest received on the CD during the holding period the difference between the total amount of accrued interest *paid* and the total amount of accrued interest *received*. Of course, the holder of the CD on the final maturity date receives the entire interest payment.

Since interest paid on a CD is computed on the basis of a 360-day year rather than a 365-day year, to convert a CD yield to its bond equivalent yield the investor must annualize the yield by multiplying it by $^{73}/_{72}$ (365 days/360 days), or a factor of 1.014. Thus a stated yield on a CD of 7 percent is equal to a yield of 7 × 1.014, or 7.098 percent on a 365-day basis. The spread between the bid and ask prices in the secondary market for CDs averages about 10 basis points, with wider spreads found on shorter maturities. For example, the investor might find a 6-month CD quoted in the secondary market at 7 percent bid, 6.90 percent asked, and a 1-month CD quoted at 6.70 percent bid, 6.50 percent asked. Normal settlement on CD trades takes place the next business day following the transaction, with payment due in Federal funds. To facilitate settlement, CDs of many non-New York banks are often issued and redeemed through a New York correspondent bank of the issuer.

In early 1975, a new type of negotiable certificate of deposit was issued, with a minimum term of 360 days and a variable, or "floating," interest rate which is changed every 90 days. The interest rate on the variable rate CDs is pegged at a certain interest spread over the bank's then-current rate on conventional certificates of deposit with a 90-day maturity. Other types of variable rate notes are discussed later in this chapter.

Commercial Paper

Commercial paper consists of short-term promissory notes which large corporations sell at a discount to institutional and individual investors, other corporations, and commercial paper dealer firms. Since commercial paper is almost always unsecured and represents borrowing done on the strength of the company's creditworthiness alone, commercial paper issuers are usually large, well-known concerns whose financial soundness has been assumed to be above question. However, on occasion in the past, a company has run into difficulty paying off its bank loans or its commercial paper.

The total amount of commercial paper outstanding has shown rapid growth in recent years. As of December 1974, $53.3 billion of commercial paper was outstanding, up 63 percent from $32.6 billion at the end of 1969, and up 780 percent from $6.0 billion at the end of 1962. Among the reasons for this increase have been benefits to both the issuer of, and the investor in, commercial paper.

From the issuer's standpoint, commercial paper represents a lower cost of short-term funds than bank borrowings, since the commercial paper rate is usually below the prime commercial lending rate of the banks. The fact that banks usually require a borrower to keep 10 to 20 percent of the loan on deposit with the bank as compensating balances also makes commercial paper more attractive from a cost savings standpoint.

Investors have been attracted to commercial paper by its higher interest returns relative to Treasury bills and other short-term money market instruments. Historically, commercial paper has offered a 25 to 100 basis point (0.25 to 1.00 percent) rate advantage over 91-day Treasury bills. In times of very tight money, and in times of investor concern over safety, the yield spread between commercial paper and 91-day Treasury bills has widened considerably, to 200 to 500 basis points (2.00 to 5.00 percent), as occurred in mid-1974. In addition, investors favor the flexibility in choosing the size, date of issuance, and date of maturity of commercial paper. While commercial paper has been available in amounts as low as $5,000, in practice $25,000 is virtually the smallest amount which can be found (and there is usually a $25 fee charged when an amount this small is purchased). It is much more common to encounter commercial paper sold in much larger amounts—$100,-000, $500,000, $1 million, or even higher. The normal minimum round-lot transaction in commercial paper is $250,000. The investor can generally select any maturity date he desires, from 5 to 270 days after the commercial paper is issued. Most commercial paper has an original maturity of somewhere between 30 and 120 days. Commercial paper with a maturity in excess of 270 days is very rarely encountered, since a corporate security with over 270 days' maturity must be registered with the Securities and Exchange Commission in order to be offered to the public.

Standard & Poor's, Moody's, and Fitch Investors Service all rate commercial paper according to the following rating systems:

Standard & Poor's	*Moody's*	*Fitch Investors Service*
A-1: Highest investment grade	Prime-1	F-1: Highest grade
A-2: High investment grade	Prime-2	F-2: Investment grade
A-3: Medium investment grade	Prime-3	F-3: Good grade
B: Medium grade	Not	F-4: Not recommended
C: Speculative	rated	
D: Expected to default		

As a matter of practice, commercial paper in the lower classifications of the above rating services is generally unacceptable to investors. Many commercial paper dealers require their issuers to maintain open unused bank lines of credit to support most, if not all, of their commercial paper outstanding. In recent years, some banks have backed commercial paper through the use of so-called standby letters of credit, and an insurance company has also guaranteed commercial paper of one issuer. Moody's rating service has a separate rating category for commercial paper issuers backed by a letter of credit—Prime-1 LOC.

The large dollar amounts involved in commercial paper imply that very large investors with excess cash to invest have been by far the principal purchasers of commercial paper—primarily corporations. In recent years, some investment institutions and individuals have begun buying commercial paper. For the individual investor with a small amount of money to invest, commercial paper is probably not the best short-term investment for his needs because of the large dollar amount of normal purchases and the lack of established secondary trading facilities for commercial paper. The reduced liquidity of commercial paper is offset somewhat by the ability of the purchaser to select the exact maturity date which best suits his requirements. As is described below, selling commercial paper before its scheduled maturity date is the exception rather than the rule. Consequently, *before* the investor purchases commercial paper, he should *be sure* that any funds placed in this instrument will not be needed prior to maturity. If the possibility exists that the money will be needed for other purposes before the scheduled maturity of the commercial paper, the investor should consider other short-term money market securities which can be traded in the secondary market.

Commercial paper is generally divided into two categories— directly placed commercial paper and dealer-placed commercial paper—both of which refer to the method by which it is sold to the investor. During the period 1969–1974, about two-thirds of all commercial paper issued was directly placed paper and one-third was dealer-placed paper. Directly placed commercial paper, some-times referred to as "finance company paper," is issued by a variety of firms, including (1) captive sales finance companies of large industrial corporations, such as Ford Motor Credit, General Electric Credit Corporation, and General Motors Acceptance Corporation; (2) personal and business loan companies, such as CIT Financial and Commercial Credit Corporation; and (3) in recent years several large bank holding companies and REITs. Directly placed commer-cial paper is sold through the issuer's own sales organization directly to investors and generally sells at a somewhat higher price (lower yield) than dealer-placed commercial paper because of several fac-tors: (1) the strong financial condition and size of direct issuers as a group; (2) the ability to select the exact issuance date and maturity date on directly placed paper, whereas for dealer placed paper the investor may not always be able to obtain the *exact* maturity date desired, since the commercial paper may sometimes be sold from the dealers' inventories; (3) the usual practice of most direct issuers of offering rate protection to the investor for 3 to 4 days after the commercial paper has been purchased (if interest rates rise during this period, the direct issuer may adjust the interest rate on the commercial paper upward to conform with market yields); and (4) direct issuers will generally repurchase outstanding commercial paper from an investor if unusual circumstances cause the investor to need his funds before the scheduled maturity date of the paper. In addition, investors can sometimes buy directly placed paper with a maturity as short as 3 days, and some issuers offer directly placed paper in small amounts. For example, an investor can purchase commercial paper directly from General Motors Acceptance Corporation in amounts as low as $25,000, with the maturity to be chosen by the investor (between 30 and 270 days).

Dealer-placed commercial paper is sold by over 600 corporations to investors through nine commercial paper dealers, all of which are securities brokerage and investment banking firms. After a corporation has issued commercial paper, the dealer firm may resell the paper immediately to investors, or it may hold the commercial paper in inventory for subsequent resale. As compensation for their selling efforts and for the market risk which dealers assume by holding commercial paper in inventory (if interest rates move up, the commercial paper inventory will be sold at a lower price than the price at which it was purchased from the corporation), dealers usually offer commercial paper at ⅛ percent higher yield than the interest rate at which it was purchased from the corporate issuer. Unlike directly placed paper, "unusual circumstance" arrangements for repurchasing commercial paper from an investor who needs his funds before maturity are generally not available on dealer-placed commercial paper. Commercial paper rates on both dealer-placed and directly placed paper are quoted in the daily newspaper, with rates shown for various maturity intervals from 30 to 270 days.

Similar to bankers' acceptances and Treasury bills, commercial paper trades on a discount yield basis, using a 360-day year. Once in a while, interest-bearing commercial paper is found, similar to certificates of deposit, but this is very rare. To find the bond equivalent yield and the dollar price of commercial paper if the discount yield is known, the investor uses the same formulas which are described in Chapter 6 for converting Treasury bill discount yields to dollar prices and to their bond equivalent yields. The bond equivalent yield of commercial paper is somewhat higher than the stated yield. For example, 30-day commercial paper with a stated yield of 7 percent has a bond equivalent yield of 7.14 percent. Commercial paper is most often found in bearer form, though it is occasionally encountered in a form payable to the order of the investor. All income on commercial paper is fully taxable at the federal, state, and local income tax levels.

Settlement on commercial paper transactions takes place in Federal funds on the same day or the business day following the trade. For same day settlement, trades have to be executed by 12:30 P.M. Eastern time. Commercial banks located in New York and Chicago usually act as the issuing agent for the corporation, and final payments of principal and the earned discount interest are also collected from the bank named as payment agent on the front of the commercial paper note.

Cash Management Funds

Two new types of short-term investments have been created in recent years in response to high short-term interest rates and the desire of many individual investors to avoid tying up their funds for a long period of time. The *cash management fund* is simply a mutual fund which invests in short-term money-market instruments, and the *variable interest rate note* gives the investor the option (after a certain time period) of redeeming his investment on specified maturity dates every 6 months or at the end of the note's life, several years from its original issue date.

Cash management funds enable the small investor, in conjunction with other investors, to earn interest on many of the short-term money market instruments which have large minimum purchase requirements and which would otherwise not be able to be purchased by the individual investor with modest funds. As of January 1975, there were over 20 of these funds operating, and a current list of the available cash management funds can be obtained from any securities brokerage firm. Generally, the minimum investment in a cash management fund is $1,000 to $5,000, although some funds will accept dollar amounts as low as $100 in certain cases. Most, but not all, of the cash management funds are "no load" funds; that is, there is no initial sales commission charge, and each fund usually charges a management fee of up to ½ percent or more of the individual's money being managed, with up to an additional ½ percent of the money for expenses of the fund as they are incurred. Other benefits of a cash management fund include the ease of getting into and out of the fund quickly, since they have no minimum investment period, and the fact that the investor does not have to concern himself with reinvesting his money continually.

However, in analyzing cash management funds and deciding whether they are appropriate investments, the investor should be aware of several factors. First, the rates of return on cash management funds change daily, and there is no guarantee of a minimum return over a period of time. Since federal regulations prohibit the publication of the yields being earned on the funds on a day-to-day basis, the investor has to call the fund to find out exactly what his annualized yield is at any one point in time. Second, a cash management fund is only as safe as the fund management and the types of instruments in which the fund invests. If the fund invests in relatively illiquid or poor-quality short-term securities in order to maximize yields, problems could develop if the issuer of the securities runs into financial difficulty or if a large number of the cash management fund's shareholders attempt to withdraw their money at once, forcing the fund to sell any illiquid holdings at a substantial discount in price. Finally, if the fund invests in instruments of long maturity within a rising-interest-rate environment, the net asset value of the fundholder's shares may decline. This might be of concern if the investor decides to redeem his investment before the long-maturity securities have matured and been paid off at par.

In sum, while the cash management fund offers many advantages to individuals, the investor should carefully analyze the fund's prospectus *before* putting his money into the fund in order to judge (1) the character and investment ability of the fund's management; (2) what types of instruments the fund is able to buy and what instruments it has purchased in the past; and (3) the average maturity of the fund's investment portfolio and the percentage of the fund's assets which are invested in long-term securities, if any. Another factor to be investigated is how the funds account for interest income and portfolio price changes. Virtually all cash management funds declare and distribute accrued interest on a daily basis, after expenses. In some funds, the net asset value per share, at which the investor buys into and sells out of the fund, reflects realized and unrealized gains and losses *as they occur,* whereas on other funds, the net asset value per share is held constant at a certain amount (usually $1 per share), with unrealized and realized gains or losses distributed at the end of the fund's accounting year.

Variable Rate Notes

Another type of security which can be considered an outlet for short-term investment money is the variable rate note, initially offered to the public in mid-1974. The variable rate, or "floating" rate, note as it is sometimes called refers to the fact that after a certain initial period of time, the coupon interest rate on the notes will be moved upward or downward at 6-month intervals, according to fluctuations in the yield on a certain type of widely quoted and traded money market instrument. In the case of a large number of the note issues, the rate is set at 1 percent above the bond yield equivalent of the average of the weekly rates for 91-day Treasury bills, as published on a discount basis by the Federal Reserve Bank of New York during the 21 days prior to the semiannual period for which the interest rate is being determined.

While the variable rate notes have a *final* maturity several years or more after their original offering date, they are looked upon as possible investments for the short-term because of a feature, also called a "put" option, which allows the holder of the notes the right, on 30 days' notice, to redeem the securities at 100 percent of their face value plus interest, on any interest payment date starting roughly 2 years after the securities were initially offered. The issuer must receive the notes not less than 30 days prior to the semiannual repayment date, if the investor decides to "put" the notes back to the issuer. Thus, starting 2 years after issue date the investor has the option of "selling" the securities back for par after a holding period of 6 months or holding the securities for several years, thus having many of the advantages of a 6-month note combined with the features of a security with a longer maturity. Of course, the investor can also sell his notes in the open market before the 6-month put-back dates, with the price set not by its long maturity but by its short (6 months') maturity, since the buyer can get par for the notes within 6 months after purchasing them from the investor. Thus, if interest rates rise, these notes will not tend to drop as rapidly in price as would long-term securities, since investors would be treating them as 6-month securities rather than as a security with several years' maturity. (Chapter 3 pointed out that short-term securities change less rapidly in price than long-term securities for a given interest rate rise). The minimum initial purchase requirement on the notes is usually $5,000, and they can be purchased and sold in the secondary market (often, they have been listed on the New York Stock Exchange and can be bought and sold for a normal broker's commission) in multiples of $1,000.

While variable rate notes with a put option have many advantages for the individual investor, he should keep in mind that interest paid on these securities is fully taxable at the federal, state, and local levels. In the case of several bank-related offerings, the notes are *unsecured* obligations, not of the particular commercial bank (or industrial firm), but of their parent holding companies, and they are thus *not insured* by the Federal Deposit Insurance Corporation. Also, 10 years after the original issue date, the notes are usually callable at the option of the issuer upon 30 to 45 days' notice. Finally, if 91-day Treasury bill rates drop to unusually low levels relative to other short-term instruments because of technical or psychological factors, the investor might be better off owning other types of short-term investments rather than the notes, since the interest rate on the latter can be adjusted *downward* as well as upward.

Therefore, before purchasing variable rate notes with a put option feature, the investor should compare their yields on an aftertax basis with other types of securities of the same maturity for which the investor contemplates holding the notes. In addition, the investor should try to ascertain the outlook for the interest rate on which the variable rate is being based; if it is expected to be lower than normal relative to other short-term money market instruments, the investor should carefully examine the other investment alternatives to see whether he might be able to earn a higher return elsewhere for the maturity he desires.

Repurchase Agreements and Other Instruments

Just as the Federal Reserve enters into various types of repurchase agreements with government securities dealers to implement monetary policy according to the procedures described in Chapter 5, repurchase agreements can also be used by large investors as a short-term investment outlet. For example, corporations and other large institutional investors use repurchase agreements (also known as RPs) to purchase Treasury securities, Federal Agency issues, certificates of deposit, commercial paper, or tax-exempt securities from a securities dealer who agrees to buy them back from the investor within a certain period of time at a stated price. This arrangement provides the investor with a specified interest return and protection from adverse price movements owing to possible interest rate level changes during the investor's holding period.

The normal minimum size on repurchase agreements of this type is $1 million, with payment made in Federal funds and interest paid to the investor at maturity, generally 1 day but sometimes ranging up to 30 days. On some RPs, no specific maturity is set, with the agreement able to be terminated by either the dealer or the investor at any time. Interest rates on repurchase agreements are generally above the Treasury bill rate for a similar maturity security and below the interest rate the dealer firm must pay to borrow money from commercial banks.

As mentioned earlier in this chapter, individuals and institutions have also profitably invested their short-term funds through the purchase of government, agency, corporate, tax-exempt, or international bonds and notes which have less than a year remaining to maturity. Also, certain corporate bonds and preferred stocks which have been called for redemption in the near future may on occasion be bought to earn attractive yields over a short period of time. Before investing in such specialized issues, the investor should analyze the security carefully, using the worksheet provided at the end of Chapter 4 and the other worksheets in this book, while relying upon the advice of a qualified securities broker, commercial banker, or investment adviser.

NINE

Tax-Exempt Securities

In this chapter, we will review the broad group of fixed-income securities whose interest payments are exempt from federal income taxes. As a class, these investments are generally called *tax-exempt* securities, even though, as we have seen earlier, many U.S. government and agency securities are also exempt from taxation, but at the state and local level, rather than the federal level. Tax-exempt securities are issued by city, county, state, and other types of local governmental bodies and are often referred to as *municipal* securities. In our analysis, we will employ the terms "tax-exempt" and "municipal" interchangeably when describing this group of securities as a whole.

The total of tax-exempt securities issues has shown remarkable growth during the past 20 years; municipal securities currently represent about one-quarter of the total of new long-term issues of all types of fixed-income securities which are brought to market each year. In 1973, $47.6 billion worth of new short- and long-term tax-exempt securities was issued, up 206 percent from the $15.6 billion issued in 1963, and up 474 percent from the $8.3 billion marketed in 1953. A substantial part of the growth in new tax-exempt issues during the 1963–1973 period was accounted for by short-term issues (with less than 12 months' original maturity) which grew 350 percent, from $5.5 billion in 1963 to $24.7 billion in 1973. All this new issue activity brought the total amount of state and local government debt outstanding to $181.9 billion (of which $167.3 billion was long-term and $14.6 billion was short-term) at the end of 1973, up 96 percent from $92.9 billion (of which $88.0 billion was long-term and $4.9 billion was short-term) 10 years earlier.

Tax-exempt securities are issued by an incredibly heterogeneous group of entities, with over 20,000 separate governmental bodies having more than 50,000 different issues outstanding. By far, the largest dollar amount of tax-exempt securities are accounted for by obligations of municipalities and the 50 states. Other types of issuers include counties, school districts, townships, and special bodies such as park districts and sewer agencies. Municipal securities are offered by these issuers in order to finance projects of a lasting nature which will benefit the citizens of the area. Such projects include schools; highways, bridges, and tunnels; sewer, water, electric, and gas facilities; aid to veterans and public housing; and most recently, pollution control equipment.

The great variety of issuers and purposes make it imperative for investors to approach the municipal securities area with deliberate caution. It is similar to the experience of walking into a clothing store with an enormous selection to choose from—the individual has to exercise care and diligence in finding the right article which is properly suited to his needs. Therefore, to an even greater degree than in other areas of the fixed-income securities field, the investor should be careful, patient, and precise in selecting tax-exempt securities. In this regard, it may be helpful for the investor to review the process of setting investment objectives, as described in Chapter 2.

Tax Benefits of Tax-Exempt Securities

Municipal investments have many benefits, first and foremost of which is their tax-exempt status for federal income tax purposes. For this reason, state and local government securities have traditionally been attractive to commercial banks and to wealthy individuals who are subject to high incremental tax rates. In recent years, a broader number of investors of various income levels have become aware of the value of the tax-exemption feature. For example, Table 9-1 shows that for a married couple whose annual income if $44,000, a municipal security yielding 5 percent gives the same aftertax return as a fully taxable investment yielding 10 percent. Generally speaking, from a tax standpoint, municipal securities are generally appropriate for individuals or couples whose taxation rate on additional income (also called the *incremental* tax rate) is 36 percent or over. For single taxpayers, this incremental tax rate is reached at an income level of $18,000 (with tax rates rising steadily to 70 percent for an annual income of $100,000 and above). For married taxpayers filing a joint return, the 36 percent incremental tax bracket is reached at an income level of $24,000 per year (with rates also rising to 70 percent on annual income level of $200,000 or more).

Thus, generally speaking, the higher the annual income tax bracket, the greater the tax-free yield equivalent of municipal securities. For example, from Table 9-1 it can be seen that for a couple earning $101,000 per year, a 5 percent tax-free yield returns the same aftertaxes as a fully taxable yield of 13.16 percent (see the arrows in the table and the explanation to find how this result was reached).

To use the table, locate your level of annual taxable income in the left-hand column, and across the top of the table find the tax-exempt yield nearest to the yield on the tax-exempt security being evaluated. Tracing across the row which shows your own income, find the yield for a taxable fixed-income security to equal the same after taxes as the tax-free yield. The table does not take into account the fact that capital gains on tax-exempt securities are taxable, and thus the taxable equivalent yield of a municipal security selling at a discount from par value is slightly lower. For practical purposes, however, the table is valid for comparing all types of taxable and tax-exempt investments with similar price terms and maturities.

In addition to the federal income tax exemption, municipal securities usually offer exemption from the state income taxes and often from the local (county or city) income taxes of the state and locality of the issuer of the securities. When this exemption occurs, tax-exempt securities exhibit an even greater net aftertax yield advan-

TABLE 9-1 Taxable Equivalent Yields of Tax-Exempt Yields

Taxable Income (Single Return)	Taxable Income (Joint Return)	Tax-Exempt Yields — Taxable Equivalent Yields									
		2.50	3.00	3.50	4.00	4.50	5.00	5.50	6.00	6.50	7.00
$ 8,000 – 10,000	$16,000 – 20,000	3.47	4.17	4.86	5.56	6.25	6.94	7.64	8.33	9.03	9.72
10,000 – 12,000	20,000 – 24,000	3.68	4.41	5.15	5.88	6.62	7.35	8.09	8.82	9.56	10.29
12,000 – 14,000	24,000 – 28,000	3.91	4.69	5.47	6.25	7.03	7.81	8.59	9.37	10.16	10.94
14,000 – 16,000	28,000 – 32,000	4.10	4.92	5.74	6.56	7.38	8.20	9.02	9.84	10.66	11.48
16,000 – 18,000	32,000 – 36,000	4.31	5.17	6.03	6.90	7.76	8.62	9.48	10.34	11.21	12.07
18,000 – 20,000	36,000 – 40,000	4.55	5.45	6.36	7.27	8.18	9.09	10.00	10.91	11.82	12.73
20,000 – 22,000	40,000 – 44,000	4.81	5.77	6.73	7.69	8.65	9.62	10.58	11.54	12.50	13.46
22,000 – 26,000	44,000 – 52,000	5.00	6.00	7.00	8.00	9.00	(10.00)	11.00	12.00	13.00	14.00
26,000 – 32,000	52,000 – 64,000	5.32	6.38	7.45	8.51	9.57	10.64	11.70	12.77	13.83	14.89
32,000 – 38,000	64,000 – 76,000	5.56	6.67	7.78	8.89	10.00	11.11	12.22	13.33	14.44	15.56
38,000	76,000										

Income range	Income range										
44,000–50,000	88,000–100,000	16.67	15.48	14.29	13.10	11.90	10.71	9.52	8.33	7.14	5.95
50,000–60,000	100,000–120,000	17.50	16.25	15.00	13.75	12.50	11.25	10.00	8.75	7.50	6.25
60,000–70,000	120,000–140,000	18.42	17.11	15.79	14.47	13.16	11.84	10.53	9.21	7.89	6.58
70,000–80,000	140,000–160,000	19.44	18.06	16.67	15.28	13.89	12.50	11.11	9.72	8.33	6.94
80,000–90,000	160,000–180,000	20.59	19.12	17.65	16.18	14.71	13.24	11.76	10.29	8.82	7.35
90,000–100,000	180,000–200,000	21.88	20.31	18.75	17.19	15.63	14.06	12.50	10.94	9.38	7.81
100,000	200,000	22.58	20.97	19.35	17.74	16.13	14.52	12.90	11.29	9.68	8.06
over 100,000	over 200,000	23.33	21.67	20.00	18.33	16.67	15.00	13.33	11.67	10.00	8.33

tage over fully taxable fixed-income investments. For example, a couple living in New York City with a combined annual income of $50,000 is subject to a 50 percent incremental federal income tax rate, a New York State incremental tax rate of 15 percent, and a 3.5 percent incremental New York City tax rate. For this couple, a New York City security with a current yield of 5 percent would be equal to a yield of 15.8 percent, which is fully taxable at the federal, state, and city levels. The general formula for finding the fully taxable equivalent yield of a municipal security is as follows:

$$\text{Fully taxable equivalent yield} = \frac{\text{tax-exempt yield}}{1 - \left(\begin{array}{c} \text{investor's incre-} \\ \text{mental federal} \\ \text{tax rate} \end{array} + \underbrace{\begin{array}{c} \text{investor's incre-} \\ \text{mental state} \\ \text{tax rate} \end{array} + \begin{array}{c} \text{investor's} \\ \text{incremental} \\ \text{local tax rate} \end{array}}_{\text{only if applicable to the security}} \right)}$$

This formula can be used by couples filing a joint income tax return or by an individual filing a single return—all that is needed is to know one's incremental tax rate at the federal, state, and local levels, and this information is contained in the income tax preparation forms given out by states, cities, and the United States government at the start of each year. When buying fixed-income securities, the investor should always compare available tax-exempt yields with the *aftertax* returns on fully taxable securities, taking into account his own incremental tax rates at *each* taxation level.

Three caveats should be mentioned in using the preceding formula. First, the formula does not take capital gains taxes into account (this will be reviewed later in this chapter). Second, the investor should find out whether the income on a specific security is exempt at *both* the city and the state income tax level, *just one* of them, or *neither* of them. Third, virtually all states and cities do not exempt income derived from holding the obligations of another state or city. Thus, a New York City resident holding a municipal bond issued by the Los Angeles Department of Water and Power would *not* receive tax exemption on the interest at the New York State and City income levels. According to the formula, for a New York City individual taxpayer in the 40 percent incremental federal tax bracket, the fully taxable equivalent yield on a Los Angeles

Department of Water and Power bond currently yielding 5 percent would be:

$$\begin{array}{l}\text{Fully taxable} \\ \text{equivalent} \\ \text{yield}\end{array} = \frac{5 \text{ percent}}{1 - (40 \text{ percent} + 0 + 0)} = \frac{5 \text{ percent}}{1 - (0.40)} = \frac{5 \text{ percent}}{0.60} = \begin{array}{l}8.33 \\ \text{percent}\end{array}$$

The investor will note that the New York State and City tax brackets do not apply, since the security being evaluated was of a Los Angeles entity.

It should also be noted that some municipal issues are automatically exempt from *all* federal, state, and local income taxes; such securities would include the obligations of all Puerto Rican municipal issuers, as well as certain securities issued by local housing and urban renewal agencies under the auspices of the U.S. Department of Housing and Urban Development. Because municipal securities' aftertax yields are equivalent to much higher fully taxable returns on corporate bonds, commercial paper, and other types of fixed-income securities, municipal yields are generally lower than yields on other fully taxable securities of comparable quality and maturity—as was mentioned in Chapter 4. For example, during the past 15 years, municipal securities have usually yielded from 65 to 70 percent of the yields on high-grade corporate utility bonds.

Another advantage of state and local government securities is their safety. In general, tax-exempt securities are considered to rank very high in quality, although low-grade, speculative municipal issues can also be found. During the depression years of the 1930s, less than 2 percent of all municipal securities had a delinquency of any sort in the timely payment of principal and interest, and of this total most issuers ultimately paid off their debts in full. In expansionary economic periods, defaults by municipal issuers have been extremely rare.

Because of the strong security of many high-quality tax-exempt issues, they have a high collateral value. Unlike corporate bonds and stocks, Federal Reserve Board margin requirements do not set special collateral or margin requirements on municipal obligations. This permits the investor to obtain credit up to a large portion of the total value of his municipal investments, if so desired. However, it should be mentioned that interest expenses on loans used to purchase municipal securities, or on loans with municipal securities used as collateral, are *not* deductible for federal income tax purposes. From Chapter 6, the investor may recall that interest expenses on margin loans used to purchase government, agency, or corporate issues *are* tax deductible on federal returns.

A final important benefit of municipal securities is the flexibility which they provide an investor in structuring his portfolio. Tax-exempt securities are available with maturities from 1 month to 50 years or more, and a substantial majority of issues are offered in serial form, with a portion of the issue maturing each year until final maturity. If the investor knows exactly when he needs his principal back over a period of time, he can purchase staggered maturities of one single issue or a number of issues. If the investor needs all his capital at one specific moment in time, it is often best to tailor his investment to that exact time period by choosing a tax-exempt security which matures on or close to the date the funds will be required. A short-term example of how a maturity might be tailored to specific needs involves the selection of a short-term tax-exempt note which is scheduled to mature on or shortly before an individual's income taxes fall due. A long-term example might involve the investment of a specific amount of money in tax-exempt bonds which mature just prior to a child's entrance into college some years in the future.

As a general rule of thumb, if the investor wants his principal back in 12 years, for example, but does not need high current tax-free income, he might consider investing in low-coupon bonds selling at a discount and maturing in 12 years' time. However, it should also be remembered that the difference between the purchase price and the par value of the bonds repaid at maturity is taxable at capital gains rates (which could also be altered by Congress). On the other hand, it the investor needs maximum current tax-exempt income for living expenses, he should purchase municipal securities with high-interest coupons.

In investigating the tax-exempt securities area, the investor should also be aware of some of the specialized aspects of investing in municipal securities. Most municipal issues have many different serial maturities, with separate coupon rates and interest yeidls, so that even if a tax-exempt security offering is of large size, actually it is effectively composed of many smaller issues with varying lives. The many maturities and coupon rates for tax-exempt securities are one of the principal reasons why municipal securities are quoted on a yield basis, rather than on a percentage-of-par or dollar price basis. The mechanics of yield basis quotations will be covered later in this chapter.

Another feature of municipal securities markets is the practice of many municipal investors of purchasing a particular tax-exempt security and holding it in their portfolios until final maturity. Also, municipal securities markets exhibit a dispersion of trading activity among a very large number of dealer firms, well over 600, located throughout the United States. Municipal securities are not quoted on a daily basis in the newspaper, except for certain bonds which have one standard coupon and maturity for a large part or all of an issue; these are called "term" bonds and are usually quoted on a percentage-of-par basis rather than a yield basis, hence their other name, "dollar bonds." The absence of easily available price and trading information should be kept in mind by the investor, although he can obtain prices for a specific issue merely by contacting a commercial bank or securities broker.

The municipal securities market tends to display a somewhat greater degree of price fluctuation than comparable corporate, agency, or U.S. government securities whenever interest rates move up or down. This is partly because of the commercial banks' practice of buying a sizable portion of new municipal issues when money is readily available (interest rates trending downward) and in turn selling their municipal holdings to satisfy their customers' loan demands in period of credit stringency (interest rates moving upward).

Although a large number of individual and institutional investors in municipal securities are not affected by this phenomenon, since they buy tax-exempt securities and hold them until maturity, the occasional greater tendency toward price fluctuation of tax-exempt securities underscores the need for the investor to carefully review his objectives (using the worksheet at the end of Chapter 2) *before* embarking on a program of investing in tax-exempt securities.

In the following sections, we will review the various types of long-term and short-term tax-exempt securities which are available to the investor. In addition, we will discuss the mechanics of purchasing and selling state and local government issues. At the end of this chapter, a section on tax-exempt bond funds has also been included.

Long-Term Tax-Exempt Securities

Generally, municipal securities are classified as long-term (bonds) if they mature in over 1 year and as short-term (notes) if they mature in less than 1 year. All long-term state and local government securities, as well as most short-term issues, can be classified into one of two major categories: general obligation issues and revenue bonds.

General obligation bonds   General obligation bonds are backed by the full faith and credit of the issuer and are considered a general credit obligation of the state or local government which issued them. In 1974, $13.2 billion worth of general obligation securities were brought to market. Timely payment of principal and interest on the bonds is secured by the unlimited ability of the issuer to tax property or other items within the community or the state involved. Unlimited-tax general obligation bonds are distinguished from certain general obligation issues which, even though they are guaranteed by the full faith and credit of the state or local government issuing the securities, *do not* carry the backing of *all* the taxing power of the issuer. These bonds are called *limited-tax* general obligation bonds, and they are secured by the pledge of a tax which is limited in amount or rate, such as a maximum property tax. Before buying a limited-tax general obligation bond, the investor should find out from his securities broker or commercial bank how much of the limited taxing power behind the bonds remains unused, in order to pay off the principal and interest of the bonds when due. If the limited taxation power of the state or local government issue has already been completely utilized, there is no extra margin of safety to protect the bondholder. For this reason, limited-tax general obligation bonds often sell at a lower price (higher yield) than unlimited-tax general obligation bonds of the same quality and maturity. Both limited- and unlimited-tax general obligation bonds are usually judged according to the strength of the tax base of the area being taxed to pay off the bonds.

Revenue bonds   There are several different types of revenue bonds, all of which have one feature in common: they are generally secured primarily by payments from some special source or sources of income. In 1974, $10.0 billion in revenue bonds of all types were issued. The source of income-backing revenue bonds could either be a revenue-producing enterprise or a special tax of some sort, such as a tax on alcoholic beverages or cigarettes. This latter group of bonds is frequently referred to as *special tax* bonds, and they are considered revenue bonds since they do not carry the general credit backing which general obligation bonds have.

What most people refer to as revenue bonds in the truest sense of the word are securities whose principal and interest are paid from the operation of specific income-producing facilities. Traditionally, these facilities have included water, electrical, and gas systems and toll bridges, tunnels, and expressways. In recent years, the types of facilities financed by revenue bonds have expanded, partly because of a broadened concept of governmental enterprise and partly because most revenue bonds are not usually subject to the same sort of constitutional and statutory debt limitation provisions· with which general obligation bonds must ordinarily apply. Revenue bond–financed facilities now include college dormitories and other educational projects, airports, parking garages, hospitals, port facilities, sports complexes, rapid transit systems, and hydroelectric power projects, to name the most prominent examples.

Often, a special *agency, commission,* or *authority* is established by a subdivision of, or directly by, a state government, a local government, or a combination of several state and local governments. The wide diversity of revenue bonds and their dependence on a certain source of income makes it important for the investor to exercise care in checking the quality ratings on revenue bonds before purchasing them. As was mentioned in Chapter 5, the investor should also be aware of the various psychological factors and fundamental changes which can cause particular types of revenue bonds to be affected favorably or adversely in price relative to other similar issues. An example would be the lower-than-normal prices (higher yields) reached by the Los Angeles Airports Department bonds and other airport-related revenue bonds, which occurred as a result of investors' concern in late 1973 and early 1974 that the energy crisis would curtail air travel and reduce the ability of issuers of airport facilities revenue bonds to repay their obligations because of decreased fees and other receipts.

This example brings up the subject of what would happen if the revenue derived from a specific project or facility were not sufficient to pay back interest and principal on the securities. In most cases, the bonds would go into arrears and trade at a substantially reduced price until the necessary revenues were again earned and the interest and principal could be repaid. Fortunately for investors, to date this has been very rare, and bond investors' confidence in these securities in general is evidenced by the large amounts of money which are invested in them each year. Nevertheless, the investor should be aware of the consequences and the course of action which would result if the revenues were inadequate to meet interest and principal payments.

In some cases when revenues are inadequate, there may be some commitment of aid from a state or local government to provide additional funds to help meet debt service payments in the event that revenues from a project or facility fall short of scheduled interest and principal obligations. This state or local government commitment may be in the form of a *legally binding contract* between the government and the issuer of the revenue bonds, or it may take the form of a *"moral obligation,"* under which the state or local government does not guarantee to aid the revenue-producing enterprise but instead will provide such funds *only* if the necessary appropriation is approved by the lawmakers of the state or local government which is providing the moral backing. While this appropriation most probably would pass, it is not a 100 percent certain form of assistance, and the investor should keep this in mind in evaluating securities whose ultimate backing involves some sort of moral commitment. One other type of backup arrangement for revenue bonds takes the form of a *lease* of the facility involved to a state or local government, with the governmental lease payments sufficient to cover interest and principal on the revenue bonds issued by a specific revenue authority or agency. The *lease* and the *legally binding contract* forms of backup are felt to be more secure than the *moral obligation* form.

One type of tax-exempt revenue security which carries a special form of guarantee is the *public housing agency bond*. These bonds, issued by local housing authorities throughout the country to finance the construction of low-rent housing projects, are primarily backed by the project's revenues. In addition, they are secured by the full faith and credit of the U.S. government, and any shortfall in revenues from the housing projects to pay interest and principal on the bonds is made up by Congressional appropriations. In 1973–74, over $1.5 billion of new public housing authority bonds were issued. An added benefit of these bonds is their normally tax-exempt status not only from federal income taxes but also from state and local taxes in the state and locality where the bonds were issued.

Two other types of tax-exempt revenue bonds carry the further backing of a corporation: *industrial revenue bonds* and *pollution control bonds*. Each of these securities involves the issuance of bonds by a municipality or authority, the proceeds of which are used to construct facilities or to purchase equipment which is leased to a corporation. The lease payments from the corporation are structured to pay all costs of servicing the bonds, including principal and interest. Since these bonds pay interest on a tax-free basis, they usually carry a coupon about 150 to 200 basis points lower than fully taxable bonds issued by the same corporation, thus providing the company with a lower net interest cost than otherwise possible.

Industrial revenue bonds were originally created by state and local governments to attract industry to their communities through the benefit of the interest cost savings mentioned above. In recent years, however, the use of industrial revenue bonds has declined somewhat, since Congress has limited the total size of each new issue which can be sold.

Pollution control bonds, however, were exempted from the

Congressional ceiling on the size of industrial revenue bonds, and several individual issues to date have exceeded $50 million in amount. The proceeds from the sale of pollution control bonds must be used to finance pollution abatement facilities. The issuance of pollution control bonds has expanded rapidly, from $88 million in 1971 to over $2 billion in 1974.

In concluding this discussion of the various types of revenue bonds, several points should be made. Revenue bonds are judged a bit differently than general obligation bonds, which focus primarily on the taxing power of an issuer. In judging revenue bonds, analysts evaluate the financial soundness of the project behind the securities, specifically with regard to (1) the interest coverage ratio, which is the ratio of annual net revenues available for debt service to the annual interest charges on the total securities outstanding of the issuer and (2) the size and nature of any reserves which the issuer has set aside for payments of principal and interest in the event that unforeseen contingencies occur. Any "makeup," guarantee, contracts, leases, or moral obligation arrangements on the part of governmental bodies other than the issuer are also considered.

Some revenue bonds are not rated by the major bond rating agencies. The investor should always check the rating on revenue bonds before making a purchase. If the investor decides to buy revenue bonds, he should select only those tax-exempt revenue bonds which have adequate security from a revenue or guarantee standpoint and whose price (yield) is commensurate with any additional risk involved relative to stronger revenue bonds or to general obligation bonds. Further details on the mechanics of buying and selling long-term tax-exempt securities of both the revenue and the general obligation type are provided in the following sections.

Initial Offering Procedures, Price Quotations, and Secondary-Market Trading

Initial offerings　Municipal securities are initially sold to the public by underwriting syndicates usually composed of a combination of small municipal dealer firms, larger securities brokerage and investment banking firms, and commercial banks, who have purchased (underwritten) the bonds from the issuer for reoffering to investors. The larger the issuer and the more widely known the state or local government which is offering the bonds, the more likely it is that nationally oriented securities brokerage firms and commercial banks will participate in the issue's underwriting group. On the other hand, for smaller and more locally known issues, small and medium sized, regionally oriented securities firms and banks will normally handle the underwriting. The underwriting firms' compensation is derived from the difference between the price at which the securities were bought from the issuer and the price at which they were reoffered to the investor. This amount is known as an *underwriting spread*.

A high proportion of all tax-exempt offerings is done through the *competitive bidding* method, whereby the state or local government formally announces its intent to raise money and invites bids on the securities to be sold. The official bidding notice also states any coupon rate restrictions and other conditions of the sale, such as the time, place, and date for bids to be entered. Usually, several underwriting groups compete with each other in submitting bids, with the winning bid awarded to the underwriting syndicate which has bid the highest price (the lowest net interest cost) to the issuer before reselling the securities to the public.

Under the *negotiated* method of underwriting, no bids are submitted to the issuer; rather, representatives of the underwriting group meet with the issuer in advance of the offering and negotiate a coupon rate on the bonds in the light of current market conditions. Numerous revenue bonds are offered by the negotiated underwriting method. When deciding whether to purchase municipal securities of any type in an initial offering (or in secondary trading, for that matter), the investor should *always* ask his commercial bank or securities broker for a copy of the *offering circular* or the *official statement* describing the bonds and the issuer's financial condition in much greater detail. In negotiated offerings, a *preliminary offering circular* is usually prepared and made available before the offering, and the investor should request a copy for review prior to purchasing the securities involved.

Because most municipal bonds are offered in serial form, with several different maturities for separate amounts of the total issue, not all the securities have the same coupon or reoffering yield. Generally, the short maturities have higher-interest coupons and are offered at a premium over par, and the intermediate and longer maturities generally are offered to the investor at or near par. This normally results in an upward-sloping yield curve, with short-term yields to maturity lower than long-term yields to maturity. As was mentioned in Chapter 4 (and will be further discussed in Chapter 13), the normal slope of the yield curve is upward, with short-term yields lower than long-term yields.

In order to compare the yields on numerous maturities of one tax-exempt issue with another, many underwriters and investors in municipal securities look at the reoffering yields for the 5-, 10-, 15-, 20-, 25-, and 30-year maturities of the issue. Another widely followed indicator of municipal securities prices in general is the *Bond Buyer* 20-bond index, published by the daily newspaper of the same name, which is devoted to fixed-income securities. The 20-bond index gives the average weekly yield for the 20-year maturity issues of 20 medium- and high-grade municipal bonds. The all-time lowest price (highest yield) for the index was reached in December of 1974, when its yield was 7.15 percent and the highest price for the index (its lowest yield) was attained in February 1946 when the yield was 1.04 percent. The *Bond Buyer* also publishes an 11-bond index, which comprises the 11 highest-quality issues within the 20-bond index. As was seen in Chapter 5, two important influences (among others) on the level and direction of municipal securities yields, and thus on the initial prices set on newly offered issues, are (1) the visible supply of tax-exempt securities which will be brought to market during the next 30 days and (2) the placement ratio, or the amount of bonds distributed as a percentage of that week's total new issue offerings over $1 million in size. The investor should remember to keep these factors in mind as they relate to interest rate pressures when purchasing new issues of tax-exempt securities, or when buying them in the secondary market.

New municipal issues are generally offered to investors on a *when issued* basis. This means that payment for the securities does not have to be made until the bonds are delivered, which can take anywhere from 15 to 45 days or more, to allow for the bond certificates to be printed and approved by the state or local government. In addition, a legal opinion on the bonds has to be rendered by bond counsel for the issuer.

Legal opinion   The last point mentioned above is very significant, both in initial offerings and in secondary-market trading. Before the tax-exempt securities are issued, a reputable firm of attorneys specializing in municipal borrowing must be employed by the state or local government to carefully analyze the manner of authorization for issuing the bonds and to give a legal opinion on the legality of the bonds. When buying municipal securities of any type in either primary or secondary trading, the investor should *make sure* the bonds are accompanied by the legal opinion. Otherwise, if the investor does not have the legal opinion when the securities are to be sold, their marketability is significantly impaired, causing a substantial discount in the price the investor will receive for the bonds, if he is even able to sell them at all. Most, *but not all,* of the tax-exempt securities issued during the past few years avoid this potential problem by having the legal opinion printed on the bond certificate when the bonds are originally prepared. The investor should find out whether the legal opinion is printed on the securities, and if not, he should obtain and protect the legal opinion as carefully as he would safeguard the bonds themselves.

Ratings   The following paragraphs review the bond rating process and descriptions of the meanings of the letter classifications used by two of the major rating services in judging municipal debt. For example, some of the factors which influence the rating of a general obligation tax-exempt security, in addition to those mentioned earlier in this chapter, include (1) the size and the growth rate of the state or locality issuing the bonds; (2) the stability and diversity of the area's population and commercial resources; (3) the net debt of the community, both on a per capita basis and relative to the assessed value of the property; (4) the local property and income tax rates; and (5) any debt limits imposed by the state or local governments themselves.

The rating of a municipal security can definitely influence how the security trades relative to other tax-exempt issues. For instance, during the past 15 years, 20-year-maturity general obligation municipal bonds carrying a rating of Aaa by Moody's have sold at a 50-basis-point (0.50 percent) lower yield (higher price) than similar securities carrying Moody's Baa rating.

The investor should pay close attention to the rating on a security, keeping in mind that it relates to the *issuer* of the securities as well as to the security itself. For example, a lower-rated *long*-maturity bond carries more credit risk than a lower-rated *short*-maturity bond on account of the greater length of time until the investor receives his money back, and thus the higher degree of uncertainty associated with the security. During the past 5 years, two insurance related organizations, the MGIC Investment Corporation and the Municipal Bond Insurance Association (composed of four large insurance firms), have begun to guarantee unconditionally certain municipal issues which ordinarily would receive a low quality rating. If the issuing government decides to pay for this insurance service, the insured securities receive a double-A or triple-A rating, resulting in a lower net interest cost for the issuer over the life of the bond.

In addition, a subsidiary of the MGIC Investment Corporation, called MGIC Indemnity Corporation, has recently begun a portfolio credit insurance program for investors with over $50,000 in three or more municipal investments, of which 75 percent must carry a rating of BBB by Standard & Poor's (Baa by Moody's) or better. Depending on the risk of the investor's portfolio holdings, the annual insurance premiums range from 0.05 to 0.35 percent of the portfolio's total face value. While these two types of insurance programs (issuer insurance and portfolio credit insurance) are still in their early stages, it is advisable for the investor to stick to bonds rated *at least* Baa/BBB or better, and preferably with a rating of A or higher. Unless the individual's total assets are large enough to permit the partial or total loss of money invested in lower-rated bonds, he should avoid them altogether, unless he is very familiar with the issuer and its debt-paying ability. If the investor sticks with higher-rated bonds, the issuer insurance and portfolio insurance programs should rarely concern him.

The many municipal securities with similar names, coupon rates, and maturities, but with different ratings, make it imperative for the investor to use the worksheet at the end of Chapter 4 in checking carefully the *exact name* of the issue and its rating by Standard & Poor's and/or Moody's rating services *before* buying the bond. The investor should also find out the *issue date* of the security to distinguish it from other issues offered at other times by the same state or local government body. At the same time, the investor should also check whether the issue is a general obligation or revenue bond and confirm that the coupon rate and maturity are the ones he has specified. Otherwise, if an error occurs, delays and additional expenses will result, or even worse, the investor may not notice that he is holding the wrong security until some date far into the future. As has been mentioned several times earlier in this book, the investor should also find out if the issue being purchased is callable and, if so, under what conditions and at what price.

STANDARD & POOR'S MUNICIPAL BOND RATINGS*

AAA-Prime – These are obligations of the highest quality. They have the strongest capacity for timely payment of debt service.

General Obligation Bonds – In a period of economic stress, the issuers will suffer the smallest declines in income and will be least susceptible to autonomous decline. Debt burden is moderate. A strong revenue structure appears more than adequate to meet future expenditure requirements. Quality of management appears superior.

By permission of Standard & Poor's Corporation.

*To provide more detailed indications of credit quality, bond letter ratings may be modified by the addition of a plus or minus sign, when appropriate, to show relative standing within the major rating categories, the only exceptions being in the **AAA**-Prime Grade Category and the lesser categories below **BB**.

Revenue Bonds – Debt service coverage has been and is expected to remain substantial. Stability of the pledged revenues is also exceptionally strong, due to the competitive position of the municipal enterprise or to the nature of the revenues. Basic security provisions (including rate covenant, earnings test for issuance of additional bonds, debt service reserve requirements) are rigorous. There is evidence of superior management.

AA-High Grade – The investment characteristics of general obligation and revenue bonds in this group are only slightly less marked than those of the prime quality issues. Bonds rated **AA** have the second strongest capacity for payment of debt service.

A-Good Grade – Principal and interest payments on bonds in this category are regarded as safe. This rating describes the third strongest capacity for payment of debt service. It differs from the two higher ratings because:

General Obligation Bonds – There is some weakness, either in the local economic base, in debt burden, in the balance between revenues and expenditures, or in quality of management. Under certain adverse circumstances, *any one such weakness* might impair the ability of the issuer to meet debt obligations at some future date.

Revenue Bonds – Debt service coverage is good, but not exceptional. Stability of the pledged revenues could show some variations because of increased competition or economic influences on revenues. Basic security provisions, while satisfactory, are less stringent. Management performance appears adequate.

BBB-Medium Grade – This is the lowest investment grade security rating.

General Obligation Bonds – Under certain adverse conditions, several of the above factors could contribute to a lesser capacity for payment of debt service. The difference between **A** and **BBB** ratings is that the latter shows *more than one fundamental weakness,* or *one very substantial fundamental weakness,* whereas the former shows only one deficiency among the factors considered.

Revenue Bonds – Debt coverage is only fair. Stability of the pledged revenues could show substantial variations, with the revenue flow possibly being subject to erosion over time. Basic security provisions are no more than adequate. Management performance could be stronger.

BB-Lower Medium Grade – Bonds in this group have some investment characteristics, but they no longer predominate. For the most part this rating indicates a speculative, non-investment grade obligation.

B-Low Grade – Investment characteristics are virtually nonexistent and default could be imminent.

D-Defaults – Payment of interest and/or principal is in arrears.

NCR – No contract rating. No ratings are assigned to new offerings unless a contract rating is applied for.

Provisional Ratings – The letter "p" following a rating indicates the rating is provisional, where payment of debt service requirements will be largely or entirely dependent upon the timely completion of the project.

MOODY'S MUNICIPAL BOND RATINGS*

Aaa – Bonds which are rated **Aaa** are judged to be of the best quality. They carry the smallest degree of investment risk and are generally referred to as "gilt edge." Interest payments are protected by a large or by an exceptionally stable margin and principal is secure. While the various protective elements are likely to change, such changes as can be visualized are most unlikely to impair the fundamentally strong position of such issues.

Aa – Bonds which are rated **Aa** are judged to be of high quality by all standards. Together with the **Aaa** group they comprise what are generally known as high grade bonds. They are rated lower than the best bonds because margins or protection may not be as large as in **Aaa** securities or fluctuation of protective elements may be of greater amplitude or there may be other elements present which make the long-term risks appear somewhat larger than in **Aaa** securities.

A – Bonds which are rated **A** possess many favorable investment attributes and are to be considered as upper medium grade obligations. Factors giving security to principal and interest are considered adequate, but elements may be present which suggest a susceptibility to impairment sometime in the future.

Baa – Bonds which are rated **Baa** are considered as medium grade obligations; i.e., they are neither highly protected nor poorly secured. Interest payments and principal security appear adequate for the present but

Reprinted with written permission of Moody's Investors Service, Inc.

*Those bonds in the **A** and **Baa** groups which Moody's considers to possess the strongest investment attributes are designated by the symbols A-1 and Baa-1. Other A and Baa bonds comprise the balance of their respective groups.

certain protective elements may be lacking or may be characteristically unreliable over any great length of time. Such bonds lack outstanding investment characteristics and in fact have speculative characteristics as well.

Ba – Bonds which are rated **Ba** are judged to have speculative elements; their future cannot be considered as well-assured. Often the protection of interest and principal payments may be very moderate, and thereby not well safeguarded during both good and bad times over the future. Uncertainty of position characterizes bonds in this class.

B – Bonds which are rated **B** generally lack characteristics of the desirable investment. Assurance of interest and principal payments or of maintenance of other terms of the contract over any long period of time may be small.

CAA – Bonds which are rated **Caa** are of poor standing. Such issues may be in default or there may be present elements of danger with respect to principal or interest.

Ca – Bonds which are rated **Ca** represent obligations which are speculative in a high degree. Such issues are often in default or have other marked shortcomings.

C – Bonds which are rated **C** are the lowest rated class of bonds, and issues so rated can be regarded as having extremely poor prospects of ever attaining any real investment standing.

Con.(   ) – Bonds for which the security depends upon the completion of some act or the fulfillment of some condition are rated conditionally. These are bonds secured by (a) earnings of projects under construction, (b) earnings of projects unseasoned in operating experience, (c) rentals which begin when facilities are completed, or (d) payments to which some other limiting condition attaches. Parenthetical rating denotes probable credit stature upon completion of construction or elimination of basis of condition.

Price quotations   With the exception of certain revenue bonds (the dollar bonds mentioned earlier), all municipal securities are quoted on a yield to maturity basis rather than on a percentage-of-par basis. This means that instead of hearing a municipal bond's price quoted as "98½ bid, 99 offered," as might be the case with corporate, agency, or U.S. government bonds, the investor might hear 5 percent coupon municipal bonds with 15 years to maturity quoted "5.40 percent bid, 5.30 percent offered." What does this price quotation mean in dollar terms? To find this out for municipal bonds, we need to refer to a *basis book* (which gives *dollar prices* if the *yield* is known), similar to the *yield book* (which gives *yields* if the *dollar prices* are known) which we encountered earlier in connection with most nonmunicipal securities. Price lists for various types of basis books are available from the Financial Publishing Company, 82 Brookline Ave., Boston, Massachusetts 02215. Looking in a basis book on the page for 5 percent coupon issues, we see that a 15-year maturity issue yields 5.40 percent at a price of 95.92 (or $959.20 per $1,000 bond), and a yield of 5.30 percent on this same security is equal to a price of 96.92 (or $969.20 per $1,000 bond). The dealer's spread in this example is $10 per bond, equivalent to the difference between the price at which the dealer would *buy* the bonds *from* an investor (on a 5.40 percent yield basis), and the price at which the dealer would *offer* the bonds *to* the investor (on a 5.30 percent yield basis).

On average, the dealer's market spread in dollar terms usually works out to between ½ to 1 point ($5 to $10 per $1,000 bond), although on smaller, longer-maturity, inactively traded issues, the spread in dollar terms could be even wider, up to 2 full points ($20 per $1,000 bond) or more. The investor should also keep in mind the fact that spreads are also wider for smaller-than-normal trades, so that excessive trading into and out of municipal securities in small amounts will cost money and reduce the investor's effective yield to maturity from holding the security. This also underscores the necessity of buying and selling through a reputable dealer who will not widen his spreads on individual investors' orders when he knows that they are not "comparison shopping," i.e., checking the price quotations of several dealer firms. When feasible, it is a good idea to do this type of comparison shopping when buying or selling municipal securities, but if this is impractical, the investor should be certain that he is dealing with a reputable firm.

Secondary-market trading Secondary-market trading in tax-exempt securities can be done through securities brokers, municipal bond dealers, and commercial banks which generally trade with each other and the public at large on a net (noncommission) basis. As mentioned earlier, it is a highly fragmented market with an absence of easily accessible price quotations or trading volume figures for the general public. Municipal traders communicate with each other by telephone and private teletype networks, and each day a publication called the *Blue List* shows the securities that are owned by dealers in their inventory positions and which are offered for resale, as well as the yield at the dealer's offering price. The *Blue List* also shows unsold balances remaining on any under-writing syndicate accounts which have not been disbanded. A normal round-lot trade of tax-exempt securities is $100,000 par value of securities.

Almost all municipal securities issued in recent years pay interest on a semiannual basis and come in denominations of $5,000 and up, although some bonds are still available in $1,000 denominations. Unless the investor plans to hold his securities to maturity, he is better off buying at least $25,000 worth to enhance their marketability when they are sold. Marketability is also influenced by the fact that the primary market for many of the very small municipal securities is limited to the immediate geographical vicinity of the issuer. Thus, the investor should avoid small issues of obscure localities that are unknown to him and located a great distance from his own home town—it might be difficult to find a buyer for these bonds in the future. Marketability is usually enhanced if the investor owns securities of a well-known and well-regarded state or local government for which financial information is readily available.

Another feature affecting the marketability and ease of trading municipal bonds is whether they are in bearer or registered form. Bonds which are in *bearer* form, also known as *coupon bonds,* since interest is collected by clipping the coupon and forwarding it to the paying agent of the issuer, are more easily marketable and trade at slightly higher prices than bonds in *registered* form. If the investor does decide to keep his tax-exempt securities in bearer form, he must remember to safeguard them as carefully as cash or Treasury bills.

Discount bonds Earlier in this chapter, the point was mentioned that any capital gains on tax-exempt securities are *not* tax-exempt. Rather, they are fully taxable at the investor's applicable capital gains tax rate. Capital gains occur (1) when the investor sells after interest rates have fallen and bond prices have moved up or (2) if the investor purchases a municipal security in the secondary trading market at a discount and holds it until the bond matures at its par value. Most bonds selling at a moderate or deep discount from par value are low-coupon issues which have fallen in price as interest rates have risen. For example, if the general level of tax-exempt interest rates were 6 percent, a 4 percent coupon issue with 20 years to maturity would sell at a price of $768.90 per $1,000 bond in order to provide a yield to maturity of 6.00 percent. However, this 6.00 percent yield to maturity includes $231.10 of *taxable* capital gain at the end of 20 years' time and is *not* the same as a 6 percent coupon 20-year municipal issue purchased at par, which gives a completely tax-exempt yield to maturity of 6.00 percent. To compensate for this tax disadvantage, discount municipal bonds tend to sell at a slightly lower price and a somewhat higher yield than bonds purchased at par or at a premium. As a result, in a 6 percent tax-exempt interest rate environment, the 4 percent coupon 20-year bonds might sell at a price *below* their theoretical value of $768.90 per $1,000 bond, in order to produce a 6 percent tax-exempt yield to maturity (after capital gains taxes)— perhaps at a 6.40 to 6.50 percent yield to maturity or thereabouts.

The investor should recall that this works *just the opposite* for *fully taxable securities* such as corporate bonds at a discount, which tend to sell at a slightly *higher* price (lower yield) than other issues with higher coupons selling near or above par. This is because of the fact that the capital gains taxes (on the increase to par value at maturity) are *lower* than ordinary income taxes on interest, but still *higher* than *no* income taxes on tax-exempt issues' income. Tax-exempt discount bonds are appropriate for investors who do not have high current income needs, they can be a good trading vehicle for possible capital gains if interest rates decline, and they can also be useful to those individuals whose incremental tax bracket (and thus possibly their capital gains tax rate) will be lower some years in the future, when the bonds mature and the capital gain is earned.

Settlement procedures Payment for and delivery of municipal bonds takes place 5 business days after the transaction, in clearing-house funds. The purchaser must also pay to the seller the accrued interest on the bonds, which represents the interest earned on the securities from the last interest payment date through the settle-ment date. If the buyer of the bonds sells the securities before the next interest payment date, he will also receive the total accrued interest, and his actual interest earned for the period he held the bonds will be the difference between the total accrued interest he paid and the total accrued interest he received when the bonds were sold. Whoever holds the bonds at the time of the regular interest payment date collects the entire coupon interest earned since the last interest payment date. If the bonds are in default as to payment of interest at the time a transaction is made, the bonds are traded *flat*, or without accrued interest, and any unpaid interest coupons which are past due must also be attached to the bonds unless other arrangements are made.

Short-Term Tax-Exempt Securities

Numerous alternatives exist for the individual to invest his capital on a tax-free basis for periods of less than 1 year. Often, the effective aftertax yield of such investments exceeds the yields which can be earned on short-term government agency securities, U.S. Treasury bills, or other fully taxable short-term money market instruments such as those described in the previous chapter. Most short-term tax-exempt investments can be divided into two principal categories: (1) those which are solely backed by the state and local governments which have issued the securities and (2) those which also carry the additional backing of the United States government (commonly known as *project notes*).

Short-term securities backed by state and local governments Many state and local governments issue short-term securities to provide working capital until an expected receipt of funds, such as (1) the payment of taxes (these securities are often called *tax anticipation notes,* or TANs), (2) the receipt of other types of revenues (*revenue anticipation notes,* or RANs), and (3) the inflow of money from the issuance of a longer-term security (*bond anticipation notes,* or BANs). In addition, a few bond issues with serial maturities include some securities which mature in less than 1 year, and the investor can also consider these as possible tax-exempt short-term investments. Finally, several states have housing assistance programs which use short-term financing (in anticipation of longer-term issues) to fund construction expenditures. These securities virtually always represent either a guarantee or the direct obligation of a state. In total, short-term tax-exempt securities issued by state and local governments of all types amounted to $29.0 billion in 1974. Beginning in 1974, Moody's Investors Service, Inc., began to rate short-term municipal obligations, and a description of the rating classifications is contained below.

MOODY'S SHORT-TERM MUNICIPAL SECURITY RATINGS*

MIG 1 – Notes and other short-term loans which are rated **MIG 1** are judged to be of the best quality, carrying the least degree of risk.

MIG 2 – Notes and other short-term loans which are rated **MIG 2** are judged to be of high quality, bearing little risk that all terms as to time and amounts will be met.

MIG 3 – Notes and other short-term loans which are rated **MIG 3** are judged to be of favorable quality, with all security elements accounted for but lacking the undeniable strength of the preceding grades.

MIG 4 – Notes and other short-term loans which are rated **MIG 4** are judged to be of adequate quality, carrying specifiable risk but generally protected into investment status.

Reprinted with written permission of Moody's Investors Service, Inc.

*Not all short-term municipal issues are rated by Moody's. The rating of any given issue carries no implications as to any other similar issue of the same obligor. Ratings terminate at the retirement of the short-term issue and may be withdrawn for failure to provide current information or for other reasons.

Almost all short-term tax-exempt notes issued by state and local governments are in bearer form, with interest paid back with principal at maturity. The lowest denomination of these securities is $5,000, with larger sizes and denominations available, depending on the investor's preference and the total size of the issue. For practical purposes, the minimum amount of these notes which can be traded without price concessions is $25,000. Short-term tax-exempt notes are traded on a yield basis, with dealers' spreads between their bid and ask quotes varying, based on the type of short-term tax-exempt security, its maturity, and the technical and fundamental conditions affecting short-term money markets at the time.

Quotation practices on short-term tax-exempt notes are based on a 360-day year. This means that the investor has to multiply the stated yield on a short-term tax-exempt security by a factor of $^{365}/_{360}$, or 1.014, in order to arrive at the bond equivalent yield of a certain stated yield. A short-term tax-exempt note might be quoted 5.00 percent bid, 4.75 percent offered, meaning the dealer would sell the notes to an investor at a yield to maturity of 4.75 percent, which on a bond equivalent basis equals 4.75 percent × 1.014, or 4.82 percent, *tax-free*. Similar to long-term tax-exempt securities, the purchaser of short-term tax-exempt notes always pays to the seller the total accrued interest since the securities were issued. If the securities are held to maturity by the investor, he collects the entire amount of interest earned.

Settlement on short-term tax-exempt notes takes place 5 business days after the transaction in Federal funds. However, prior arrangements can be made for settlement in fewer or more than 5 business days.

Project notes   Twice each month, the U.S. Department of Housing and Urban Development competitively auctions short-term notes issued by local government bodies which provide urban renewal and housing assistance within their own communities. The notes generally range in maturity from 3 months to 1 year, and while they are the primary obligations of the public housing agencies (also known as *local housing authorities*) or the local urban renewal agencies (also known as *local public agencies*) which have issued them, they are also secured by the full faith and credit of the United States government. The United States government is obligated to pay off any deficiency in fund when the notes fall due. Interest on both types of project notes is exempt from federal income taxes, and in most cases, from state and local taxes in the state and local community in which they were issued. Project notes are considered to be of the highest quality, and as of mid-1974 there had never been a default in the timely payment of principal and interest on any of the more than $90 billion of notes sold since the inception of these programs over 20 years earlier. In recent years, project notes have accounted for an increasing share of total short-term municipal securities offerings. In 1973, local housing authority issues totaled $6.6 billion, up 144 percent from the $2.7 billion issued 5 years earlier, and local public agency issues to finance urban renewal projects amounted to $4.4 billion, up 37.5 percent from $3.2 billion in 1969.

Project notes are issued in bearer form, on an interest-bearing basis. Interest is payable when the notes mature. Denominations include $1,000, $5,000, $10,000, $25,000, $50,000, and $100,000, but pieces below $25,000 in amount are not often encountered. At the time of the initial offering, the investor specifies (1) the specific denominations of the notes being purchased by him, since after the notes have been issued the denominations cannot be changed; and (2) the paying agent (any bank which is a member of both the Federal Reserve System and the Federal Deposit Insurance Corporation) where he would like the interest and principal to be paid at the time the project notes mature. Validation of the notes is effected by the paying agent's signature on the face of each note. Similar to other tax-exempt securities, the legality of the respective project notes must be passed on by lawyers designated and paid for by the investor, unless the offering notice for the notes indicates that an approving opinion will be provided by the General Counsel of the Department of Housing and Urban Development.

Several commercial banks and securities brokerage firms maintain secondary trading markets in project notes, and secondary-market prices and offerings on various issues are contained in the daily *Blue List.* Quotations and settlement procedures are virtually the same as those followed in transactions involving short-term tax-exempt securities backed by state and local governments.

Tax-Exempt Bond Funds

Tax-exempt bond funds are funds formed to invest in municipal securities and to pay out the interest income received to fundholders on a completely tax-free basis. Each fund is of the closed-end trust type, meaning that once the fund has been formed, the fund cannot sell new shares (sometimes called *units,* or *certificates*) to the public. If the investor wishes to sell his holding in the fund, it can either be sold in the secondary trading market for fund units maintained by the securities firm which originally sponsored the fund offering, or the holding can be redeemed by the fund itself. Since tax-exempt bond funds were first created in 1961, over 160 funds totalling over $3 billion in value have been offered primarily to individual investors. For a few funds, the minimum investment is $1,000, but most require a minimum purchase of $5,000.

After the initial investments for the fund have been selected, no further trading is allowed by the Securities and Exchange Commission, which regulates tax-exempt bond funds. Usually, the fund invests in 20 to 25 different issues ranging from 15 to 50 years in maturity. The funds themselves do not have a final maturity date, but as a fund's bond holdings mature (or as the bonds held are paid off by the state or local government through sinking funds or other redemption operations), the proceeds are distributed on a pro rata basis to fund holders, and when the fund reaches a certain percentage of its original size (e.g., 20 percent), it is liquidated and the remaining funds are proportionately distributed to fundholders.

The funds do not charge an annual management fee. The fund sponsor's compensation comes instead from the initial sales charge, which ranges between 3.5 to 4.5 percent of the fund's assets, depending on the fund. This is one of the drawbacks of tax-exempt bond funds, in that only 95½ to 96½ percent of the investor's capital is working for him. To some degree, however, this is offset by some of the advantages of these types of funds: (1) diversification, as the investor is able to own a proportionate share of several municipal securities by making a single investment as small as $1,000 or $5,000; (2) the fact that the fund holdings were selected by professionals in the municipal securities field; and (3) convenience and freedom from the details of safekeeping and coupon collection—on some funds, interest receipts are paid out monthly.

On the other hand, the funds also have some disadvantages. First is the fact that most of the funds have no sliding scale of sales charges for large-size purchases of the fund. In addition, the investor loses some flexibility by investing in a tax-exempt bond fund, since he cannot select the exact maturity of his investment or predict when part of his principal may be returned to him. It is true that he can sell or redeem his units when he desires, but this could be difficult if the fund sponsor for some reason decides to stop making a secondary market in the issue (they are not required to do so), or if several other fundholders decide to redeem their units at the same time. If this happens, the fund may be forced to liquidate some of its investments in order to pay off the investors who want their money returned. Although the funds generally are restricted by their charters from purchasing securities rated below BBB or Baa, many have sought to maximize income by heavy concentration in higher-yielding issues. If these issues have to be sold prior to maturity or if defaults occur, significant discounts or capital losses might have to be accepted by the fund. Finally, if the investor's state and local governments provide income tax exemption from securities of their own state and local area, the investor will lose this possibility of double or triple tax exemption if he invests in a fund which purchases securities from all over the country. Some firms have sponsored funds aimed only at the residents of certain states—California, Florida, Michigan, New York, or Pennsylvania—and these do provide some state and local tax advantages to residents of these respective states.

With the aid of this book, with some study, effort, and experience, and with the advice and assistance of an intelligent and reputable securities broker or commercial banker, the individual should be able to take advantage of the benefits of investing in tax-exempt securities without purchasing tax-exempt bond funds. However, if the investor decides to purchase units in a bond fund, he should inquire about the judgment of the fund's portfolio selection group and the quality of the portfolio they chose. In addition, the investor should find out if a fund exists which invests solely in the obligations of issuers within his own state, in order to gain any additional tax exemption privileges at the state and local level.

TEN

Corporate Securities

The range of fixed-income securities issued by corporations is quite broad, encompassing several types of bonds, notes, and preferred stock issues, in addition to some of the short-term money market instruments discussed in Chapter 8. Companies utilize long-term fixed-income securities as an important source of capital for plant construction, purchases of equipment, and working capital, and to retire other forms of long-term and short-term debt. For individual and most institutional investors, the interest income from corporate bonds and notes, as well as the dividend income from preferred stocks (with one exception for preferred stocks) is fully taxable at the federal, state, and local levels. Because of this full taxability, and because corporate securities are considered to have somewhat more credit risk than the obligations of federal, state, and local governments and agencies, corporate issues usually return higher yields than governmental or agency securities having similar characteristics. These higher yields make corporate fixed-income securities particularly attractive to tax-free institutional investors, such as pension funds, state employee retirement systems, and foundations. Other large buyers of corporate securities include life insurance companies and individuals whose total annual income does not place them in a high enough incremental tax bracket to benefit from the tax-exemption feature of municipal issues. Figure 10-1 compares corporate bond yields with yields on long-term governmental and tax-exempt securities during the past 50 years.

In this chapter, our analysis will focus on publicly offered corporate securities, rather than private placements, which are primarily intended for large institutional investors. The first section reviews the various types of corporate bonds, the differences in securities issued by particular industry groups, coupon classifications, the evaluation of corporate securities, trading practices for these issues, and corporate bond funds. The second section treats preferred stocks, and the third section covers those bonds and preferred stocks which are convertible into the common stock of the same company.

Types and Major Issuers of Corporate Bonds

Corporate bonds, often referred to simply as "corporates" or "straight" bonds, represent the obligation of a company to pay a specified amount of principal and interest to the investor at specified times in the future. The specific rights of the bond holders and the obligations of the corporation are spelled out in a document called the *bond indenture,* which is a contract between the company and the *bond trustee,* usually a bank acting on behalf of the investors in the security. In addition, there may be restrictions contained in the indenture, called *protective covenants,* which might be designed, for example, to keep the company from issuing additional debt or paying dividends to common stockholders unless specified financial conditions are met. For a review of how corporations pay back principal and interest, and other features of corporate fixed-income securities, the investor should refer to Chapters 3 and 4. Generally, corporate bonds have an original maturity of 15 years or more, while corporate notes (also treated in this section) mature in 5 to 10 years, though this designation is not always strictly applied—the investor will sometimes encounter 15-year notes or 5-year bonds.

In total, $250.5 billion worth of corporate bonds, representing

FIGURE 10-1. *Bond yields. (By permission of the Board of Governors of the Federal Reserve System.)*

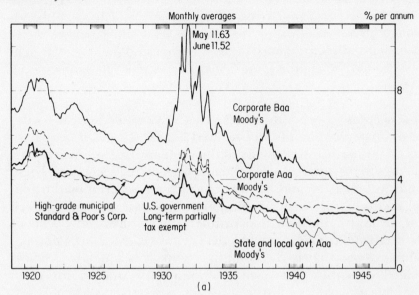

(a)

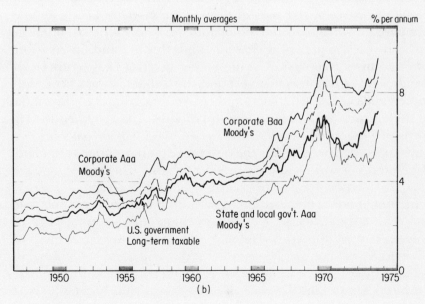

(b)

over 5,000 different issues, was outstanding at the end of 1974, up 92.3 percent from $130.4 billion at year-end 1967. The aggregate gross vólume of all newly issued nonconvertible corporate bonds averaged $28.3 billion per year in the 1970–1974 period. After deducting bond retirements, the average net amount of new straight bonds issued during the same 5-year period was $20.8 billion each year.

Types of bonds   Corporate bonds usually fall into one of two categories: unsecured bonds and secured bonds. *Unsecured* bonds are backed primarily by the ability of the company to generate enough earnings to pay interest and principal back on the securities. These bonds include *notes* and *debentures*, which are secured by the general credit of the corporation, and *subordinated debentures*, which rank behind bank debt and ordinary debentures but ahead of preferred and common stockholders in any claim made against the company's property in the event the company is liquidated. Subordinated debentures have become frequently utilized in recent years, particularly by industrial issuers. Nevertheless, the investor should be aware of the risks of owning an unsecured obligation as compared with a secured obligation, in the event of financial difficulty on the part of the issuer. With this in mind, in choosing among unsecured issues, unless the investor has consciously decided to own a speculative bond, he should always seek only those bonds which will maintain their creditworthiness in favorable as well as unfavorable economic conditions. An infrequently seen form of unsecured bond is the *income* bond, which pays interest only if it is earned, whereas the indenture on most bonds stipulates that interest is owed, on a cumulative basis, whether or not the company produces operating earnings in a given year.

  Secured bonds are backed by a guaranteed right to some specified property of the issuer, such as certain equipment, plant facilities, or land owned by the corporation. For example, this right may be evidenced by a mortgage on a power plant, and if the issuer defaults on principal or interest payments, the bond trustee can foreclose on the mortgage and sell the plant in order to repay the bondholders all or part of their money. A substantial portion of utility and railroad issues are *mortgage bonds*. Another type of secured bond is the *collateral trust bond*, which is backed by certain assets (usually securities) which are pledged by the company to the trustee, who is empowered to sell the collateral to pay off the bonds in case of default. A well-regarded type of secured bond is the *equipment trust certificate*, usually sold by railroads to finance the purchase of rolling stock. Airlines employ a similar security to buy aircraft, called a *guaranteed loan certificate*. Equipment trust certificate holders actually own a share of the railroad's rolling equipment, which can be sold to another railroad if the issuer of the certificates defaults. Because of the necessity of owning and operating rolling equipment to run a railway, railroads, despite their occasional financial problems, have *very rarely* defaulted on any equipment trust certificates during the past 100 years. An unusual feature of equipment trust certificates is the fact that they are issued in serial form, similar to many municipal issues.

As mentioned earlier, *corporate notes* generally have an initial maturity of 10 years or less and are often sold by a company in anticipation of issuing long-term bonds at lower interest rates some time in the future. Notes may be either secured or unsecured, and they may or may not be callable or redeemable during their life. A number of note issues have sinking funds designed to retire a portion of the issue prior to its final maturity, effectively shortening the average life of the notes. Although a sinking fund for a note issue may give it a degree of price support in the secondary trading market and reduce the company's credit risk slightly, the investor should be aware that his notes can be called away from him by lot to satisfy sinking-fund requirements, particularly if the note is trading above its sinking-fund call price. Notes have historically been used extensively by banks and finance companies, and more recently, by utilities which at times have experienced difficulty in raising long-term funds at reasonable interest rates. The investor can also purchase the notes of some of the largest finance companies, such as the General Motors Acceptance Corporation, directly from their own offices rather than through a securities brokerage firm. When this procedure is followed, there is normally a $25,000 minimum purchase requirement.

If interest rates are low and expected to rise, the investor wanting to purchase a fixed-income security should consider investing in very-short-maturity notes or in short-term money market instruments, rather than in longer-term bonds, to protect his capital while the increase in market yield levels is taking place. If interest rates are high and expected to fall, the investor stands to gain more by buying longer-maturity bonds instead of notes. If the investor is not sure which way interest rates will move, short- and intermediate-term notes are somewhat safer, in that prices for notes will neither rise nor fall as fast as for long-term securities for an equivalent change in interest rates. In general, note issues are primarily suitable for the investor who knows he will need his funds back at some definite time in the future, between 1 and 10 years from the date of the notes' issuance.

Major issuers of corporate bonds Traditionally, investors have divided corporate bonds into three primary classifications: public utility, industrial, and railroad securities. In recent years, many investors have further subdivided some of these groupings, so that numerous investors and traders distinguish between electrical, gas, and telephone types of utility issues, and between finance company, bank and other industrial bonds. For a given maturity and quality rating, each group exhibits similar trading characteristics and yield patterns relative to other groups. *Utility* issues account for the largest portion of total corporate bond issues outstanding. In 1974, total gross new issues of electrical, gas, and water utility bonds amounted to $12 billion, up from $4.2 billion offered in 1967. Average yields on double-A rated utility bond issues have generally served as the benchmark against which other corporate bond yields are compared. From 1964 through early 1975, double-A rated utility bonds have yielded on average between 4.46 percent and 9.17 percent. Of the major groups of utility bonds, the securities of Bell Telephone Company and its subsidiaries, often called *telephone* bonds, are generally considered to be the most liquid and most easily tradeable in view of the usual large size of these issues and their high quality ratings. Gross new issues of bonds in the communications industry (principally telephone bonds) grew from a total of $1.8 billion in 1967 to $3.6 billion in 1974.

Typical utility bonds have traditionally had a maturity range of 30 to 40 years, 5-year protection from refunding, and no sinking-fund provisions. From Chapter 4, the investor will recall that even when bonds are noncallable or nonrefundable, they generally may be called in by lot or otherwise for sinking-fund purchases, if the market price of the bonds is above the sinking-fund call price. If the market price of the bonds is below the sinking-fund call price, the corporation will generally repurchase the bonds it needs for sinking-fund purposes on the open market. Some very large utilities, and all subsidiaries of the Bell Telephone System do not have sinking funds for their issues. Those utility-related securities which do have sinking funds normally commence sinking-fund purchases 4 to 5 years after the bonds have been issued. Double-A rated utility issues have usually yielded the same as triple-A Bell Telephone subsidiary bonds; but in 1974, investors' fears over possible downward quality rating revisions on electric utility securities caused *telephone* issues to sell at *higher* prices (lower yields) than other types of utility bonds. This also caused several utility companies to alter the normal terms of their bond issues in order to make their securities appeal to investors. For example, on some bonds maturities were shortened from 30 or more years to 20 years, and the customary nonredemption period was lengthened, from 5 to 10 years, and sinking funds were added to attract investor interest. Several utilities issued notes with maturities of 5 to 10 years and with nonredemption periods of 5 to 7 years. On rare occasions, other utility issuers granted purchasers of their newly offered bonds the option, upon 6 months' prior notice, to cash in their bonds at face value at a specified time (usually 15 years) prior to maturity. *Gas* utility securities normally have sinking funds, and because of the limited life of the gas supplies behind a number of these issues, they have in normal times sold at 20 to 25 basis points (0.20 to 0.25 percent) greater yield (lower price) than *electrical* utility securities.

During the past 40 years, even though they are considered to have a somewhat higher overall risk than utilities, *industrial bonds* have generally sold at a lower yield (higher price) than similarly rated utility bonds. One reason for this is the somewhat shorter average maturities of industrial bonds, and the use of more active sinking funds on industrial bonds as compared with utilities—about three-quarters of all industrial bonds have sinking funds, versus a much lower proportion for utilities. In 1974, gross new issues of industrial bonds of all types were $20 billion, a gain of 49 percent over the 1967 figure of $13.4 billion. Within these totals, finance companies' new bond issues went from $1 billion in 1967 to $1.9 billion in 1974, and banks' bond offerings rose from $300 million to $2.3 billion over the same time period.

Industrial issues usually carry refunding protection for 10 years from the date of issuance, and sinking funds which start sometime between 5 and 10 years from the initial offering. Finance company issues have a special provision which allows bonds to be called ahead of the regularly scheduled refunding date if the finance company's receivables (money owed to them by their customers) decline below certain levels; however they also usually carry refunding protection for 10 years from the date of issuance. The bond issues of banks and bank holding companies are usually of 10 to 30 years' maturity. Several bank-related bonds have sinking funds and are not redeemable for 5 to 10 years after the issue date. The sinking-fund provisions on bank issues are similar to those on industrial issues, and long-term bank bonds usually have 10 years' refunding protection, with 5 to 7 years' refunding protection on the notes of bank issuers.

Since the mid-1920s, because of a higher perceived credit risk by investors, *railroad bond* issues have usually traded at higher yields (lower prices) than utility bonds of the same quality rating and maturity, although at times they have traded at lower yields (higher prices) than similar utility issues. This type of exceptional yield relationship was particularly evident in late 1973 and early 1974, when it was felt that the nation's energy shortage would have a beneficial effect on railroads' operating earnings and a detrimental effect on the prospects of many utilities. Gross new issues of transportation companies (which include airlines as well as railroads) have declined in the 1967–1974 period, from $2.0 billion in 1967 to $0.9 billion in 1974.

From this brief review of the major groups which issue corporate bonds, the investor should not attempt to memorize the exact yield spreads between one type of issue and another, because these relationships can and do change very dramatically over time. Instead, the investor should try to get a *general* grasp of how one category of bonds trades relative to another; for instance, railroad issues would normally be expected to sell at a higher yield (lower price) than industrial bonds of the *same maturity and quality rating.* The investor should keep these relationships in mind and he should also be sensitive to *possible changes* in these relationships on account of economic factors, fundamental developments, and psychological attitudes and perceptions when deciding whether to purchase or sell a particular bond. Finally, the investor should try to develop an appreciation for the *normal* maturity, sinking-fund provisions, and call features for each type of bond. If a specific bond lacks normally included features which are advantageous to investors, it will affect that security's price and marketability.

Coupon classifications   Many professional investors refer to corporate, agency, and U.S. government bonds by names which relate to their coupon rate compared with current interest rate levels. Many of these names have already been encountered earlier in other contexts. *Discount bonds* is another term for low-coupon issues selling at a discount from par, after interest rates have risen since the time of the bonds' initial offering. Discounts are further classified into *moderate discounts* (bonds selling in the low 70 to mid-80 price range) and *deep discounts* (those issues trading at a price in the low 70s or below). Some bonds, particularly bonds arising out of corporate recapitalizations, tender offers, and merger deals, trade at high yields to maturity and sell at substantial discounts to par, even though they have coupons close to prevailing interest rate levels. This is because of the fact that these bonds are low-rated securities carrying considerable credit risk. The average investor, who cannot afford to lose that portion of his funds committed to this type of investment, should avoid these bonds altogether. These bonds are best left to specialized investors who can analyze and withstand the risks inherent in these issues. No extra yield advantages are worth the possible protracted delays in interest payments and capital losses which will occur if the company should default on its obligations. Low-coupon long-maturity discount bonds of good quality can be an attractive investment in a period of declining interest rates because of their greater protection against being called and the greater upward price movement they will experience relative to higher-coupon securities of similar maturity.

Current coupon bonds refer to bonds with coupon rates close to current general interest levels. Usually, current coupon bonds can be expected to trade a few points above or below par, in the 90 to 105 range. The relative attractiveness of a current coupon issue depends on *when* it is callable and at *what size call premium.* If rising overall interest rates are expected, current coupon issues without call protection can be purchased, since there would be little likelihood of the bonds being called unless the interest rate outlook changed. If falling interest rates are foreseen, current coupon issues should be purchased only with call protection, and if possible, with a sizable call premium to be paid by the issuer if in fact the bonds are called.

Premium bonds trade at prices of roughly 105 or more, and carry higher-interest coupons than current interest rate levels, interest rates having fallen since the time these securities were originally issued. The current yield is always higher than the yield to maturity on premium bonds, since the investor pays above par for premium bonds and only receives par at maturity. Under certain conditions, some premium bonds which trade above their call price are cushioned from an immediate price decline if interest rates begin to rise again. For example, an 8 percent bond with 20 years left to maturity may be callable (currently or at some point in the future) at a price of 108. If interest rates drop to 6 percent, this bond should theoretically sell for 123⅛, but in fact, it will not rise much above 108 on account of the risk of its being called at that price. However, if interest rates rise from the 6 percent level to the 7 percent level, these bonds, unlike low- and intermediate-coupon bonds which would decline in price under these conditions, are still worth more than 108—in fact, 110⅝. Thus many high-coupon bonds enjoy a "cushion" against price declines as interest rates rise to a certain point, and they are called *cushion bonds*. After interest rates rise past this specific point (in our example that point is 7.24 percent, since 7.24 percent is the yield to maturity for an 8 percent 20-year bond at a price of 108), cushion bonds will decline in price just like any other bonds. Premium bonds are attractive to the investor seeking maximum current income, and to investors seeking to limit their capital losses in the event of a further rise in interest rates.

Many investors in cushion bonds compute a *yield to call price*, which assumes that the security is called by the issuer at the end of a specified period of time at the stated call price. This helps determine whether the investor should buy a different issue instead of the premium bond under consideration. For example, if the yield to call price is lower than the yields available from issues whose maturity matches the expected call date, the investor should purchase the shorter-maturity issue.

Quick Formulas for Finding the Yield on Bonds

In Chapter 3, we demonstrated the method of finding a security's yield to maturity through the use of yield tables. If the investor does not have yield tables or a yield to maturity calculator handy, a close approximation can be derived through the use of the following formulas:

$$\begin{array}{l} \text{Yield to maturity} \\ \text{for a security} \\ \text{selling at a} \\ \textit{discount} \end{array} = \frac{\text{total dollar amount of annual interest per bond} + \text{total discount divided by years left to maturity}}{(\text{discount bond cost} + \text{par value}) \div 2}$$

$$\begin{array}{l} \text{Yield to maturity} \\ \text{for a security} \\ \text{selling at a} \\ \textit{premium} \end{array} = \frac{\text{total dollar amount of annual interest per bond} - \text{total premium divided by years left to maturity}}{(\text{premium bond cost} + \text{par value}) \div 2}$$

For example, to find the approximate yield to maturity of a 7 percent coupon bond with 10 years left to maturity, if bought at a price of 90, the following operation would be performed:

$$\text{Yield to maturity (discount bond)} = \frac{\$70 + (\$100 \div 10 \text{ years})}{(\$1,000 + \$900) \div 2} = \frac{\$80}{\$950} = 8.42 \text{ percent}$$

Checking this yield to maturity against the exact yield to maturity as shown in the yield book (8.42 percent as calculated under our formula versus 8.50 percent as listed in the yield book) we find the two values fairly close. If the same 7 percent coupon bond with 10 years to maturity had instead been purchased at a price of 108, the yield to maturity would work out as follows:

$$\text{Yield to maturity (premium bond)} = \frac{\$70 - (\$80 \div 10 \text{ years})}{(\$1,000 + \$1,080) \div 2} = \frac{\$62}{\$1,040} = 5.96 \text{ percent}$$

The 5.96 percent yield to maturity as computed by the formula is only 3 basis points (0.03 percent) different from the yield book number of 5.93 percent.

Analysis of Corporate Bonds

Ordinarily, the average investor will rely upon the advice of his securities broker and the bond rating assigned by the rating services to evaluate whether a securities credit standing is high enough to meet his objectives. (Included in this section are descriptions of the credit rating classifications of corporate bonds by Moody's and Standard & Poor's.) Nevertheless, the investor should be aware of three types of analytical ratios which can supplement the opinions of the rating agencies and the investor's securities broker.

The first ratio measures the margin of safety of the issuer in meeting interest payments, and it is called the *overall interest coverage ratio*. This ratio computes a single coverage figure for all of the company's bonds outstanding (as well as any private placements) and assumes that a default on a subordinated debt issue is as unsatisfactory as a default on more senior secured obligations, such as a mortgage bond. The ratio is calculated according to the following formula (additional formulas are included after the bond ratings):

$$\begin{array}{l} \text{Overall interest} \\ \text{coverage ratio} \end{array} = \dfrac{\begin{array}{l}\text{total annual} \\ \text{interest charges}\end{array} + \begin{array}{l}\text{aftertax net income (excluding} \\ \text{any extraordinary gains or losses)}\end{array}}{\text{total annual interest charges}}$$

For example, if a company had \$1 million in annual interest charges on all its bonds (and private placements, if any) outstanding, and if its aftertax net income amounted to \$4.5 million, the overall interest coverage ratio would equal:

$$\begin{array}{l} \text{Overall interest} \\ \text{coverage ratio} \end{array} = \dfrac{\$1 \text{ million} + \$4.5 \text{ million}}{\$1 \text{ million}} = \dfrac{\$5.5 \text{ million}}{\$1 \text{ million}} = 5.5 \text{ times coverage}$$

Several caveats should be pointed out in calculating the above coverage ratio. First, there are several methods of computing interest coverage ratios. Some analysts calculate the ratio on a pretax, rather than an aftertax, basis, using pretax net income (exclusive of any extraordinary gains or losses) in the formula; some analysts add one-third of the total annual rental charges payable by the company to both the numerator and denominator of the ratio; and some analysts compute a coverage ratio for interest obligations plus preferred stock dividends by adding preferred stock dividend requirements to both the numerator and the denominator of the ratio. The investor should be aware of the variety of these methods; and when someone quotes an interest coverage ratio to him, he should find out exactly what method of calculation has been utilized, and particularly whether *all* interest charges have been included. Coverage ratios are calculated and published for all new issues by Moody's and Standard & Poor's in the monthly review publications described in Chapter 15.

The second caveat is that the investor should not merely derive the interest coverage ratio for 1 year only. If possible, ratios should be calculated for several recent years, under both favorable and unfavorable economic conditions for the company. And third, although a coverage ratio of 10 times interest charges is almost always better than a coverage ratio of 4 times interest charges, it is very difficult to set an absolute "threshold ratio" figure below which a company's interest coverage is "bad," and above which it is "good."

Different industries can withstand different debt levels depending on the variability and stability of their income flows. Because of this, the investor is better off inquiring how the ratio of the company being evaluated compares with the ratios of other companies in its *own as well as other* industries. In general, the higher the overall interest coverage ratio, the more able the company is to pay off its debt service obligations in a timely fashion. Of course, the investor should always be on the alert to avoid the exceptions to this general statement.

The next ratio measures the strength of the company's financial condition, computing long-term debt as a percentage of the total capitalization of the issuer, as shown below:

$$\text{Capitalization ratio} = \frac{\text{long-term debt}}{\text{total capitalization}}$$

In this formula, long-term debt includes all debt of the company which matures in greater than 1 year (both privately and publicly held debt), and total capitalization includes not only long-term debt but also the total balance sheet value of common stock, capital surplus, retained earnings, and the par value (or liquidation value) of any preferred stock outstanding. For example, if a corporation has $50 million of long-term public and private debt outstanding, and the balance sheet value of its common stock is $25 million, its capital surplus $175 million, and its retained earnings $500 million, with no preferred stock outstanding, the capitalization ratio is calculated as follows:

$$\text{Capitalization ratio} = \frac{\$50 \text{ million}}{\$50 \text{ million} + \$700 \text{ million}} = 0.067, \text{ or } 6.7 \text{ percent}$$

This means that long-term debt accounts for 6.7 percent of the total capitalization of the hypothetical company. Again, some people compute the capitalization ratio differently than others, and it is impossible to generalize about specific ratios which are "good" or "bad," without knowing more about the industry that the company is in and the trend of the capitalization ratio for several years. Usually, the lower the percentage of debt in a company's capital structure, the stronger and more able that company is to repay the principal and interest on its notes and bonds under adverse economic conditions.

Finally, two ratios which gauge the working capital position of a company, and thus its level of cash resources, are the *current ratio* and the *quick ratio* (also known as the "acid test"). These ratios are computed as follows:

$$\frac{\text{Current}}{\text{ratio}} = \frac{\text{current assets}}{\text{current liabilities}}$$

and

$$\frac{\text{Quick}}{\text{ratio}} = \frac{\text{current assets} - \text{inventories}}{\text{current liabilities}}$$

For example, if a company had current assets of $3.0 million, of which inventories amounted to $1.5 million, and current liabilities amounting to $1.5 million, these two ratios would be:

$$\frac{\text{Current}}{\text{ratio}} = \frac{\$3.0 \text{ million}}{\$1.5 \text{ million}} = 2.0$$

and

$$\frac{\text{Quick}}{\text{ratio}} = \frac{\$3.0 \text{ million} - \$1.5 \text{ million}}{\$1.5 \text{ million}} = 1.0$$

As with the overall interest coverage ratio and the capitalization ratio, it is very difficult to state what are acceptable and unacceptable figures for the current ratio and the quick ratio, though a widely used standard for the current ratio is 2.0, and for the quick ratio, 1.0. Again, it is best to compare one company's current and quick ratios to those for other companies in its own and other industries, and the investor should be sure that these ratios are being computed in the same manner whenever making comparisons because of slight differences in the ways some analysts compute the ratios compared with others' methods.

The use of the ratios mentioned in this section is by no means mandatory in order to achieve profits and success in fixed-income investing. However, for those investors who desire to probe further and quantify the margin of safety and quality in a company's financial condition, ratio analysis can be a useful and significant aid. After some experience in computing these ratios, the investor will begin to develop the ability to differentiate between a financially strong company and a weaker one. In making these judgments, the investor should remember to draw upon the resources of his securities broker and the major security rating services.

STANDARD & POOR'S CORPORATE BOND RATINGS*

AAA – Bonds rated **AAA** are highest grade obligations. They possess the ultimate degree of protection as to principal and interest. Marketwise they move with interest rates, and hence provide the maximum safety on all counts.

AA – Bonds rated **AA** also qualify as high grade obligations, and in the majority of instances differ from **AAA** issues only in small degree. Here, too, prices move with the long term money market.

A – Bonds rated **A** are regarded as upper medium grade. They have considerable investment strength but are not entirely free from adverse effects of changes in economic and trade conditions. Interest and principal are regarded as safe. They predominantly reflect money rates in their market behavior, but to some extent, also economic conditions.

BBB – The **BBB**, or medium grade category is borderline between definitely sound obligations and those where the speculative element begins to predominate. These bonds have adequate asset coverage and normally are protected by satisfactory earnings. Their susceptibility to changing conditions, particularly to depressions, necessitates constant watching. Marketwise, the bonds are more responsive to business and trade conditions than to interest rates. This group is the lowest which qualifies for commercial bank investment.

BB – Bonds given a **BB** rating are regarded as lower medium grade. They have only minor investment characteristics. In the case of utilities, interest

By Permission of Standard & Poor's Corporation.

*To provide more detailed indications of credit quality, bond letter ratings may be modified by the addition of a plus or minus sign, when appropriate, to show relative standing within the major rating categories, the only exceptions being in the **AAA** category and the lesser categories below **BB**. Canadian corporate bonds are rated on the same basis as American corporate issues. The ratings measure the intrinsic value of the bonds, but they do not take into account exchange risks and other uncertainties.

is earned consistently but by narrow margins. In the case of other types of obligors, charges are earned on average by a fair margin, but in poor periods deficit operations are possible.

B – Bonds rated as low as **B** are speculative. Payment of interest cannot be assured under difficult economic conditions.

CCC-CC – Bonds rated **CCC** and **CC** are outright speculations, with the lower rating denoting the more speculative. Interest is paid, but continuation is questionable in periods of poor trade conditions. In the case of **CC** ratings the bonds may be on an income basis and the payment may be small.

C – The rating of **C** is reserved for income bonds on which no interest is being paid.

DDD-D – All bonds rated **DDD, DD** and **D** are in default, with the rating indicating the relative salvage value.

NR – Not Rated.

MOODY'S CORPORATE BOND RATINGS

Aaa – Bonds which are rated **Aaa** are judged to be of the best quality. They carry the smallest degree of investment risk and are generally referred to as "gilt edge." Interest payments are protected by a large or by an exceptionally stable margin and principal is secure. While the various protective elements are likely to change, such changes as can be visualized are most unlikely to impair the fundamentally strong position of such issues.

Aa – Bonds which are rated as **Aa** are judged to be of high quality by all standards. Together with the **Aaa** group they comprise what are generally known as high grade bonds. They are rated lower than the best bonds because margins of protection may not be as large as in **Aaa** securities or fluctuation of protective elements may be of greater amplitude or there may be other elements present which make the long term risks appear somewhat larger than in **Aaa** securities.

A – Bonds which are rated **A** possess many favorable investment attributes and are to be considered as upper medium grade obligations. Factors giving security to principal and interest are considered adequate but elements may be present which suggest a susceptibility to impairment sometime in the future.

Baa – Bonds which are rated **Baa** are considered as medium grade obligations, i.e., they are neither highly protected nor poorly secured. Interest payments and principal security appear adequate for the present but certain protective elements may be lacking or may be characteristically unreliable over any great length of time. Such bonds lack outstanding investment characteristics and in fact have speculative characteristics as well.

Ba – Bonds which are rated **Ba** are judged to have speculative elements: their future cannot be considered as well assured. Often the protection of interest and principal payments may be very moderate and thereby not well safeguarded during both good and bad times over the future. Uncertainty of position characterizes bonds in this class.

B – Bonds which are rated **B** generally lack characteristics of the desirable investment. Assurance of interest and principal payments or of maintenance of other terms of the contract over any long period of time may be small.

Caa – Bonds which are rated **Caa** are of poor standing. Such issues may be in default or there may be present elements of danger with respect to principal or interest.

Ca – Bonds which are rated **Ca** represent obligations which are speculative in a high degree. Such issues are often in default or have other marked shortcomings.

C – Bonds which are rated **C** are the lowest rated class of bonds and issues so rated can be regarded as having extremely poor prospects of ever attaining any real investment standing.

Initial Offerings and Secondary-Market Trading Practices

Corporate bonds, notes, and preferred stocks are brought to market by either the competitive or negotiated offering method, similar to initial offering practices in tax-exempt securities. An underwriting syndicate of securities brokerage and investment banking firms is formed to purchase the issue from the company and reoffer the securities to institutional and individual investors (commercial banks are not permitted to underwrite, or act as securities brokers in, corporate securities).

The competitive bidding method usually involves two or more

competing syndicate groups submitting sealed bids by a specified time to the corporation, which awards the issue to the underwriting group that submits the bid with the lowest net interest cost to the company. Competitive bidding is employed frequently by utility companies and in the equipment trust certificate offerings of railroads. Virtually all industrial and finance company issues are handled by the negotiated offering method, in which one or more investment banking firms, acting as manager on behalf of the underwriting syndicate, negotiate the coupon rate, offering terms, and other details of the issue with the company, taking into account the buying interest which investors have expressed in the issue. The underwriting firms are compensated by the spread between the price per security paid to the issuing corporation and the price paid by the investors to the underwriters. Over the past few years, the underwriters' average spread in competitive offerings has been around $8 per $1,000 bond, and about $8.75 per $1,000 in negotiated issues.

As mentioned earlier, the total size of a debt issue has an influence on its marketability, with more active trading and greater liquidity in larger issues, particularly those in the $100 million range and over. Although a substantial number of corporate bond issues are listed on the New York Stock Exchange and many small trades are executed there on a commission basis, most corporate bond trading is done off the stock exchange in over-the-counter trading among securities broker-dealer firms and between these firms and the general public. Corporate bond prices are usually quoted on a net basis in percentage-of-par terms, in points and one-eighth point fractions. Bond trading activity on the New York Stock Exchange is reported in most daily newspapers. The following excerpt is a sample quotation taken from the morning newspaper of July 31, 1974:

Bond	*Current Yield*	*Sales in $1,000s*	*High*	*Low*	*Last*	*Net Change*
General Electric 7½ 96	8.5	55	88⅛	88	88	−⅛

This quotation means that, at the close of trading on July 30, 1974, the General Electric 7½ percent coupon bonds maturing in 1996 were trading at a price of 88 ($880 per $1,000 bond), representing a price decrease of ⅛ point ($1.25 per $1,000 bond) from the previous day's closing price. At a price of 88, the General Electric 7½s of 1996 had a *current yield* of 8.5 percent. If the investor wants to know the bond's yield to maturity at that price, he can consult the yield book or utilize the quick formula presented earlier:

$$\text{Yield to maturity} = \frac{\$75 + (\$120 \div 22 \text{ years})}{(\$1,000 + \$880) \div 2} = \frac{\$80.45}{\$940} = 8.65 \text{ percent}$$

The newspaper price quotation also shows that these General Electric bonds traded on the New York Stock Exchange at a high of 88⅛ and at a low of 88 on July 30, and a total of 55 bonds ($55,000 principal amount) traded.

Although corporate bonds generally come in denominations of $1,000 and above, it is difficult and expensive for the investor to trade in small amounts of these securities. A round lot for trading corporate bonds is $100,000 par value, and many brokerage firms do not like to accept an over-the-counter order for as few as 10 to 20 bonds, although most of the nationally oriented securities brokerage firms which deal with the general public will handle orders for under 20 bonds. The minimum commission charged for trading most bonds, whether executed on the stock exchange or not, is $2.50 per $1,000 bond (¼ point). This minimum commission is sometimes lowered for notes and certain soon-to-mature or low-priced bonds. However, most firms charge a commission *above* the minimum commission rate, usually $5 to $10 per $1,000 bond (½ to 1 point), or an odd-lot charge is added to the minimum commission which has the same net effect of increasing transactions costs. In addition, buying or selling bonds in small amounts can take a few days to accomplish. Sometimes the bond dealer making a market in the issue, normally with a ¼ to ½ point spread between the bid and offered prices on actively traded issues, will *lower his bid price* (to an odd-lot *seller*), or *raise his offered price* (to an odd-lot buyer) by ¼ to ½ point from the prevailing quotation for a round lot transaction.

What does this mean for the small investor? Generally, it means that the investor's effective yield from holding corporate bonds is reduced when they are traded. For example, assume that the investor purchases $10,000 worth of 7 percent coupon bonds on their initial offering. No commission is charged on a purchase made in an underwriting, since the underwriting spread is deducted from the proceeds remitted to the company. One year later, the investor sells the bonds at a price equal to his purchase price, as interest rates are assumed to be at the same level as at the time of the initial offering. For holding the bonds 1 year, the investor collects $70 per $1,000 bond in interest, but from this amount he has to *subtract* commissions, odd-lot charges, and any dealer trading discount deducted from the current market price of the bonds. These expenses might amount to $7.50 to $15 per $1,000 bond, reducing the interest received, $70, to the $55 to $62.50 range, which makes the investor's effective yield somewhere between 5.5 and 6.25 percent.

For these reasons, the investor should not try to trade corporate bonds actively in small amounts. If the investor purchases small amounts of corporate bonds, he should try to do this on the initial offering if possible, and with money which will not be needed until the bonds mature. Also, it is important for the investor with a small amount of money to invest to deal through a firm which is accustomed to executing bond trades in odd-lot amounts and which will not overcharge for trades of small size.

Settlement procedures Delivery of and payment for corporate bonds normally takes place in clearinghouse funds 5 business days after the transaction. If the investor desires to arrange earlier or later settlement, or payment in Federal funds, this must be set up beforehand. Accrued interest from the last coupon payment date through the day prior to the delivery date must be paid by the purchaser of the bonds to the seller. As with other fixed-income securities, the holder of the bonds on the interest payment date is entitled to collect the entire amount of the interest since the previous coupon date.

Corporate Bond Funds

As with tax-exempt securities, numerous mutual funds have been formed to invest primarily in straight and convertible bonds. Some of these funds are of the *open-end* type, meaning that new shares can be offered to the public or redeemed at the fund itself by an investor who has a holding in the fund. Many of the bond funds started in recent years are of the *closed-end* type, in that if an investor wishes to buy into or sell out of the fund, his purchase or sale transaction would have to be with another investor, since the total number of shares in a closed-end fund are fixed.

Open-end bond funds usually can be sold back to the fund at their net asset value per share. If the investor purchases shares of an open-end fund from the fund, he buys them at the *offered* price, which is usually 8 to 8½ percent above the bid price, i.e., the net asset value per share. On the other hand, closed-end bond funds can trade at a premium or discount from their net asset value per share, the size of the premium or discount depending on investors' expectations for bond market price performance in general (interest rate outlook) and their estimation of the quality of the fund's management and its portfolio of bond holdings.

Bond funds are attractive to investors for several reasons. First, they provide the investor with a share of a much wider, more flexible, and more diversified portfolio of bonds than could be bought with a small amount of money. Second, since the bond fund executes its transactions in large size, the investor avoids the payment of odd-lot charges which are levied on small trades. Third, many bond funds have high-quality, professional managers making portfolio decisions which the investor may not have the time or knowledge to carry out. Fourth, bond funds are convenient for the person who does not wish to attend to records maintenance, safe-keeping, and the other administrative details associated with bond investing. In addition, a few bond funds pay interest on a monthly basis, rather than semiannually.

Together with these advantages, some bond funds may also have certain features which can be drawbacks under certain conditions. The 8 to 8½ percent sales charge paid on the initial offering of some bond funds (or the 8 to 8½ percent premium over net asset value paid to purchase shares of open funds) and the ½ to 1 percent annual management fees and other charges reduce the amount of money the investor actually has working for him by around 9 percent or more. Closed-end funds, if bought after the initial offering, involve the payment of a normal stock brokerage commission, which is less than the 8 to 8½ percent on open-end funds, but closed-end funds may at times lack marketability because another buyer must be found when the shares are to be sold—they cannot be redeemed at the fund itself.

In addition, some bond funds are allowed to (1) invest in low-quality bonds, restricted securities, and private placements; (2) borrow money to leverage themselves; and (3) carry out other operations designed to increase income. In an environment of credit stringency and concern over quality such as that experienced during 1974, these maneuvers can subject the portfolio to undue risks and can impair the fund's liquidity position. This impairment can possibly result in a capital loss over and above any risks of capital loss caused by rising interest rates. Also, numerous bond funds are permitted to place a substantial percentage of the fund's assets in the stock market, which may not be what the investor had in mind when purchasing a bond fund. On the other hand, *under certain circumstances,* investing in stocks and performing the other maneuvers described above can be construed as *advantageous* for a bond fund. Finally, in order to earn a high current yield, some funds may invest in bonds with little remaining or no current call protection, although the income earned by the fund may thus be substantially reduced if interest rates fall and the bonds held by the fund are called.

Almost all investors have the ability to invest in bonds on their own, without placing their money in a bond fund. This book and a substantial number of securities brokerage firms are oriented toward making the investor knowledgeable enough to profitably invest in corporate bonds and other fixed-income securities. Nevertheless, for some individuals who are not disposed toward managing their own securities portfolio, a bond fund is the easiest and most attractive way of investing in corporate fixed-income securities.

If the investor decides to purchase a bond fund, he should seek first of all to find one whose managers are highly capable and conservative in the way they invest the fund's assets. This means not only following sound investment practices, but also avoiding undue risks in managing the fund's portfolio. In addition, for several *quality* funds the investor should carefully examine the sales charges, management fees, and other expenses deducted from his investment. Some funds charge no "load" or sales fee at all. Before purchasing a bond fund, the investor should investigate the market-ability of his investment when it will be sold. For example, in some bond funds it is possible to sell fund shares at the offered, rather than the bid, side of the market, thus obtaining a higher overall price for the investment than otherwise. However, not all funds offer this feature, and the investor should weigh this positive aspect against other characteristics of the fund which may be less advantageous.

Preferred Stocks

Preferred stocks are corporate fixed-income securities that carry a certain fixed dividend, which is usually stated in dollar terms or as a percentage of the preferred's original issue price. While the dividend is a fixed amount, it can be omitted under certain conditions. Usually, the preferred dividends are cumulative, meaning that any dividends not paid in 1 year are carried over and owed in the next year, and so on until all dividends are paid. The corporation normally must pay its preferred stock dividends before it can grant any dividends on its common stock. If preferred stock dividends are not paid for a certain period of time, holders of the preferred issue are entitled to elect a certain number of directors to the company's board of directors in order that their rights and interests can be protected.

In the event that the issuing company is liquidated, the preferred stockholders have a claim on assets *after* the company's debtors (including its bondholders and noteholders), but *before* its common stockholders. The preferred shareholders' claims are usually limited to the par value of the preferred stock, which has traditionally been $100 per share, although in recent years preferred stock issues with a $25 or $50 par value per share have also been marketed to the public.

Preferred stock is an expensive form of corporate financing because preferred stock dividends paid out by a company are not deductible from its pretax income, whereas interest payments on a corporation's debt issues are deductible from pretax income. Because of this, preferred stock issues are not widely used, though the total of new issues of preferred stock has grown from $885 million in 1967 to $3.4 billion in 1973.

Because of an Internal Revenue Service regulation which sets a tax ceiling of 15 percent on dividends *received* by one corporation from another corporation, yields from preferred stocks are particularly attractive to *corporate* investors. For example, insurance corporations have been major purchasers of preferred stocks, in large part because of the 85 percent tax-exempt income from preferred stock dividends at the federal tax level. It should be mentioned that a few public utility preferred issues, called "old money" preferreds, provide approximately only a 60 percent federal tax exemption. A substantial majority of preferred issues, called "new money" preferreds, provide the usual 85 percent federal tax exemption, to corporate investors only.

If we assume a 48 percent corporate tax rate, the aftertax yield of a 7 percent preferred stock to a corporate investor is 6.50 percent. This is derived by the following method. Since only 15 percent of the dividend is taxable, and the corporate investor currently pays taxes at a 48 percent maximum incremental rate, the total tax rate paid equals 15 percent $\times$ 48 percent, or 7.2 percent of the stated dividend rate. Subtracting taxes at a 7.2 percent rate from a 7.0 percent yield, the tax payment is 0.50 percent and the aftertax yield is 6.50 percent. This procedure, though seemingly a bit complicated and confusing at first, can be followed for any preferred stock yield level and corporate income tax rate, by using the formula below:

$$
\begin{array}{l}
\text{Aftertax} \\
\text{equivalent} \\
\text{yield of a} \\
\text{preferred} \\
\text{stock to a} \\
\text{corporation}
\end{array}
=
\begin{array}{l}
\text{pretax} \\
\text{preferred} \\
\text{dividend} \\
\text{yield}
\end{array}
\left[1 - \left(\begin{array}{l} \text{corporate} \\ \text{incremental} \\ \text{tax rate} \end{array} \times \begin{array}{l} \text{rate of taxation} \\ \text{on preferred} \\ \text{stock—15\% on} \\ \text{"new money" preferreds,} \\ \textit{or } 40\% \text{ on "old} \\ \text{money" preferreds} \end{array} \right) \right]
$$

If we insert the numbers from the example above, the formula becomes:

Aftertax equivalent yield
of a preferred to corporation = 7.0% − (7.0% × 48% × 15%)
= 7.0% − 0.5% = 6.5%

Pretax yields on newly offered preferred issues are usually similar to long-term corporate bond yields on comparably rated companies, but preferreds can also trade on occasion at significantly higher or lower yields than similar straight debt securities, depending upon internal trading conditions in preferred markets. A listing of Moody's preferred stock ratings is contained on this page.

In October 1974, President Ford proposed that corporations be allowed to deduct from *pretax* income the dividends paid on preferred stock issued after December 31, 1974. Under this proposal, if a corporation elects to follow this alternative rather than pay preferred stock dividends out of *aftertax* earnings, the 85 percent tax saving for corporate purchasers of this type of preferred would not be allowed. Individual investors may in certain cases be attracted to some of the preferred stocks issued under this proposal (if passed).

Most preferred stocks have no maturity date, but are generally callable at the issuer's option at a periodically declining premium over the original issue price. A few older preferred stock issues and most of the recently issued preferred stock issues have sinking funds, which give them a final maturity date (since, at some point, the sinking fund has retired the entire issue), and thus an average life. The no-final-maturity feature on older preferreds causes them to trade like very-long-maturity bonds, fluctuating widely in periods of changing interest rates. Another factor contributing to the wide price swings sometimes seen on preferreds relative to corporate bonds of similar coupon rate and quality rating is the small size of numerous preferred issues, in terms of total shares, and the tendency of many corporate investors to buy preferred stocks and hold them for very long periods of time, thereby reducing the total tradeable supply and liquidity of the issue.

MOODY'S PREFERRED STOCK RATINGS*

"aaa" – An issue which is rated **"aaa"** is considered to be a top-quality preferred stock. This rating indicates good asset protection and the least risk of dividend impairment within the universe of preferred stocks.

"aa" – An issue which is rated **"aa"** is considered a high-grade preferred stock. This rating indicates that there is reasonable assurance that earnings and asset protection will remain relatively well maintained in the foreseeable future.

"a" – An issue which is rated **"a"** is considered to be an upper-medium grade preferred stock. While risks are judged to be somewhat greater than in the **"aaa"** and **"aa"** classifications, earnings and asset protection are, nevertheless, expected to be maintained at adequate levels.

"baa" – An issue which is rated **"baa"** is considered to be lower-medium grade, neither highly protected nor poorly secured. Earnings and asset protection appear adequate at present but may be questionable over any great length of time.

"ba" – An issue which is rated **"ba"** is considered to have speculative elements and its future cannot be considered well assured. Earnings and asset protection may be very moderate and not well safeguarded during adverse periods. Uncertainty of position characterizes preferred stocks in this class.

"b" – An issue which is rated **"b"** generally lacks the characteristics of a desirable investment. Assurance of dividend payments and maintenance of other terms of the issue over any long period of time may be small.

"caa" – An issue which is rated **"caa"** is likely to be in arrears on dividend payments. This rating designation does not purport to indicate the future status of payments.

Reprinted with written permission of Moody's Investors Service, Inc.

*Because of the fundamental differences between preferred stocks and bonds, a variation of the Moody's bond rating symbols was used when Moody's extended its ratings services to include quality designations on preferred stocks as of October 1, 1973. The new symbols, presented above, are designed to avoid comparison with bond quality in absolute terms. It should always be borne in mind that the preferred stock occupies a junior position to the bond.

Most preferred stock issues are listed on the New York Stock Exchange and quoted in the *stock* price sections of the newspaper. Settlement procedures are similar to those described in the previous section which are in effect on corporate bonds. One difference stems from the fact that preferreds pay interest *quarterly,* not semiannually, and they usually fall somewhat (by the amount of the dividend) when each quarter's dividend is issued. Therefore, preferred stocks are not traded on an accrued interest basis, similar to corporate bonds. Since interest income on preferred stocks is *fully* taxable at the federal, state, and local levels for individual investors, they have not been purchased in large amounts by individuals. For corporate investors who are not oriented toward trading into and out of preferred stocks, these securities provide a very high aftertax return. The investor in preferred issues should always be aware of their tendency to fluctuate more widely than most similarly rated corporate issues of roughly equivalent quality and coupon rates for a given change in the level of interest rates. In addition, the corporate investor should choose only from among those preferreds rated A or higher, and with at least 300,000 or more of $100 par value (or its equivalent) in preferred shares outstanding.

Convertible Securities

Certain corporate bonds and preferred stock issues can be converted, at the option of the investor, into a specified number of shares of the issuing company's common stock per $1,000 bond or per share of preferred stock. These *convertible securities* appeal to investors because they offer many of the benefits of fixed-income securities, while at the same time allowing the investor to participate in price movements in the underlying common stock. Convertible bonds are usually issued in large amounts during periods of rising stock prices, as is evidenced by the average of $3.9 billion of gross new issues of convertible bonds offered in each of the relatively bullish years 1967, 1968, and 1969, compared with less than $500 million offered in 1974, a year of lackluster stock market performance. Convertible preferred stocks are generally issued by a corporation in connection with the acquisition of another company because of the favorable tax treatment which this specialized type of transaction receives.

In the remainder of this section on convertible securities, we will concentrate primarily on convertible bonds. Convertible preferred stocks are virtually the same as convertible bonds, with the same differentiating features as exist between straight debt securities and preferred stocks holding true for their convertible counterparts. Unless otherwise mentioned, trading practices and settlement procedures are the same for convertible bonds as for straight bonds. As was mentioned in Chapter 4, the coupon rate on convertible bonds is *lower* than the coupon on equivalent nonconvertible securities of the same issuer because of the potential capital gains opportunities arising out of the convertibility feature. At the same time, the coupon rate on a convertible security is usually *higher* than the dividend rate on the underlying common stock. Convertible bonds, because of their normal subordinated status, are generally rated one classification below straight bonds of the same company.

Since a convertible bond is a hybrid security, combining the elements of both common stock and straight debt, investors often evaluate the stock *conversion value* of a convertible security, as well as its bond *investment value*. To comprehend these concepts better, the following example may be helpful. With long-term interest rates at 7 percent, assume that a company issues a 5 percent 20-year maturity convertible bond which is convertible into 40 shares of the company's common stock at $25 per share for each $1,000 bond ($1,000 = 40 × $25). The convertible security's bond investment value may be computed by looking in the yield book to find the price at which a 5 percent bond with 20 years to maturity would have to sell in order to have a 7 percent yield to maturity. This price turns out to be 78½, or $785 per $1,000 bond, and this is the price at which the convertible issue would probably sell if it were not convertible. As might be intuitively expected, the bond investment value of a convertible will move down or up as interest rates rise or fall.

The conversion value of a convertible bond is simply the number of shares into which the bond is convertible (this is usually fixed for the entire life of the bond) multiplied by the market price per share of the common stock. For example, if the stock price of the company which issued the convertible described above moved up to $30 per share, the bond's conversion value would be 40 shares × $30 = $1,200 per $1,000 bond, or 120 in percentage-of-par terms. Since the bonds can be converted into 40 shares of common stock, they will generally move up in price as the common stock price rises. Similarly, if the common stock price falls, the convertible bonds will decline. However, as the conversion value of the bond approaches its investment value, it will tend to behave more like a *straight bond* than a *common stock*. Thus, if the common stock price falls from $25 to $18 per share, the bond's conversion value is 40 shares × $18 = $720, or 72. Generally, since the convertible is worth 78½ on its bond features alone (because it has a 5 percent coupon in a 7 percent general interest rate environment), it would tend to resist decline and trade above 78½, even though the common stock price has fallen by a much greater percentage. This relationship sometimes holds true even if the stock price continues to decline further.

If the convertible is trading at 80 while its conversion value is 72, the bond is said to be selling at a *premium over conversion value* of (80 − 72)/72, or $8/72$, which equals an 11 percent conversion premium. If the bond trades at 80 when its conversion value is 80, it is said to be selling at a 0 percent conversion premium, or *on parity* with conversion value. Except in very rare cases, convertible securities do not trade at a *discount* to parity—this would have the convertible selling at below its conversion value, or 80 when its conversion value is 82. This does not happen for long, because investors can buy the bonds and convert them into common stock worth more money than they paid for the bonds. When convertible securities are selling at a small-to modest-sized conversion premium, holders of the common stock will sometimes want to sell their common stock and buy the convertible, particularly if there is a sizable yield advantage in favor of the convertible securities relative to the total dividends paid on the underlying common stock.

We have dwelled at some length on the conversion premium and parity concept because it leads us to some general observations about the price behavior of convertibles. If a convertible bond is selling on parity or at a small to moderate conversion premium, it will tend to move up in price as the common stock appreciates. If the convertible security is selling at a very large conversion premium, it will tend to move up slowly if the price of the common stock rises, until the conversion premium narrows to more normal levels as it approaches conversion parity, at which point the convertible bond will tend to move up in unison with the common stock. Convertible securities selling above their call price will tend to sell at little or no conversion premium, and they will rise proportionally in price only as the price of the common stock rises.

Convertible securities are usually not purchased for their high yields alone, but also by investors who desire to participate in any upward price movement of the common stock. While convertible bonds usually have greater opportunity for price appreciation than similar straight bonds, they are also subject to more risks, since they can decline because of *two* factors: (1) a fall in the price of the underlying common stock or (2) a rise in the general level of interest rates, or both of these at once.

ELEVEN

International Securities

The international fixed-income securities of United States and foreign corporations, governments, and government agencies are available in a wide variety of forms, currencies, and maturities. Subject to certain legal limitations which will be described later, it is possible for an American investor to buy foreign bonds, notes, and other instruments in an initial offering or in the secondary trading market of another country, and in some cases, right here in the United States. For example, the investor may decide to purchase a Canadian government bond in Canada, denominated in Canadian dollars, or a Canadian government bond in London, denominated in British pounds, or a Canadian government bond in the United States, denominated in American dollars. In this chapter, we will not attempt to review all the major currencies, issuers, and trading markets for international fixed-income securities. Instead, our analysis will concentrate on the principal types of international fixed-income securities and the risks and rewards of buying these issues.

Reasons for and Risks of Investing in International Securities

The primary reason why United States investors purchase international securities is to earn a higher return through (1) higher interest

252

rates abroad; (2) an expected decline in interest rates in the foreign country, causing fixed-income securities prices to rise; (3) an anticipated currency change in the investor's favor; or (4) some combination of these factors. However, investing in international fixed-income securities also entails numerous risks.

First, it is difficult to judge the absolute or relative credit standing of international debt obligations. Even though the rating services have begun to rate new foreign bonds, the average investor will probably find it difficult to properly evaluate a foreign country's political, social, and economic climate, particularly as they relate to the willingness and ability of governmental and corporate issuers in that country to repay their debts to investors from outside their borders. Second, a further complication arises from the fact that accounting and disclosure requirements differ among nations, and very few existing foreign issues have been rated by the rating services in the United States. Third, although defaults on international fixed-income securities have been relatively rare in recent years, when viewed through a longer time perspective their credit record has been somewhat mixed, with several defaults occurring in times of economic hardship or political change within a particular country. Fourth, if the American investor buys a fixed-income security denominated in a currency other than dollars, he assumes a *currency risk* as well as the normal risk that interest rates in that country will rise, causing fixed-income securities prices to fall. As was mentioned in Chapter 5, it is a formidable enough task to try to predict accurately the level and direction of interest rates in the United States, not to mention attempting to estimate what will happen to interest rates *and* exchange rates in foreign countries. Fifth, the liquidity and ease of trading in many international fixed-income securities is usually considerably reduced compared with similar securities in the United States. This lessened marketability can pose a problem for the investor desiring to move into or out of a securities holding rapidly, and it can reduce the effective yields on international fixed-income securities. Finally, the investor in international fixed-income securities must be aware of, and abide by, special regulatory, legal, and tax constraints of both foreign countries and the United States. In many cases, these restrictions are relatively simple, or their effect is reduced because of reciprocal treaties between the particular foreign country and the United States. However, at certain times and for certain countries, these regulations can be quite stringent from a taxation standpoint and otherwise.

American investors who are considering the purchase of international fixed-income securities should keep these regulations in mind throughout their decision process. For example, at various times in the past 10 years, the United States and other foreign governments have imposed taxes, capital controls, currency restrictions, or other measures designed to prevent funds from leaving or entering certain foreign countries. In the United States from 1963 to early 1974, an *interest equalization tax* was applied to United States citizens' new investments in international debt and equity securities—for fixed-income securities, the tax rate depended on the maturity of the issue and ranged as high as 18 percent of the market value of the purchase.

The investor should also be aware of the practice of many major foreign governments whereby a *withholding tax* is levied on dividend or interest payments made to investors who reside outside that particular country. In many cases, the effective withholding tax rate for American investors in that country's securities has been reduced (often to 0 percent) as a result of treaties between the foreign country and the United States. In situations where the withholding tax is applied by the foreign tax authorities, the investor is usually allowed to deduct these foreign taxes paid on his United States income tax returns. If an investor is concerned about the tax treatment of certain foreign interest income, he should check with his counsel or the Internal Revenue Service *before* making any investment.

With the exception of a few issues, most foreign fixed-income securities have not been registered with the U.S. Securities and Exchange Commission or subjected to any other form of review procedure by an American regulatory body. In some cases, the investor may not be able to purchase an international fixed-income security until certain conditions are met. The investor should ask his securities broker how the unregistered status of any foreign securities not passed upon by the SEC will affect his intended purchase and the future marketability and liquidity of his investment.

In view of the numerous risks, the legal and regulatory issues, and the reduced amount of information on international fixed-income securities generally available to individual investors, these securities are more appropriate for institutional investors and, occasionally, for very wealthy individuals. Nevertheless, the investor should be aware of how developments in international fixed-income securities can influence United States domestic fixed-income securities' prices. For example, interest rates abroad can attract interest-sensitive funds outside the United States, while lower yields overseas can cause funds to flow into our money and capital markets from abroad in search of higher returns. These capital flows can affect the nation's balance of payments situation, since United States investors' purchases of foreign securities from foreign investors tend to reduce our balance of payments surplus or cause a deficit, whereas foreigners' purchases of U.S. securities from American investors tend to reduce any balance of payments deficit or cause a surplus.

For the investor who desires to know more about international fixed-income securities, the remainder of this chapter reviews representative short-term and long-term overseas issues and the mechanics of trading in these securities.

Short-Term International Securities in Dollars and Other Currencies

Short-term international fixed-income securities have a maturity of less than 1 year and can be divided into two main groups: dollar-denominated investments and those securities denominated in currencies other than dollars.

Dollar-denominated securities   Most of the short-term international securities denominated in dollars were created so that owners of Eurodollars, i.e., dollars deposited in foreign commercial banks (which include the United States branches of foreign banks and the overseas branches of United States banks), might be able to earn a return on their funds while owning an instrument which could be bought or sold in a secondary trading market. The Eurodollar market has shown significant growth in recent years, rising from a total net size of $12 billion in 1964 to $140 billion (of which the dollar-denominated portion amounted to $85 billion) in the second quarter of 1974.

Until the past few years, almost all trading in the Eurodollar market was done between banks, as deposits were lent from bank to bank, similar to the Federal funds market network in the United States, to satisfy the borrowing needs of these banks' corporate, governmental, and individual customers. From the investor's standpoint, a higher rate of interest than available in the United States can often be earned on *Eurodollar time deposits,* which have standard maturities of 30 days, 60 days, 90 days, 180 days, and 1 year, with other "customized" maturities under 30 days and from 1 to 2 years also available. Most transactions in this institutionally dominated market are of very large size, and deposits of $500,000 to $1 million and over are not uncommon.

Similar to time deposits in the United States, Eurodollar time deposits lack liquidity. If the owner of a Eurodollar time deposit needs his funds prior to the scheduled maturity date, he either has to accept a lower interest rate on his deposit or else *borrow* money until his time deposit matures. The great majority of Eurodollar activity is handled by the London branches of United States commercial banks and other banking institutions in London, where transactions also take place in the deposits of other currencies outside of their home country, such as Euro-Swiss francs, Euro-German marks, or Euro-French francs. These banks are compensated by the interest spread between what they pay to attract deposits and what they earn on loans made to governments, other banks, and major multinational corporations. Interest on Eurodollar deposits of 1 year or less is normally paid back with principal at maturity. On long-term deposits, interest may be paid annually, and in some cases the interest may be a variable rate, adjusted upward or downward according to fluctuations in some selected base interest rate.

In the mid-1960s, the *negotiable* Eurodollar-denominated certificate of deposit was created to provide investors with a greater degree of liquidity than otherwise available in conventional Eurodollar time deposits. In early 1974, total Eurodollar certificates of deposit outstanding amounted to over $10 billion, up 112 percent from $4.8 billion in 1971. Eurodollar certificates of deposit are issued in bearer form, with maturities ranging from 30 days to as long as 5 years. Roughly half of the Eurodollar certificates of deposit are issued by the overseas affiliates of United States commercial banks, with the remainder issued by British overseas banks and the branches of other foreign banks operating in London. A substantial majority of secondary-market trading activity is accounted for by between 10 and 15 banks, with settlement effected in London in clearinghouse funds 2 business days after the transaction. As a convenience to American investors in Eurodollar certificates of deposit, several banks have developed plans to establish settlement facilities in New York, for which Federal funds could also be used in making payments.

Another dollar-denominated short-term instrument is *Eurocommercial paper*, which like domestic U.S. commercial paper, represents short-term promissory notes offered through and traded in the secondary-market dealer firms on an unsecured, discounted basis by corporations of substantial size and widely accepted financial strength. As of late 1973, 18 corporations, all of which are American companies, have sold Eurocommercial paper, and total outstandings amounted to approximately $200 million. Settlement is 2 business days after the trade in clearinghouse funds. American investors should also remember that U.S. dollar-denominated commercial paper of some European corporations or their United States subsidiaries is also sold in the U.S. domestic commercial paper market. Interest earned on Eurocommercial paper, as well as Eurodollar certificates of deposit, is paid free of withholding taxes from any foreign country, though income received from these sources is fully taxable for American investors at the federal, state, and local levels.

Non-dollar-denominated short-term securities   Whenever an American investor purchases short-term international securities denominated in a currency other than dollars, he normally has to convert his dollars into the specific currency involved in order to pay for the security on settlement date. One method of acquiring the necessary currency is to deal with a reputable currency trading firm, but the small investor should take notice that this can be costly when dealing in small amounts.

As has been mentioned earlier, when the investor holds an asset denominated in a foreign currency, he becomes subject to a currency risk, in that each unit of the foreign currency may be worth less (or more) in dollar terms when the short-term instrument matures and the investor reconverts into dollars. This point is important enough that we will digress for a moment to discuss the currency risk aspect of foreign investing, and ways of securing protection against these risks.

As a simplified example, suppose that an American invests $500,-000 in a 1-year 7 percent money-market instrument denominated in British pounds while the pound/dollar exchange rate is £1 = $2.60. The investor's cost would be $500,000 ÷ $2.60 = £192,000. If, at the end of the 1-year holding period, the pound/dollar exchange rate had become £1 = $2.40, the investor's holding, plus interest, would be worth £192,000 plus 7 percent of £192,000, or £192,000 + £13,400. Multiplying this total of £205,400 by 2.40, the new exchange rate, we arrive at a dollar total of $493,000, producing a net *loss* on the investment in dollar terms, although the investment *earned* 7 percent interest in terms of British pounds over the same 1-year holding period.

Generally speaking, unless the investor will need a certain amount of foreign currency at the end of the investment period, for example, to settle a debt or to pay for goods, *or* unless the investor desires to speculate that the currency will gain in value relative to the dollar, it is best to secure protection against currency price variations through a *forward exchange* transaction. A forward exchange contract guarantees the holder the right to buy or sell a particular currency for a specified amount of another currency at a predetermined exchange rate. In our example above, the investor might have protected, or *hedged,* his investment in the pound-denominated money-market instrument by entering into a forward exchange contract, allowing him to buy back dollars with pounds at a certain exchange rate at the end of 1 year.

For instance, an investor might have been able to secure a *forward exchange contract* to buy dollars at an exchange rate of £1 = $2.574, so that, at the end of 1 year, his pound-denominated investment would be worth £205,400 × 2.574 = $526,000, which equals a return of 5.2 percent in dollar terms on the original investment. If the exchange rate had stayed at £1 = $2.60, the investor would have earned the pound equivalent of $35,000 in interest, producing the 7 percent return quoted on the certificate of deposit. If the forward contract had been arranged and the pound/dollar exchange rate had not deteriorated, or had moved above £1 = $2.60, the "insurance" protection purchased by the investor would have cost him money— roughly $9,000, or the difference between $535,000 and $526,000. In our example, to highlight the effects of the currency changes, we have not considered any transactions costs or safekeeping fees which might be associated with the investment, and the investor should remember that these charges may also reduce his yield to some degree.

The exact currency exchange rate used in making up a forward exchange contract with a bank or foreign exchange dealer depends on the size of the transaction, the currency traders' estimates of the possibility that the currency might be devalued or revalued during the time period covered by the contract, and most importantly, the differences in Eurocurrency interest rate levels between the two countries whose currencies are involved in the forward exchange contract. In general, if a currency is expected to be worth less at the time of the contract's expiration, the bank or foreign exchange firm making the contract will allow for this in the exchange rate which is used in the forward agreement. If this is the case, the investor may lose the same amount as he might lose if the expected devaluation of the pound occurred and he had no forward protection, but he has at least limited his loss to that amount and no more. If the currency value declines more than the expected amount, the investor is protected against further loss. In our example, the rate of £1 = $2.574 quoted in the forward cover contract assumes that the bank or foreign currency trading firm did not expect the pound to lose value from £1 = $2.60 to £1 = $2.40 during the 1-year period covered by the contract.

One good reason why the contract was written with a £1 = $2.574 exchange rate is that it relates to the difference between 1-year interest rates in the Eurodollar market as compared with the Euro-sterling market at the time the forward cover was arranged. If short-term interest rates in the Eurodollar market were 6 percent at the time that similar rates were quoted at 7 percent in the Eurosterling market, and if currency traders were not anticipating a major change in the pound/dollar exchange rate, the continuous action of traders and investors would usually cause a 1 percent difference in the forward exchange rate compared with the current, or "spot," exchange rate. In our example, this is in fact the case, since the forward exchange rate of £1 = $2.574 is 1 percent less than the £1 = $2.60 spot rate in force when the contract was entered into. In many cases, the cost of hedging cancels out all or part of the interest gain resulting from investment in an instrument denominated in another currency.

Unless the investor desires or needs to own a foreign currency at some future date, he should buy foreign currency—denominated fixed-income investments for yield purposes only when the *cost* of forward exchange in percentage terms is *less* than the *yield advantage* obtained by buying the foreign currency security. Another disadvantage of investing in foreign securities is the fact that if the security is sold before maturity, the foreign exchange coverage has to be cancelled or offset by another transaction, often costing the investor in terms of decreased net yields or even losses on his investment.

The range of short-term foreign currency fixed-income securities is quite broad, including Belgian, British, Canadian, Dutch, German, Japanese, and Swedish Treasury bills, among other governmental issues. The interest rate structure on these securities is equally varied, being influenced partly by domestic considerations, such as fiscal or monetary policies to stimulate or restrain the economy, and partly by international considerations, such as a desire to discourage or encourage the inflow of capital through lower or higher interest rates. Since 1971, for example, yields on Treasury bills in various countries have ranged from 2.01 percent in Sweden to 12.85 percent in the United Kingdom.

In addition to Treasury bills, many countries have other short-term money market instruments, such as commercial paper, bankers' acceptances, and certificates of deposit. Traditionally, the bulk of large American investors' activity in foreign short-term fixed-income securities has been concentrated in hedged purchases of

Canadian and British instruments, particularly Treasury bills, when interest rates, forward exchange costs, and the currency outlook were in favor of such transactions. In making investments in foreign securities of any maturity, short-term or long-term, the investor should refer to the evaluation worksheet at the end of Chapter 4. In addition, particular attention should be given to transactions costs (including foreign exchange and forward cover costs), the tax treatment of interest paid on these securities, and their marketability.

Long-Term International Securities in Dollars and Other Currencies

Long-term international securities can also be divided into two groups: those which are dollar-denominated and those which are denominated in other currencies. Both bonds and note issues (with 3 to 10 years' maturity) are available, though notes are somewhat less frequently encountered than bonds. In the discussion which follows, bonds and notes are discussed together, and unless mentioned otherwise, international notes should be considered the same as international bonds. It is also worthwhile to make the distinction between indigenous foreign bonds, external foreign bonds, and Eurobonds.

Indigenous foreign bonds are underwritten and sold in the home country and currency of the borrower. For example, if the German automobile manufacturer Daimler-Benz sold bonds denominated in German marks within Germany, this would be an indigenous foreign bond from the United States investor's point of view. To a German investor, this security would of course be a domestic bond issue, just as a Ford Motor Company dollar-denominated issue sold in the United States is a domestic security from the American investor's standpoint. An *external foreign bond* issue involves a company or government issuing bonds outside its home country in another country, where the bond is underwritten and sold to that country's investors in their own currency. An example would occur if Volvo, the Swedish automobile manufacturer, offered Swiss franc–denominated bonds in Switzerland to Swiss investors. *Eurobonds* are underwritten and marketed in several nations at once by a syndicate composed of securities brokerage and banking firms from numerous countries. The currency of Eurobonds is usually, but not always, different from the currencies of the countries where the issue is offered. An example might involve a company such as Exxon or Matsushita Electric issuing dollar-denominated bonds in several European countries simultaneously.

Dollar-denominated Eurobonds A large proportion of the Eurobonds offered by a wide range of American and foreign corporations and governments are denominated in dollars because of the dollar's broad acceptability and the large supply of dollars on deposit in foreign banks as Eurodollars. The total annual amount of newly offered Eurobonds denominated in dollars (also called Eurodollar bonds) rose from $921 million in 1966 to $3.9 billion in 1972, before declining to $1.0 billion in 1974. In the following paragraphs, we will discuss some of the features and trading procedures for dollar-denominated Eurobonds. Except where noted, these characteristics also apply to foreign currency–denominated Eurobonds, which will be discussed later on in this chapter.

Although most Eurobonds are listed on the London or Luxemburg stock exchanges, the secondary market for Eurobond securities is primarily an over-the-counter market whose center of activity is in London, with numerous traders also located in other financial centers throughout Europe. Straight Eurobonds are not as carefully analyzed as U.S. bonds. Very little historical data exist to give the trading values of various securities relative to each other, and in many cases international investors buy and sell dollar-denominated Eurobonds based on currency considerations, as much as on fundamental investment factors or interest rate considerations. The normal trading spread between the bid and offered prices on straight Eurobonds is usually 1 point or more ($10 and up, per $1,000 bond), and traders will generally deal in only 50 to 100 bonds on their quoted prices. Larger trades normally involve price concessions by the investor.

For Eurobond convertible securities, trading markets are also not as liquid as their United States domestic counterparts, with spreads between the bid and asked prices ranging up to 2 or 3 points in some cases ($20 to $30 per $1,000 bond). All but a handful of Eurobond convertible securities have been issued by United States corporations and are convertible into the United States company's common stock. Although a few issues have been as large as $75 million, most of the issues have been of small size, between $15 and 25 million, which has hindered active trading in the secondary market and contributed to the wide price spreads in price quotations.

Interest on most Eurobonds is paid on an annual rather than a semiannual basis, free of any withholding taxes which might be collected on interest paid on certain foreign bonds. Dollar-denominated Eurobonds are issued in denominations of $1,000 and up, in bearer form with coupons attached. Usually, straight Eurobonds rank as unsecured obligations and have equal status with all other senior unsecured domestic debt of the company. Similar to common practice in the United States, almost all Eurobond convertible issues are subordinated to the company's senior debt.

Most Euronote issues are callable after 3 years, and Eurobonds usually have call protection for 5 to 8 years after the date of issue, except that they may be called on short notice in the event that withholding taxes are imposed on the bonds' interest payments. Almost all straight Eurobonds and a few convertible Eurobonds have sinking funds. A typical issue generally has a 15-year maturity, which works out to a 10-to-11-year average life if the sinking fund is factored in. Often, when the sinking fund is purchasing bonds in the open market, because of their lack of liquidity prices tend to move sharply higher and fall just as sharply when that year's sinking-fund requirement has been satisfied.

Dollar-denominated foreign bonds Dollar-denominated foreign bonds offered in the United States by non-American issuers have averaged slightly over $1.5 billion per year in the period 1971 through 1974. By far, the largest proportion of these issues have represented securities offered by Canadian governmental, provincial, and corporate borrowers. Trading practices on foreign issues which are dealt in within the United States are the same as those employed for United States companies' corporate bonds, and interest received on dollar-denominated foreign bonds is fully taxable at the federal, state, and local level.

After the interest equalization tax was reduced to zero in early 1974 (Canadian issues have always been exempt from this tax), many observers felt that a large number of foreign companies and governments would issue dollar-denominated bonds in the United States capital markets. However, this expected spate of new foreign issues did not materialize because of (1) stringent SEC reporting and disclosure requirements, (2) legal restrictions limiting many investment institutions in their ownership of foreign securities, and (3) large amounts of domestic U.S. corporate and governmental issues offering attractive interest rates. Should any or all of these conditions change over time, the amount of non-Canadian dollar-denominated foreign bonds could be expected to rise somewhat.

One small and specialized category of foreign dollar–denominated bonds underscores the reasons why the average investor should generally avoid foreign fixed-income securities. This group of bonds is made up of the defaulted securities of certain countries such as China, Cuba, Russia, and several of the Eastern European Communist bloc nations. Some of these securities have aroused much publicity in recent years with the easing of tensions between these countries and the United States. Even though large gains were achieved by some speculators in the defaulted bonds of Japan and Germany when they were repaid in the early 1950s, it is recommended that the investor avoid investing in defaulted foreign bonds except with funds earmarked for extremely speculative, long-shot gambles.

Other foreign currency—denominated bonds Foreign bonds not denominated in dollars include internal foreign bonds, external foreign bonds, and foreign currency–denominated Eurobonds. Treating the last group first, new issues of Eurobonds denominated in foreign currencies have increased from $221 million in 1966 to $1.0 billion in 1974, with a high of $2.4 billion reached in 1972. The most widely utilized nondollar currency for Eurobond issues has been the German mark, followed by the Dutch guilder and the French franc. In general, the sinking-fund and redemption terms, trading practices, and other characteristics of foreign currency Eurobonds are the same as those described earlier for dollar-denominated Eurobonds, except that they are usually less liquid than Eurodollar bonds. One important difference stems from the fact that all foreign currency bonds are quoted on a percentage-of-par basis, so that the investor must remember that a quotation of 98 on a German mark–denominated bond means 98 percent of 1,000 German marks, or 980 German marks.

New *external foreign bonds* issued in various countries' capital markets by companies and governments located outside that particular country have risen from $378 million in 1966 to $2.6 billion in 1973. A substantial portion of these issues have been Swiss franc–denominated securities, followed by securities denominated in German marks, and to some extent, in Japanese yen.

Precise figures are difficult to obtain on the total amount of new issues of *internal foreign bonds* sold by non-United States companies and governments of a particular country primarily to investors within that same country. In some markets, particularly the United Kingdom, Japan, Germany, and Switzerland, the local issues can often be much more liquid than the straight dollar-denominated Eurobond market. For example, the United Kingdom government securities market has in the past offered very attractive yields to non-British investors willing to assume the currency risk of British pounds. At one point in early 1974, U.K. Treasury issues were priced at a current yield of 13¼ percent and a yield to maturity of 13½ percent, compared with triple-A utility bond yields at the time of 8⅛ percent. A United States investor who purchased the U.K. Treasury issue could suffer a 5 percent devaluation of the pound relative to United States dollars for every year of the life of the bonds and still earn a higher return than the 8⅛ percent on the triple-A utility bond investment in the United States. If the investor desired to cover the foreign exchange risk for 1 year, a forward contract (similar to the one discussed in the short-term investments section of this chapter) could be entered into with protection at the then current pound/dollar exchange rate at a cost of approximately 8 percent. If this 8 percent cost is deducted from the current return of 13¼ percent, the investor would earn approximately 5¼ percent on his investment at the end of 1 year. Since this is less than the return available on triple-A utility and other bond investments in the

United States, the investor would reject this investment *unless* he expected interest rates to fall in the United Kingdom by an amount which would produce a capital gain greater than the difference between the 5¼ percent hedged United Kingdom investment and the 8⅛ percent bond in the United States, or 2⅞ percent. A 2⅞ percent capital gain would occur if long-term yields in the United Kingdom dropped from 13½ to around 13 percent. Therefore, as long as the investor expects yields to decline to 13 percent or below, the United Kingdom investment is competitive with the United States triple-A utility bond investment. For the average investor, this type of transaction involves numerous expenses which will reduce his effective yields, and it also involves substantial risks, including an interest rate risk that rates may have *risen* at the end of 1 year, resulting in a capital loss.

Similar exercises can be performed in other internal foreign currency bonds, in which a wide variety of maturities, coupon rates, and quality ranges are available. For instance, if yields in the United States bond market were at the 7 percent level and yields in the German bond market were at the 6 percent yield level, the investor in German mark–denominated 10-year bonds would earn an effective yield to maturity of 7.22 percent if the German mark were revalued 10 percent during the first year the investor held the securities. The yield to maturity would work out to 7.15 percent if the revaluation of 10 percent occurred in the second year, 7.08 percent if in the third year, 7.02 percent if in the fourth year, and so forth. Trading in foreign currency–denominated issues can be accomplished through the investor's United States securities broker or on limited occasions through the United States branch of a commercial bank or brokerage firm from the country where the securities are normally traded. Again, investing in most dollar-denominated and foreign currency–denominated international securities should not be attempted by the average investor; it is best left to professionals.

Settlement on International Securities

The settlement procedures and facilities used for Eurobonds and other foreign bonds are often different from those used for American fixed-income securities. Although the investor in foreign securities does not have to remember the differences in payment and delivery methods in various countries, *before* making any investment he should make it a practice to inquire about the specific settlement procedures which must be followed both when the security is purchased *and* when it is sold.

As a general rule, in view of the expenses and delays involved in shipping international securities of all types to the United States from abroad, it is often advantageous for the investor to arrange to receive and deliver these securities from a location overseas, without having them transported to and from this country. Some investors may decide to leave their securities in their securities broker's overseas depository system, whereas others may utilize a fiduciary banking account abroad. If this latter method is used, the investor should choose a bank which is a member of one or both of the two major central clearing associations for international securities: Euroclear and Cedel. Normal payment and delivery periods will vary from country to country and even for various types and maturities of securities within a particular country, and the investor should always find out the time allowed for payment or delivery to be made, particularly when one security is being sold to purchase another security. Generally, settlement fees, commissions, transportation charges, and insurance and custody fees are assessed at a standard rate, which in many cases will significantly reduce the overall interest return derived from owning an international security purchased abroad in small amounts. On international securities traded in the United States, settlement procedures are the same as those described in the previous chapter for corporate fixed-income securities.

TWELVE

Information Charts on Fixed-Income Securities

The purpose of this chapter is to bring together, in a brief and easily utilized format, the most commonly encountered types of the wide variety of fixed-income securities discussed in Chapters 6 through 11. The investor should use these information charts often, in conjunction with the worksheets contained in Chapters 2, 4, and 5, as an aid in evaluating and selecting the group of securities in which he might make a specific investment. To derive maximum benefit from these charts, the investor should quickly scan each of the columns as he reviews his own investment objectives in order to eliminate those groups which do not fit his needs. From the remaining securities, the investor should select that group which fulfills his requirements in terms of (1) the minimum size of the investment; (2) its maturity, quality, and liquidity; (3) whether the security is in registered or bearer form, (4) its tax status; (5) the manner and frequency in which the security earns interest; and (6) where it can be purchased and traded. Other details, such as whether the security is callable or has a sinking fund, are covered in the Chapter 4 worksheet and should not be neglected in making the final decision on a specific issue.

How to Use the Charts

In approaching these charts, several caveats should be mentioned. First, while the information listed is as up-to-date as possible, the investor should keep in mind the fact that certain items can change over a period of time. As changes occur, the investor should note any revisions in the appropriate spaces in the chart.

Second, while the charts are intended to provide a broad coverage of, and representative information on, each major group of fixed-income securities, in the interest of brevity certain less actively traded or very specialized types of securities have not been included. For example, although the details of foreign Treasury bills and other short- and long-term investments from a large number of other countries have been listed, only two types of foreign Treasury bills (Canadian and British) are shown, primarily because the major focus of this book is on securities usually traded in the United States. Also, not all U.S. government agencies are listed, since a number of them are small and relatively infrequent borrowers in the capital markets, and many of these agencies are expected to borrow money indirectly, through the Federal Financing Bank. Mutual funds formed to invest in fixed-income securities have not been listed, but information on these funds is contained in Chapters 6, 8, 9, and 10. If the investor has a special interest in a particular domestic or international fixed-income security which is not listed in the charts, space has been provided at the end of the charts for the investor to record the appropriate information.

Third, the securities have been arranged, highest quality first, into two groups according to the most frequent maturity in which the security is issued: short-term (under 1 year original maturity) and long-term (over 1 year original maturity). Nevertheless, several of the securities in each group may occasionally have maturities outside of these fairly arbitrary classifications. Also, the terms "bond" and "note" are often used differently in different sectors of the fixed-income securities markets, so that certain "bonds" are included in the short-term section.

The following paragraphs briefly describe the scope, meaning, and limitations of each of the chart column headings.

Type of Security In all, 43 different types of securities are listed in the charts. Many of the categories, such as corporate notes and bonds, or state and local notes and bonds, may contain up to 5,000 separate issues, while other categories are fairly homogeneous. The breadth of the list points up the great diversity of fixed-income investment opportunities—taxable and tax-exempt, corporate and governmental, domestic and foreign, short-term and long-term. This wide variety makes it possible, and important, for the investor to find a security which is suited to his needs, and the investor should be demanding in his search for an appropriate investment.

Restrictions on size of purchase The minimum purchase requirement for these fixed-income securities ranges from $25 to $1 million. Some of the minimum purchase sizes are slightly flexible, but in most cases these requirements are rigidly adhered to. The investor should remember that he may have to sacrifice yield and/ or liquidity when buying or selling securities in small amounts. From time to time, the minimum purchase requirements may be raised or lowered in certain groups of issues, such as U.S. government notes and bonds.

Original maturity range In this column is listed the most frequently utilized initial maturity for each group of securities. On numerous occasions, longer maturities than the ones listed may be offered. In addition, as any security approaches its final maturity, the investor will be able to purchase it with a short remaining maturity. Thus, Treasury bills of 1 week's or 1 day's maturity can be found, and the investor could purchase bonds which originally had a 25-year life with 1 year, 1 month, 1 week, or even 1 day remaining to maturity.

Quality spectrum The groups of securities in the charts are listed according to their *approximate* relative standing after U.S. government securities, which possess the highest quality ranking. Those securities which in one way or another carry the backing of the full faith and credit of the United States government, or its guarantee in any form, are listed as "Extremely High Quality." It should be pointed out that within several groups of securities (excepting governments and agencies), numerous different quality issues are available. For instance, corporate notes and bonds include triple-A rated issues as well as very speculative C- and D-rated securities in default. As a general rule, the investor should *never* compromise the quality parameters he sets for himself in order to try to obtain higher yields. This could lead to losses if the securities go into default.

Form   No hard and fast rule exists for remembering whether a certain type of security is available in bearer or in registered form, or in both. In many cases, an issuer has decided to offer only registered securities even though certain older securities issues may still be outstanding in bearer form. While the investor should safeguard *all* his securities as carefully as cash, he should be particularly careful in handling and storing securities when they are in bearer, or "coupon," form, because if they are lost or stolen, the issuer has no record of ownership and the securities are considered to be owned by their possessor.

Liquidity and marketability   The charts contain one or two securities which are virtually nonmarketable, as well as others whose trading volume amounts to hundreds of millions or even billions of dollars each day. Basically, liquidity and marketability are somewhat subjectively judged, which is further complicated by the fact that market conditions can positively or negatively influence an issue's liquidity. Certain securities normally considered to be highly marketable can prove somewhat illiquid at times (usually in times of high and/or rising interest rates), while at other times some issues of average or below average liquidity can turn out to be very easily marketable (usually in times of low and/or falling interest rates). The ratings listed in the charts should therefore be used primarily as a general guide.

Tax status   The higher an investor's incremental tax bracket, the more important it is to measure various comparable securities on an aftertax yield basis rather than a beforetax basis. The tax status column in the charts refers to the tax treatment (for individuals) of interest or dividend income in each group of securities. The chart does not cover questions relating to capital gains taxes, estate, gift, and excise taxes, the specifics of foreign withholding taxes and tax credits against United States taxes owed, or certain forms of wealth taxes imposed by a few state or local governments. The investor should not overemphasize taxes in making an investment decision, nor should he completely ignore tax considerations. If the investor is even slightly unclear about a tax question, he should always consult a competent tax advisor or the Internal Revenue Service, rather than depend on the possibly erroneous (and thus costly) advice of individuals not qualified to pass judgment on tax matters.

How interest is earned   Short-term securities can pay interest on a 360- or 365-day year, by either the discount method or the interest-bearing method. In comparing securities' yields, the investor should always convert the quoted yield to a bond equivalent basis, using the methods described in Chapter 6. Most long-term securities are based on a 365-day year, and for comparison purposes their yields should be adjusted to a semiannual equivalent basis if interest is not paid semiannually on the security. On almost all interest-bearing securities, any accrued interest earned since the last coupon date (or since the initial offering date if the first coupon has not yet been paid) must be paid by the purchaser to the seller.

Where bought and traded   It is important to remember that not all securities brokerage firms nor all commerical banks make it a practice of buying and selling all types of fixed-income securities for the investor. The investor should deal only with a reputable and financially sound commercial bank or broker (this should be carefully and diligently checked out). If possible, the individual investor should choose to buy and sell securities through a firm which is (1) oriented toward serving investors of his means and (2) involved in trading the security which the investor is interested in. Otherwise, the individual will end up paying somewhat more or receiving somewhat less for his investment. In the case of initial offerings of bills, notes, and bonds of the United States government and the Federal Financing Bank, the investor can save commission fees by submitting a competitive or noncompetitive tender at a Federal Reserve bank or branch. While this method saves money, it may involve waiting in line, particularly if the offering is heavily subscribed to by other individual investors. For certain securities of government agencies and related issuers, the New York Federal Reserve Bank (and sometimes Federal Reserve banks in other cities) performs special services, such as issuance of the securities, interest payments, and final principal payments. The investor should check with the nearest Federal Reserve bank or branch to find out exactly what services the Federal Reserve performs for specific agency issues.

Further information   The investor will derive optimal use from these charts if he simultaneously consults the chapter in this book giving further details on the security he is interested in. In addition, Chapter 15 contains a list of periodicals and other sources of information on each major group of securities.

SHORT-TERM SECURITIES

Type of security	Restrictions on size of purchase	Original maturity range	Quality spectrum	Form
U.S. Treasury bills	$10,000 minimum	90 days to 1 year	Highest possible	Bearer only
Federal Financing Bank bills	$10,000 minimum	90 days to 1 year	Extremely high	Bearer only
Project notes of local authorities and local public agencies	$1,000 minimum	90 days to 1 year	Extremely high	Bearer only
Export-Import Bank discount notes	$100,000 minimum	30 days to 1 year	Extremely high	Bearer only
Federal National Mortgage Association discount notes	$50,000 minimum	30 to 270 days	Very high	Bearer only
Tennessee Valley Authority discount notes	$1 million minimum	usually 120 days	Very high	Bearer only
Banks for Cooperatives bonds	$5,000 minimum	usually 180 days	Very high	Bearer only
Farm Credit Banks discount notes	$50,000 minimum	5 to 150 days	Very high	Bearer only
Federal Home Loan consolidated discount notes	$100,000 minimum	30 to 360 days	Very high	Bearer only
Federal Intermediate Credit Bank bonds	$5,000 minimum	usually 270 days	Very high	Bearer only
State and local government notes	$5,000 minimum	30 days to 1 year	Ranges from very high to intermediate	Bearer; some are registered
Bankers' acceptances	no minimum; can find amounts as small as $5,000	1 to 270 days	High; depends on strength of endorsing bank or banks	Bearer; some are registered

Liquidity and marketability	Tax status	How interest is earned	Where bought and traded	For further information see chapter
Excellent	Fed: taxable; State: exempt; Local: exempt	Discounted; 360-day year	Securities Brokers; Commercial Banks; Federal Reserve Banks (on new issues only)	6
Excellent	Fed: taxable; State: exempt; Local: exempt	Discounted; 360-day year	Securities Brokers; Commercial Banks; Federal Reserve Banks (on new issues only)	7
Average	Fed: exempt; state and local: possibly exempt	Interest-bearing; 360-day year	Securities Brokers; Commercial Banks	9
No secondary market; investor selects maturity	Federal, state, and local: taxable	Discounted; 360-day year	Securities Brokers; Commercial Banks	7
Good; four dealer firms; investor selects maturity	Federal, state, and local: taxable	Discounted; 360-day year	Bank of America N.T. & S.A.; Goldman, Sachs & Co.; Morgan Guaranty Trust Company of New York; Lehman CP Inc.	7
Average	Fed: taxable; State: exempt; Local: exempt	Discounted; 360-day year	Securities Brokers; Commercial Banks; TVA (on new issues only; not open to general public)	7
Good	Fed: taxable; State: exempt; Local: exempt	Interest-bearing; 360-day year	Securities Brokers; Commercial Banks	7
Good; three dealer firms; investor selects maturity	Fed: taxable; State: exempt; Local: exempt	Discounted; 360-day year	A. G. Becker & Co., Inc.; Merrill Lynch Government Securities, Inc.; Salomon Brothers	7
Good; five dealer firms; investor selects maturity	Fed: taxable; State: exempt; Local: exempt	Discounted; 360-day year	The First Boston Corp.; Discount Corp. of New York; Aubrey G. Lanston & Co., Inc.; William E. Pollock & Co., Inc.	7
Good	Fed: taxable; State: exempt; Local: exempt	Interest-bearing; 360-day year	Securities Brokers; Commercial Banks	7
Average	Fed: exempt; state and local: possibly exempt	Interest-bearing; 360-day year	Securities Brokers; Commercial Banks	9
Average	Federal, state, and local: taxable	Discounted; 360-day year	Securities Brokers; Commercial Banks	8

SHORT-TERM SECURITIES

Type of security	Restrictions on size of purchase	Original maturity range	Quality spectrum	Form	
Negotiable certificates of deposit	$100,000 minimum; sometimes smaller	30 days to 1 year, possibly longer	High to intermediate; depends on strength of issuing bank	Bearer or registered	
Commercial paper	$100,000 minimum; sometimes smaller	1 to 270 days	High to intermediate; depends on strength of company	Bearer or registered	
Repurchase agreements and reverse repurchase agreements	$1 million minimum; sometimes smaller	generally 1 day; can be up to 30 days or indefinitely	High	Bearer or registered	
Canadian Treasury bills	$1,000 minimum	180 days	High; possible currency risk	Bearer only	
United Kingdom treasury bills	$5,000 minimum	91 days	High; possible currency risk	Bearer only	
Eurodollar certificates of deposit	$100,000 minimum; sometimes smaller	30 days to 1 year, possibly longer	High to intermediate; depends on strength of issuing bank	Bearer or registered	
Eurocommercial paper	$100,000 minimum; sometimes smaller	30 to 360 days	High to intermediate; depends on strength of company	Bearer	

Liquidity and marketability	Tax status	How interest is earned	Where bought and traded	For further information see chapter
Average to good	Federal, state, and local: taxable	Interest-bearing; 360-day year	Securities Brokers; Commercial Banks	8
No secondary market; investor selects maturity	Federal, state, and local: taxable	Discounted; 360-day year	Commercial paper dealer firms or directly from some issuing companies	8
No secondary market; investor selects maturity	Federal, state, and local: taxable	Interest-bearing; 360-day year	Securities dealers; some Commercial Banks	8
Average	Federal, state, and local: taxable; Can. withholding tax possible	Discounted; 365-day year	Securities brokers; commercial banks	11
Average	Federal, state, and local: taxable; U.K. withholding tax possible	Discounted; 365-day year	Securities brokers; commercial banks	11
Average to below average	Federal, state, and local: taxable	Interest-bearing; 360-day year	Securities brokers; commercial banks	11
No active secondary market	Federal, state, and local: taxable	Discounted; 360-day year	Commercial paper dealer firms active in ECP market	11

LONG-TERM SECURITIES

Type of security	Restrictions on size of purchase	Original maturity range	Quality spectrum	Form	
U.S. Series E savings bonds	$25 minimum; $10,000 maximum each year	5 years; can be redeemed beforehand or extended	Highest possible	Registered only	
U.S. Series H savings bonds	$500 minimum; $10,000 maximum each year	10 years; can be redeemed beforehand or extended	Highest possible	Registered only	
U.S. Treasury notes and bonds	$1,000 minimum; some are $10,000 minimum	1 to 20 years or more	Highest possible	Registered or bearer	
Federal Financing Bank notes and bonds	$1,000 minimum; some are $10,000 minimum	1 to 20 years or more	Extremely high	Registered or bearer	
Local housing authority bonds	$5,000 minimum	1 to 40 years	Extremely high	Registered or bearer	
Federal Home Loan Mortgage Corporation guaranteed mortgage certificates	$100,000 minimum	Up to 30 years; 15-year repayment condition	Extremely high	Registered only	
Federal Home Loan Mortgage Corporation mortgage-backed bonds	$25,000 minimum	12 to 25 years	Extremely high	Registered or bearer	
Federal Home Loan Mortgage Corporation participation certificates	$100,000 minimum	15 to 30 years	Very high	Registered only	
Export-Import Bank debentures and participation certificates	$5,000 minimum	3 to 7 years	Extremely high	Registered or bearer	
Farmers Home Administration insured notes and certificates of beneficial ownership	$25,000 minimum	1 to 25 years	Extremely high	Registered or bearer— notes; bearer only—CBO's	
Federal Housing Administration debentures	$50 minimum	1 to 40 years	Extremely high	Registered only	

Liquidity and marketability	Tax status	How interest is earned	Where bought and traded	For further information see chapter
No secondary market	Fed: taxable; State: exempt; Local: exempt	Securities are issued at a discount; redemption value increases every 6 months until maturity	U.S. Treasury; Federal Reserve Banks; commercial banks; selected post offices and other institutions	6
No secondary market	Fed: taxable; State: exempt; Local: exempt	Semiannual interest payments	U.S. Treasury; Federal Reserve Banks	6
Excellent to Good	Fed: taxable; State: exempt; Local: exempt	Semiannual interest payments	Securities brokers; commercial banks; Federal Reserve Banks (on new issues only)	6
Good	Fed: taxable; State: exempt; Local: exempt	Semiannual interest payments	Securities brokers; commercial banks; Federal Reserve Banks (on new issues only)	6
Good	Fed: exempt; state and local: possibly exempt	Semiannual interest payments	Securities brokers; commercial banks	9
Average	Federal, state, and local: taxable	Semiannual interest payments; a part of principal is returned annually	Special group of 29 securities brokers and commercial banks	7
Average	Federal, state, and local: taxable	Semiannual interest payments	Securities brokers; commercial banks	7
Average	Federal, state, and local: taxable	Monthly interest payments	Securities brokers; commercial banks	7
Average to good	Federal, state, and local: taxable	Semiannual interest payments	Securities brokers; commercial banks	7
Average	Federal, state, and local: taxable	Annual interest payments	Securities brokers; commercial banks	7
Below average in small amounts	Federal, state, and local: taxable	Semiannual interest payments	Securities brokers; commercial banks	7

LONG-TERM SECURITIES

Type of security	Restrictions on size of purchase	Original maturity range	Quality spectrum	Form	
Government National Mortgage Association mortgage-backed securities and participation certificates	$5,000 minimum, PC's; $25,000 minimum, mortgage-backed securities	1 to 25 years	Extremely high	Registered or bearer	
Government National Mortgage Association modified pass-through certificates	$25,000 minimum	1 to 25 years; average life is 12 years	Extremely high	Registered only	
Federal National Mortgage Association mortgage-backed bonds	$25,000 minimum	2 to 25 years	Extremely high	Registered or bearer	
Federal Home Loan Banks Bonds and notes	$10,000 minimum	1 to 20 years	Very high	Bearer only	
Federal National Mortgage Association secondary-market notes and debentures, and capital debentures	$10,000 minimum	3 to 25 years	Very high	Registered or bearer, capital debentures; bearer only, secondary-market issues	
Federal Land Banks bonds	$1,000 minimum	1 to 10 years	Very high	Bearer only	
Tennessee Valley Authority notes and bonds	$1,000 minimum	3 to 25 years	Very high	Registered or bearer	
International Bank for Reconstruction and Development, Asian Development Bank, and Inter-American Development Bank notes and bonds	$1,000 minimum in dollar-denominated issues; amounts vary in other currencies	3 to 25 years	High	Registered only	
State and local government notes and bonds	$5,000 minimum	1 to 50 years	Very high to low, depending on rating	Bearer; some registered	
Corporate variable rate notes	$5,000 minimum on initial offering; $1,000 minimum in secondary market	15 to 20 years, or 6 months if "put" is exercised	Very high to low, depending on rating	Registered only	
Corporate notes and bonds	$1,000 minimum, sometimes higher	1 to 50 years	Very high to low, depending on rating	Some registered, some bearer, some both	
Corporate preferred stocks	$100 minimum or less, depending on par value of the stock	Usually no maturity	Very high to low, depending on rating	Registered only	

Liquidity and marketability	Tax status	How interest is earned	Where bought and traded	For further information see chapter
Average	Federal, state, and local: taxable	Semiannual interest payments	Securities brokers; commercial banks	7
Average to good	Federal, state, and local: taxable	Monthly interest payments	Securities brokers; commercial banks	7
Average to below average	Federal, state, and local: taxable	Semiannual interest payments	Securities brokers; commercial banks	7
Good	Federal, state and local: taxable	Semiannual interest payments	Securities brokers: commercial banks	7
Average to good	Federal, state, and local: taxable	Semiannual interest payments	Securities brokers; commercial banks	7
Good	Fed: taxable; State: exempt; Local: exempt	Semiannual interest payments	Securities brokers; commercial banks	7
Average	Fed: taxable; State: exempt; Local: exempt	Semiannual interest payments	Securities brokers; commercial banks	7
Average to below average	Federal, state, and local: taxable; on foreign currency issues withholding taxes possible	Semiannual interest payments	Securities brokers; commercial banks	7
Average to good	Fed: exempt; state and local: possibly exempt	Semiannual interest payments	Securities brokers; commercial banks	9
Good to very good	Federal, state, and local: taxable	Semiannual interest payments	Securities brokers	8
Good	Federal, state, and local: taxable	Semiannual interest payments	Securities brokers	10
Average to below average	State and local: taxable for all investors; federal: for corporate investors only, 85% or 60% exempt	Quarterly dividend payments	Securities brokers	10

LONG-TERM SECURITIES

Type of security	Restrictions on size of purchase	Original maturity range	Quality spectrum	Form	
Eurobonds and notes denominated in dollars and foreign currencies, issued by United States and foreign corporations and governmental bodies	$1,000 minimum, sometimes more	3 to 25 years	Very high to low; not often rated by United States rating services	Bearer only	
Foreign notes and bonds denominated in dollars and foreign currencies, issued by United States and foreign corporations and governmental bodies	$1,000 minimum, sometimes more; amounts vary in other currencies	1 to 30 years	High to low; not rated by United States rating services	Bearer only in most cases	

Liquidity and marketability	Tax status	How interest is earned	Where bought and traded	For further information see chapter
Below average	Federal, state, and local: taxable	Annual interest payments; sometimes semiannual	Securities brokers; overseas commercial banks	11
Below average to average	Federal, state, and local: taxable; on foreign currency issues withholding taxes may be possible	Annual interest payments; sometimes semiannual	Securities brokers; overseas commercial banks	11

THIRTEEN

Yield Curve Analysis

Up to this point in the book, we have not always clearly distinguished between two main strategies of investing in fixed-income securities. One strategy might be called the *static* approach, whereby the investor buys a particular issue, either short-term or long-term, and normally holds onto that security until it matures. Under the other strategy, sometimes referred to as the *dynamic* approach, the investor from time to time takes action to change the original positions in his portfolio. An example of this method might involve selling one security before it matures in order to buy another security.

Chapters 13 and 14 describe some techniques for executing a dynamic portfolio strategy. In this chapter, we will focus on how an investor can improve his portfolio through consciously altering the *maturity structure* of his holdings. This is done by analyzing the differences between the yields of various maturities of the same or virtually equivalent securities in order to augment profits and minimize capital losses. In the following chapter, the principal emphasis is placed on other ways of making portfolio improvements, through swapping one *type* of fixed-income security for another type.

What Yield Curves Are

Most frequently, the relationship between yields and maturities of a set of similar securities is shown in a diagram called a *yield curve*. A yield curve traces on a graph the yield to maturity of a group of securities as compared with the time remaining in each security's life. Generally, yield curves are most ·often plotted for issues of the United States government, since they are the most uniform relative to each other. In addition, yield curves can be developed for other homogeneous issues, such as securities of the same government agency, corporation, or municipal issuer, as well as certain short-term money market instruments including certificates of deposit. As will be seen shortly, yield curves are fairly easy to construct, but the investor should take special care to compare securities which are, to the maximum extent possible, equivalent in every respect except maturity. Chapter 4 makes the point that many different factors, such as quality, sinking-fund and call provisions, and taxability can also influence a security's yield to maturity. Therefore, the investor should exclude from comparison any issues which are different from the others in these or other significant features, so that the analysis can focus on the effect that maturity alone has on the yields of several securities of the same issuer.

Yield curves can be plotted by (1) obtaining the yield to maturity for several different securities of the same issuer from the newspaper or from the investor's securities broker or commercial bank, (2) placing these yields on a graph according to the maturity of the security, and (3) drawing an approximate smooth curve through the center of these points. In the following section, four sample yield curves have been drawn for U.S. government securities as of different time periods during the past several years. Before reviewing each of these yield curves in greater detail, several explanatory comments should be made about the graphs.

First, the ×'s on each graph represent the yield to maturity observations for various maturities of U.S. government issues *as of a certain fixed point in time.* The yield curve is then sketched in between these points freehand, using the eye to judge whether it "fits" the configuration of the points accurately. When the ×'s are significantly above or below this yield curve, it may indicate that the security is undervalued (if above the line, it is relatively *less* expensive than most of the securities whose yields are approximated by the yield curve) or overvalued (if below the yield curve). These aberrations may be caused by special technical or psychological factors, and they may represent possible opportunities to buy a certain security at a lower price (or sell it at a higher price) relative to its "cousins." Second, the yield curve is perishable. If a yield curve is drawn for a set of securities 2 years after the original curve was prepared, the 12-year security on the first graph will become the 10-year maturity issue on the second. Similarly, the 6-month issue on the first graph will have matured by the time the second yield curve is prepared, and the yield on a more recently issued short-term security of the same borrower will have to be substituted in its place. Third, as will be seen in the charts, yield curves can have *different shapes,* and they can be at *different positions* as they move up or down in response to changing interest rate conditions. Fourth, all yield curves not only report on yield configurations as of a specific date, they also give an indication of how other investors expect interest rates to behave in the future. This point will become clearer as each of the various yield curve shapes is reviewed. In Chapter 3, the point was made that short-term securities are *less* prone to wide *price* fluctuations than long-term securities for a given change in *yields.* At the same time, however, short-term securities are *more* prone to wide *yield* fluctuations than long-term securities for a given change in *prices.* Thus, in looking at yield curves over a period of time, the short-term portion of the curve might be expected to move around more widely than the long-term portion of the curve.

Various Yield Curve Shapes

The conventional method of charting yield curves plots time to maturity along the horizontal axis of the graph and yield to maturity along the vertical axis. In the yield curve presented in Figure 13-1, known as a *negatively sloped,* or *descending,* yield curve, short-term securities' yields are above the yields on long-term securities.

FIGURE 13-1. *Negatively sloped yield curve.*

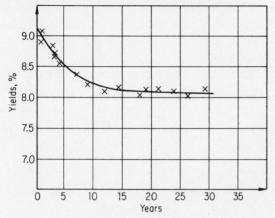

Generally, negatively sloped yield curves occur during periods of high interest rates—such as in late 1969 and during a large portion of 1974—when investors expect short-term interest rates to fall in the future relative to long-term yields. Because of this, investors are willing to accept lower-yielding long-term securities, since they believe that continuously "rolling over" short-term securities (that is, buying new short-term securities as the investor's original short-term holdings mature) will eventually produce a lower return, after short-term yields have fallen, than long-term securities with yields that are expected to drop less than those available on short-maturity securities. In a sense, a negatively sloped yield curve such as the one shown in Figure 13-1 usually comes about when investors *expect* to witness a curve similar in shape to the positively sloped yield curve exhibited in Figure 13-2, although not necessarily at the same absolute yield level. It should be mentioned that these expectations are as often as not proven wrong.

The *positively sloped,* or *ascending,* yield curve shown in Figure 13-2 occurs when the yields on short-term securities of an issuer are lower than yield levels on long-term securities of the same entity. The ascending yield pattern has been the most frequently encountered shape of the yield curve for most securities in the United States during the past four decades. Thus, the expectation of investors that

FIGURE 13-2. *Positively sloped curve.*

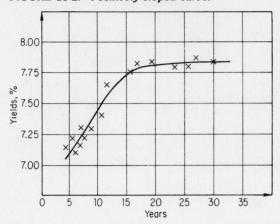

interest rates will rise in the future, which will enable the investor to reinvest at higher rates of interest, causes investors to purchase short-term securities. This in turn increases the prices of short-term securities (decreases their yields) relative to long-term issues. Under these circumstances, in order for long-term securities to attract investors, they have to sell at lower prices (higher yields) relative to short-term issues. Although not always borne out in practice, a positively sloped yield curve such as that shown in Figure 13-2

FIGURE 13-3. *Hump-backed yield curve.*

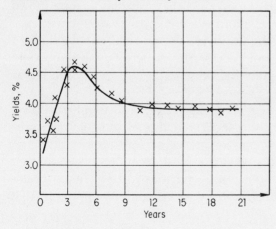

indicates that investors *expect* that securities' yields in the future may exhibit a pattern similar to the negatively sloped yield curve shown in Figure 13-1.

Two unusual yield curve shapes can also occur. In Figure 13-3, yields on very short-term maturities rise steeply and then decline gradually on longer-term securities. This type of yield curve, known as a *hump-backed,* or *humped,* yield curve, appears during periods of stringent monetary conditions, such as during the second quarter of 1970 and the third quarter of 1967. Figure 13-4 shows a *horizontal,* or *flat,* yield curve, which occurs when investors expect that interest rates in the future will be approximately the same as currently prevailing yield levels, or when the curve is shifting from a positively sloping configuration to a negatively sloping one, or vice versa.

At this point, the logical question arises regarding the underlying causes for yield curves to assume their various shapes. On this subject, there is no unanimity among economists, analysts, and professional money managers, but the role of investors' *expectations* about future interest rate levels is generally considered to be a major influence on the shape of the yield curve at any one moment in time. The normal preference of many investors for highly liquid short-term securities to earn a return on temporarily idle funds is also considered a factor in the usual pattern of short-term rates being

FIGURE 13-4. *Horizontal yield curve.*

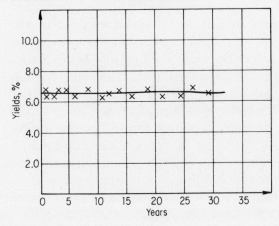

lower than long-term yields. This comes about because there is generally a greater degree of buying pressure on short- rather than long-term securities. It is also important to recognize that corporate and governmental issuers of short-term and long-term securities can affect the slope, shape, and level of the yield curve, through the degree of their demands for short-term versus long-term funds relative to investors' expectations and their momentary bias toward securities of one particular maturity as compared with other maturities.

Practical Applications of Yield Curves

Investors can derive practical use from yield curves in several ways. First, although yield curves are not highly reliable and accurate indicators of future interest rate levels, they do show how a large number of other market participants *think* interest rates will move in the future. These investors' expectations may or may not be realized. Nevertheless, construction and observation of a yield curve disciplines the investor to ask himself, in conjunction with the economic analysis described in the worksheet at the end of Chapter 5, what will happen to interest rates and when, relative to his own investment time horizon. In doing this exercise, it is often helpful to draw a current yield curve for U.S. government or other securities and then add a dotted line to the graph to represent what the investor thinks will happen to short-term and long-term yields on these issues in the future.

Second, and perhaps more important, the investor can utilize the present position and shape of the yield curve, as well as its expected future shape and position, to help select the maturity of his investments. After a certain period of time, the investor can construct new yield curves and adapt his investment strategy accordingly. For example, if an investor plans to invest a sum of money which will be needed in 10 years' time to meet expenses, numerous alternatives are available. He could buy a 10-year maturity security and hold it until it comes due; he could buy a security of 6-months' maturity and purchase another when the original investment matures, repeating the process every 6 months for 10 years; he could buy a security with 2 years to maturity, and then purchase an issue with 8 years to maturity; or he could buy a security with 15 years to maturity, and sell it after 10 years when it still has 5 years left to maturity.

In fact, the range of choices of maturity combinations is even broader than the four possibilities listed above, since each alternative could also be arranged in numerous different configurations. Yield curve analysis can aid the investor in visualizing the profit potential of various investment patterns involving several maturity choices. One reminder should be inserted here—all investors, and particularly the investor with a small to moderate amount of capital to invest in fixed-income securities, should not engage in excessive trading of his portfolio, since commission charges and other fees can significantly reduce the effective yield earned from a series of fixed-income investments.

In using yield curves to assist in the maturity decision process, the investor should also keep in mind that a yield curve can change over a period of time in several ways—either its shape or its position can change, or both of these conditions can occur. The various possibilities are reviewed briefly in Table 13-1 and more extensively on the following pages.

In the figures which follow, we show each of the possible ways a yield curve can change its shape and position, and we suggest some strategies which the investor might follow if he believes that a certain type of change will happen. In each of our examples, starting yield curve position is assumed to be an upward-sloping yield curve as of an imaginary date—June 15, 19X4. Of course, the investor will not always initially encounter an upward-sloping yield curve. Two other limitations also apply to our brief overview of possible yield curve changes. In each alternative which is considered, we only cover what

TABLE 13-1 Possible Ways a Yield Curve Can Change over Time

Alternative	Shape of the yield curve	Position of the yield curve
1	Remains the same	Remains the same
2	Remains the same	Moves upward or downward
3	Configuration changes	Remains the same
4	Configuration changes	Moves upward or downward

happens for one particular shape of the future yield curve, and for a move of the yield curve in one direction. Practically speaking, a myriad of shapes and absolute yield levels can and will be encountered. It is the task of the investor to exercise judgment in estimating the shape and position of the yield curve at a certain chosen point in the future, and to execute an optimal investment strategy to take advantage of actual conditions as well as estimates.

Figure 13-5 depicts two of the four alternative situations listed in Table 13- 1. In alternative situation 1, a positively sloped yield curve retains its original shape and holds a steady position over the 5-year period from June 15, 19X4 to June 15, 19X9. This does not necessarily mean that conditions remained static throughout that time span. What it does mean is that *at the end of the 5-year period,* the yield curve is unchanged in shape and position from its original form. When this situation occurs for a positively sloped yield curve, long-term securities will rise somewhat in price (decline in yield) as they move toward maturity. Looking at Figure 13-5, if the investor buys a 7.5 percent coupon security with 10 years remaining to maturity at a price of par ($1,000 per $1,000 bond), its yield to maturity works out to 7.5 percent (point *A* in Figure 13-5). After 5 years, when the security has 5 years remaining to maturity, its yield has declined, not because of any overall decline in interest rates, but because the former 10-year security is now a 5-year security and trades like one.

FIGURE 13-5. *Possible yield curve changes, I.*

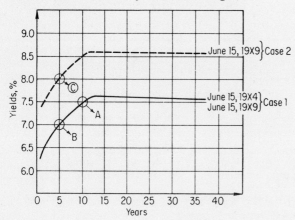

FIGURE 13-6. *Possible yield curve changes, II.*

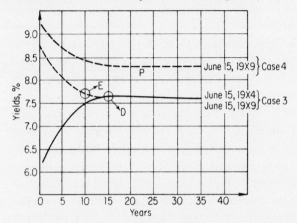

In numerical terms, point *B* on the figure shows 5-year securities yielding 7.0 percent rather than 7.5 percent. This means that the $1,000 bond is now worth $1,020. This is the classic form of *riding the yield curve,* which means taking advantage of a price gain in a security as it simply moves toward maturity, without any change in the overall level of interest rates.

Since interest rates fluctuate and the shapes of yield curves can change over time, riding the yield curve is not always as simply and easily accomplished as it may seem. Alternative situation 2 from Table 13-1, labeled as case 2 on Figure 13-5, illustrates this point. Even though the yield curve has remained positively sloped, the position of the yield curve has shifted upward as the general level of interest rates has risen between June 15, 19X4 and June 15, 19X9. If the investor had purchased the same 7.5 percent coupon 10-year maturity issue at par (point *A* on the original yield curve) and then desired to sell this security after 5 years, its yield would be higher (8.0 percent) and its price lower ($980 per $1,000 bond), represented by point *C* on the figure. If the investor sells his bonds at this point, he will suffer a loss of principal equal to $20 for every $1,000 bond. The investor might have been better off had he bought a shorter maturity issue and then reinvested the proceeds at a higher yield after interest rate levels had risen.

Figure 13-6 demonstrates what happens in situations 3 and 4 listed in Table 13-1. The third possible way yield curves can change over time involves a change in the shape of the yield curve while the overall level of the curve does not shift upward or downward. In the set of yield curves marked case 3 in this figure, riding the yield curve is impossible since, as time passes and maturities shorten, yields increase (prices decline), rather than decrease. If the investor purchased a 15-year bond at point *D* in the figure and sold it after 5 years (point *E*), a capital loss would be experienced as the positive slope changed to a negative slope. The investor would probably have done better by initially investing in short-term securities to protect against possible price declines. After interest rates have risen on securities of 12 years' maturity and under (as shown by the dotted line in case 3 of Figure 13-6), the investor would have the choice of buying either short- or long-term securities. It should be noted that in case 3, long-term yields did not change position as the yield curve assumed its new shape. Had an investor bought 30-year bonds and sold them after 5 years, his sale yield would have been roughly the same as his purchase yield level.

Case 4 shows what happens when the yield curve undergoes a change both in its slope and in its absolute interest level. The slope of the yield curve has changed from positive to negative, while the curve has shifted upward, as interest rates in general have risen (prices have fallen). The investor would probably have done best by buying short-term securities and waiting for the level of interest rates to rise while the configuration of the yield curve was also changing. This maneuver would have limited a price decline in the value of the investor's holdings and would have permitted the investor to reinvest at higher yields at a later date.

Riding the yield curve can also be done on very short-term securities with an original maturity of 1 year or less, such as Treasury bills, discount notes, or commercial paper. Figure 13-7 shows a sample yield curve for U.S. Treasury bills, with both the horizontal and vertical axes expanded to permit closer analysis. (The investor can also do this when constructing his own yield curves, if his focus is on a small yield range or a certain maturity range.) In the yield curve in Figure 13-7, a positively sloped yield curve is depicted, with 91-day Treasury bills yielding less (selling at a higher price) than 182-day bills. *Provided that the yield curve holds this shape and position* for the next

FIGURE 13-7. *Sample yield curve for Treasury bills.*

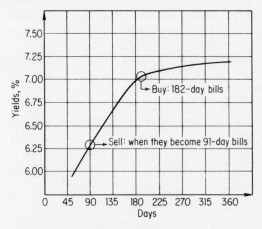

91 days or more, the short-term investor can earn a higher return by buying 182-day bills, selling them at a higher price (lower yield) when they become 91-day bills, and reinvesting the augmented proceeds in new 182-day bills. We have confined our analysis to these two maturities because they are much more marketable and liquid than the other "odd maturity" T bills. Riding the yield curve in this manner produces a higher return than merely buying 182-day bills and holding them to maturity or buying 91-day bills and rolling them over continually as they come due.

WORKSHEET: CONSTRUCTING ONE'S OWN YIELD CURVES

When the investor prepares to purchase a fixed-income security, yield curve analysis will help in making a decision among the alternatives listed below:

Alternative 1 Invest in a security with exactly the same maturity as the length of the expected investment period. This might be done if interest rates are high and are expected to remain high in the maturity range corresponding to the investor's expected investment period.

FIGURE 13-8. *Sample yield curve chart 1.*

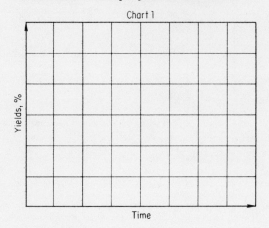

Alternative 2 Invest in a short-term security and continually reinvest the proceeds upon maturity in new short-term securities until the end of the expected investment period. This might be followed if the investor may have need for his funds on short notice, or if short-term yields are high and expected to stay high or move higher. This is the least risky alternative of those described here.

Alternative 3 Invest in a short-term security for a period of time and switch to a longer-maturity security for the remainder of the expected investment period. This alternative might be chosen if short-term interest rates are high and expected to drop, while long-term rates are low and expected to rise, or if short- and long-term rates are the same. This situation might be described as a current negatively sloped yield curve changing to a flat curve and then to a positively sloped yield curve at some point in the future. This alternative entails a moderate degree of risk.

Alternative 4 Invest in a security with a maturity longer than the expected investment period and sell it prior to its scheduled maturity. This alternative can produce an increased investment return when the yield curve is positively sloped or when the overall level of interest rates is expected to fall. However, this alternative also

FIGURE 13-9. *Sample yield curve chart 2.*

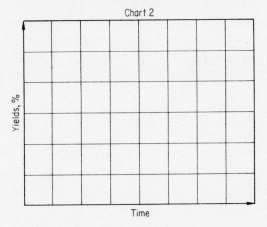

carries the greatest risk of capital loss if the investor is wrong in his predictions.

To help the investor construct current yield curves and choose among the maturity alternatives listed above, blank yield curve charts have been included in Figures 13-8 and 13-9. The investor can label the specific yields to maturity covered in his analysis along the vertical axis, and the appropriate times (in days, years, or multiples of years) along the horizontal axis. Generally speaking, the charts can be most effectively utilized if the investor: (1) selects a time period and yield range for the graph which will accent the shape of the yield curve but which will also allow for changes in the slope and the position of the yield curve; (2) ensures that a comparison is being made between the yields to maturity of equivalent or virtually equivalent securities; (3) plots not only the *current* yield curve, but also his best estimate of how the *future* yield curve will look at various times during and at the end of the projected investment period; and (4) chooses the maturity pattern of his investments from among the alternatives listed above, in concert with his own objectives and expected movements in the shape and position of the yield curve.

FOURTEEN

Portfolio Improvements

In the previous chapter, we reviewed various techniques for altering the *maturity* composition of an investor's portfolio in order to increase yield and reduce the risk of principal loss when interest rates change. In this chapter, we will concentrate on ways of changing, or switching, from securities of one *coupon* to another, one *quality* level to another, and one *yield* level to another, both within and between various types and categories of fixed-income securities. Another name for this switiching activity is *swapping,* which simply consists of selling one fixed-income security to purchase another. While all the swaps discussed here are oriented toward portfolio *improvements,* in practice, the investor must realize that not all swaps will achieve this intended objective of upgrading his holdings, since swaps involve risks as well as rewards.

Swaps are not appropriate for every investor. In general, active switching between various fixed-income securities should be attempted only by the more sophisticated investor who can devote the necessary study and time to analyzing developments in the credit and capital markets and to more aggressive portfolio management. Because of the higher transactions costs and related charges associated with executing small trades, swapping should not normally be attempted by investors with a small-to-moderate-sized portfolio. Nevertheless, since a sizable number of both small and large investors will occasionally desire to shift their investments from one area of the fixed-income securities markets to another, it is worthwhile to spend some time familiarizing oneself with the concepts and mechanics of swapping.

At this point, it should be emphasized that recognition of broad trends in interest rates and the ability to perceive shifts in investor psychology are at least as important if not more important as intensive swapping activity which takes advantage of relatively small yield differentials. All too often, investors concentrate on one aspect of a swap, while completely ignoring other areas of the fixed-income markets which are more attractive. Rather than always focusing on how closely the security to be purchased approximates the security to be sold, the investor should, with the aid of his securities broker or commercial bank, attempt to find the *best available investment* in the entire marketplace at the moment a swap is being considered. Only if this broader approach is followed will the investor be able to derive the maximum benefits from swapping.

In the sections which follow, we will explore the reasons for and the risks inherent in swapping, as well as specific examples of several different types of relatively simple swaps. At the end of the chapter, a worksheet has been provided to aid the investor in evaluating fixed-income securities swap transactions.

Reasons for and Risks Inherent in Swapping Securities

Most of the time, swaps are effected in order to gain an increased amount of current income, an increased yield to maturity, or both. A second powerful motivating factor behind swapping is to seek improved price appreciation potential in the event of an upward or a downward change in interest rates. This type of maneuver, involving such tactics as investing in short-term securities if interest rates are expected to rise and lengthening the maturity of one's investments if interest rates are expected to fall, is basic to fixed-income investing and has been stressed throughout this book, particularly in Chapters 3 and 13.

A third reason for swapping is to purchase a certain security at an historically attractive yield relative to other similar issues or groups of issues. If and when the security which the investor bought moves back to its historical relationship with other issues, the investor may "reverse swap" back into his original investment or its equivalent. This type of swap usually necessitates having, or obtaining, knowledge of current and previous yield patterns for several types of securities. Normally, most individual investors will have to rely on outside sources for this information, such as a securities brokerage firm or a commercial bank. Numerous additional motivations for swapping also exist—the investor may wish to establish a loss to offset capital gains or income on his tax return, or he may wish to upgrade the quality or improve the marketability of his holdings, to name just a few reasons.

Swapping between various fixed-income securities may also result in disadvantageous investment results. If the investor guesses wrong about the price movement of the security which he switches into relative to the price performance of the security he sold or other issues, the swap may result in lessened interest income or even a capital loss greater than might have been experienced otherwise. While the investor may believe a certain security has become less expensive relative to another security and that in time the security will regain its comparative value, this does not always turn out to be the case. In some instances, the "temporarily" cheaper security may take longer than expected to regain its relative investment value, and occasionally, the cheaper security may never again sell on a basis similar to its former patterns. To avoid this, the investor should always think carefully about the *underlying causes* behind an out-of-the-ordinary yield relationship and whether these causes will soon be eliminated or continue for a long time. An apparent bargain may be relatively cheap because its fundamental components of value have been temporarily or permanently impaired, and it is up to the investor to determine *beforehand* whether a security is priced accurately or represents true value.

Knowledge of historical yield spreads between several types and categories of fixed-income securities is difficult for the average investor to obtain. Some large investors are aided by computers in performing reviews of historical and current yield spreads between a very broad range of securities. These aids to large investors make it virtually impossible for the average individual to compete with professionals on the same terms when swapping. Nevertheless, in attempting to discover and evaluate fixed-income securities swaps, the investor can and should call upon the resources of a reputable securities broker or commercial bank. In this activity, the investor should concentrate primarily on present and future trends in the yields of various types of fixed-income securities, both on an absolute basis and relative to each other. Again, the investor's outlook should be broad; he should continually ask whether a swap should be done *within* a specific category of securities or *between* one category and another.

Specific Types of Swap Transactions

Several different types of fixed-income securities swaps are presented in the following pages, in the form of examples which use imaginary names in order to emphasize their application in the U.S. government, agency, municipal, corporate, and even the international sectors of the market. Several different yield levels are used in the sample situations, to emphasize that swaps can be done in virtually any interest rate environment and that the *underlying principles* of swapping are just as important as the specific details of the transaction. Almost all these sample swaps are relatively easy to learn. Much more complex and intricate variations can be devised by the investor as he gains experience and familiarity with the concept of swapping. For simplicity in presentation, commission costs have been omitted from the examples, but the investor should remember to include all commission expenses when evaluating specific swaps.

Swaps between equivalent securities having different prices One of the simplest and most fundamental types of swaps involves the sale of a fixed-income security and the purchase of a lower-priced security of the same or a very similar issuer which is equivalent in coupon, quality, and maturity. Often, these swaps are carried out between similar securities of the various operating subsidiaries of the Bell Telephone System, or between various government agencies having similar degrees of federal guarantee. For example, the investor might execute the following transaction:

	Price		Yield to maturity, %
SELL: 30-year maturity, 8% XXX bond at	100	=	8.00
BUY: 30-year maturity, 8% ZZZ bond at	99	=	8.09
GAIN in yield to maturity		=	0.09

Money generated from the trade = 1 point, or $10 per $1,000 bond, which can be invested or used for other purposes.

The above swap, from XXX bonds to ZZZ bonds (the bonds could have been securities of the same issuer), generates a gain of 9 basis points in yield to maturity and enables the investor to free up $10 per $1,000 bond for any desired use. An additional benefit of this type of swap comes about if the newly purchased security begins to trade on a similar basis as the security which was originally owned. If, after 1 month, 6 months, or 1 year, interest rates have fallen, to 7¾ percent for securities such as the ones above, and if both the XXX bonds and the ZZZ bonds trade in line with these new yield levels and with each other, the original bond would have gained about 3 points in price (from 100 to 103), while the newly purchased bonds would have experienced a larger price gain, of 4 points (from 99 to 103). If the two bonds begin to trade on an equivalent basis while general yield levels remain the same or trend upward, the newly purchased bonds will still perform better.

A large number of swap opportunities of this type arise from new bond offerings, when a new issue, even though it is the equivalent of seasoned issues already outstanding, declines in price after the underwriting syndicate has disbanded. In this case, the investor could sell his existing holding and purchase the equivalent security at a lower price (higher yield to maturity). Occasionally, very slight

funds from their fixed-income securities investments is to lengthen their maturities. For instance, if the overall interest rate for both 10-year securities and 20-year securities is 8 percent, the investor might sell his holdings of 10-year 7½ percent ZZZ bonds at 96⅝ (a yield to maturity of 8 percent) and purchase 20-year 7½ percent ZZZ bonds for 94½ (also a yield to maturity of 8 percent), freeing up an additional $21.25 per $1,000 bond (96⅝ − 94½, equals 2⅛ points, or $21.25 per $1,000 bond). When the investor withdraws money from his portfolio by lengthening maturities or moving from a higher-coupon security to one with a lower coupon, he should keep in mind that he is also exposing himself to larger price declines in the event that interest rates change. Generally speaking, this type of transaction is advisable principally during periods of declining interest rates.

While swap opportunities in these first two general categories of swapping can be discovered by the investor's own frequent observation of the newspaper to stay up to date on price and yield trends of various fixed-income securities, the next three types of swaps presented below usually require some knowledge of historical yield patterns and interrelationships. Thus, they generally necessitate access to, and the use of, statistics maintained by commercial banks, securities brokerage firms, or the major debt rating agencies.

Swaps between securities with different quality ratings   These swaps require a deft sense of timing, a knowledge of historical versus current yield spreads, and most importantly, an ability to forecast future interest rate movements and possible credit rating changes. For example, the normal yield pattern for a certain type of fixed-income security (such as a utility issue, an industrial security, or a general obligation tax-exempt security) may show that an A-rated issue has generally averaged 75 basis points more in yield than a triple-A-rated issue of equal coupon and maturity during the past several years. If the A-rated security happens to move up in price so that it now yields only 50 basis points more than the AAA-rated security, the investor can usually profit by selling the A-rated issue and buying the AAA-rated bond. After this swap transaction has been executed, the investor can then *swap back* into the A-rated security from the AAA-rated issue when the yield spread between the two securities has widened to well in excess of its normal 75-basis-point differential, perhaps to a 100-basis-point spread. The sample transaction below demonstrates how this works. For simplicity, we assume no change has occurred in the overall level of interest rates, even though the relationship between the yields on A-rated and AAA-rated issues does change:

STEP 1: (The normal yield differential between AAA and A securities is 75 basis points, but the existing spread is 50 basis points)

	Price		Yield to maturity, %
SELL: 20-year, A-rated, 8% XXX bonds	95¼	=	8.50
BUY: 20-year, AAA-rated, 8% ZZZ bonds	100	=	8.00
Basis point *differential* = 50 basis points		=	0.50

Additional money needed for the trade = 4¾ points, or $47.50 per $1,000 bond.

STEP 2: (At some point in the future, the yield differential between AAA and A securities has moved above normal to 100 basis points)

	Price		Yield to maturity, %
SELL: 20-year, AAA-rated, 8% ZZZ bonds	100	=	8.00
BUY: 20-year, A-rated, 8% XXX bonds	90⅞	=	9.00
Basis point *differential* = 100 basis points		=	1.00

Money generated from the trade = 9⅛ points, or $91.25 per $1,000 bond.

Thus, swapping from the A-rated security into the AAA-rated security and back again when the normal yield spread has been exceeded produced a net gain of 4⅜ points (9⅛ − 4¾), or $43.75 per $1,000 bond in the example above. Similar relative gains can be achieved even in periods of changing interest rates. This type of swap can also be done in reverse. That is, if the investor expects interest rate spreads between A and AAA securities to return to a 75-basis-point level from an existing level of 100 basis points, he should buy the A-rated bonds at a lower price (100-basis-point higher yield) than the AAA-rated bonds, and then swap back into the AAA-rated bonds when their price is higher relative to the A bonds (at or below the normal 75-basis-point higher yield).

Swaps of this type can be done between several rating classifications *within* one general type of securities, such as from A-rated railroad securities to AA-rated rail issues, and vice versa, or from Baa-rated general obligation municipal bonds to A-rated general obligation municipal securities, and the reverse. In addition, similar swaps can be done *between* one general type and another type, such as from A-rated industrial bonds to AAA-rated utility issues, and vice versa, or between AA-rated tax-exempt revenue bonds and Baa-rated tax-exempt general obligation bonds, and the reverse.

Several important caveats must be kept in mind when doing swaps between different quality ratings of the *same type* of securities or between the same or different quality ratings of *different types* of securities. First, the average differential between two groups of issues during the past several years may not necessarily be experienced again during the investor's own investment time horizon. Second, related to this phenomenon is the possibility that yield spreads owing to quality differences may continue to widen when they are expected to narrow, and vice versa. Third, a particular issue may trade differently from others within its own quality rating category because of liquidity factors or because it is about to be upgraded or downgraded in its quality ranking. Fourth, success in swapping between securities of different quality ratings is not simple to achieve, and it demands that the investor have or obtain information about historical yield spreads. Sometimes, the investor may concentrate too much on yield differentials due to quality rankings when instead he should be aware of broad emerging interest rate trends or the credit risks involved in investing in lower-quality securities.

As was mentioned in Chapter 4, during periods of easier monetary conditions (lower interest rates), differences in yields because of quality considerations tend to narrow, while during stringent monetary conditions (higher interest rates) investors tend to place more emphasis on quality differences between various fixed-income securities, causing yield spreads between high-quality and low-quality issues to widen. Generalizing from the above comments, when yield differentials between similar high-quality and low-quality securities are expected to *widen,* investors may wish to swap from low-quality securities to higher-quality issues. On the other hand, when yield spreads are expected to *narrow* between high-quality securities and low-quality issues, it may be more beneficial to switch out of the higher-quality securities into lower-quality issues, while keeping possible credit risks in line with the investor's own guidelines.

Swaps between different categories of fixed-income securities This type of swap involves switching between agency, corporate, government, and municipal issues of roughly the same maturity and the same relative coupon level on an aftertax basis. Because investors' tax brackets will differ, and because of the varying tax status of each of these categories of securities at the federal, state, and local levels, the investor should always compare the net result of these swaps on both a beforetax and an aftertax basis. In the example below, we compare yields on an historical basis before taxes, since most investors start out by analyzing yield spreads between different categories of securities in the same way:

STEP 1: (The normal yield differential between AAA-rated corporate industrial bonds and U.S. government issues is 70 basis points, but the existing spread is 50 basis points.)

	Price		Yield to maturity, %
SELL: 25-year, AAA-rated, 7½% XXX bonds	94½	=	8.00
BUY: 25-year, 7½% U.S. government bonds	100	=	7.50
Basis point *differential* = 50 basis points		=	0.50

Additional money needed for the trade = 5¹/₂ points, or $55 per $1,000 bond.

STEP 2: (At some point in the future—here assumed to be 1 year—the differential in yields between these two types of securities now exceeds the 70-basis-point norm and is at 100 basis points; in this example, we also assume that interest rate levels on long-term U.S. government securities have moved downward to 7 percent.)

	Price		Yield to maturity, %
SELL: 24-year, 7¹/₂% U.S. government bonds	105³/₄	=	7.00
BUY: 24-year, AAA-rated, 7¹/₂% XXX	94¾	=	8.00
Basis point *differential* = 100 basis points		=	1.00

Money generated from the trade = 11 points, or $110.00 per $1,000 bond.

As can be seen from the example, swapping from the AAA-rated corporate industrial bonds to the U.S. government bond and back again when the normal yield spread has been exceeded produces a net gain of 5½ points, or $55 per $1,000 bond in the example above. Although the investor has to give up some yield and pay a higher price for an equivalent amount of bonds when buying the U.S. government issue in step 1, *if the securities eventually exceed their historical yield differential* relationship, this is more than compensated for when swapping back into the corporate bonds in step 2, since the investor then receives a relatively higher yield and pays a lower relative price for the issue.

Similar swaps can be done in varying interest rate conditions and between corporate and municipal securities, U.S. government and agency securities, and numerous other combinations. At certain times, investors have been able to swap from a corporate security into a similar U.S. government agency issue at the same yield to maturity, thus obtaining a higher-quality issue at roughly the same price. Later, after the yield spread between corporate and agency issues has widened, the investor has the option of swapping back into the corporate security or holding onto the agency issue which was acquired at a bargain price relative to the corporate bond. In addition, the investor should keep in mind the caveats mentioned at the end of the section on swapping between securities with different quality ratings.

Special Situation Swaps

Special situation swaps include swaps between corporate convertible securities and their underlying common stock, and vice versa, as described in Chapter 10, and swaps between convertible bonds and nonconvertible bonds of the same or similar companies. Also included in this category are swaps, primarily for corporate investors, involving preferred stocks and corporate bonds or between various types and quality categories of preferred stocks, executed along the same lines as the various swaps presented in this chapter. Other special situation swaps may include combination switches between various maturities, coupon levels, quality ratings, and categories of securities. Thus, the investor might encounter a swap between a Baa-rated 8½ percent 15-year industrial bond into a

AAA-rated 5 percent 30-year utility bond, if the security to be purchased is trading at an attractive current price relative to the historical price of the security to be sold, *and if the expected level of interest rates in the future favors the security to be purchased,* with its maturity, coupon, and quality ranking.

Generally, keeping track of historical yield spreads for such a diverse set of securities requires the aid of a computer, as is done by several securities brokerage firms and commercial banks. Nevertheless, the average investor may occasionally make swaps similar to these for other reasons than yield spreads alone. Such reasons may include different tax treatments of various securities, a desire for improved liquidity, higher quality, greater current income, or to change the portfolio's tendency toward price fluctuation in view of an expected upward or downward change in interest rates. While these reasons may override yield spread considerations, the investor should ask his securities broker or commercial banker how the current yield differential between the security he has decided to purchase and the security to be sold compares with the historical yield differential during the past several years. This may at least give the investor an idea of the relative attractiveness of one security vis-à-vis the other, but the investor should also keep an open mind toward the full range of investment possibilities.

WORKSHEET: EVALUATING SPECIFIC SWAP TRANSACTIONS

Note: The numerous factors to be considered in evaluating a swap transaction should be carefully organized so that the investor can see the transaction within the context of other alternative investments, and so that the investor can recognize exactly what benefits and disadvantages he is receiving from the switch. The investor may want to refer to the worksheets at the end of Chapters 2, 3, and 5, as well as the charts contained in Chapter 12, while filling out this worksheet for a specific swap transaction. Again, when the investor cannot find the answer to a question on his own, he should ask his securities broker, his commercial banker, or another professional investor to assist him.

POINT 1: *What are the details of the security to be purchased, compared with the details of the security to be sold, as outlined below?* _____

Item	Feature	Security to be sold	Security to be purchased	Current differential	Historic differential
A.	Maturity	_____	_____	_____	n.a.*
B.	Quality	_____	_____	_____	n.a.
C.	Coupon	_____	_____	_____	n.a.
D.	Price	_____	_____	_____	_____
E.	Current Yield	_____	_____	_____	_____
F.	Yield to maturity (before taxes)	_____	_____	_____	_____
G.	Yield to maturity (after taxes)	_____	_____	_____	_____
H.	Marketability	_____	_____	_____	n.a.
I.	Sinking-fund provisions	_____	_____	_____	n.a.
J.	Call features	_____	_____	_____	n.a.

*n.a. = not applicable

COMMENT: The investor should consider each of these factors in deciding whether to swap between one security and another, and where applicable, he should obtain information on how the security to be purchased has traded relative to the security to be sold during an appropriate time period prior to the present. This time period will generally correspond to or exceed the investor's expected holding period for any fixed-income investments he makes. If the investor is seeking to swap between basically equivalent securities, he should make sure that there is *very little* difference between items A, B, C, H, I, and J for the two securities.

POINT 2: *Are there any other hidden factors which may account for wide differentials between the two securities being considered?* _____

COMMENT: The investor should also check to see whether certain factors which are not immediately apparent are causing a security to seem as if it is selling at "bargain" prices when there is in fact a reason for its relative price weakness. Such factors might include (1) an expected increase or decrease in the issuer's credit rating; (2) deteriorating earnings coverage or other financial indicators (such as those mentioned in Chapter 10); and (3) underlying technical, fundamental, or psychological developments which might have caused investors to sell the security below "normal" levels.

POINT 3: *What is the investor's time horizon?* _____
If the security being purchased is expected to gain in yield relative to the security to be sold, over what time period is this expected to happen, and why? _____

COMMENT: It is especially important to keep in mind the time horizon of the investment, particularly when the investor contemplates reverse swapping back into the security he originally owned after yield differentials have returned to their historical levels. However, the investor should consider what *specific* factors will cause the historical yield differential to be restored, with emphasis on any possible reasons these factors will be postponed or eliminated.

POINT 4: *What are the commission costs involved in each portion of the proposed swap transaction(s)?* _____

COMMENT: The investor should find out, before going ahead with a swap transaction, whether commission costs and any other transactions fees will substantially reduce the possible returns to be generated from the swap. Usually, it is not worth while for the investor to try to take advantage of small yield differentials in odd-lot transactions.

POINT 5: *What will the effect of an increase or decrease in interest rates be on the security to be purchased as compared with the security which is being sold?*
_____

COMMENT: This is an extremely important question, since small yield gains obtained by swapping can be completely wiped out by price changes in a security on account of interest rate changes. The investor should devote a great deal of attention to trying to estimate which way interest rates will move and then tailor his investment strategy accordingly. If the investor is unsure about the future course of interest rates, he should adopt a conservative investment strategy and buy only those securities which have features tending to *reduce* price fluctuations.

POINT 6: *What are the advantages and disadvantages of the swap under consideration?* _____

COMMENT: The investor should enumerate any current and expected gains which will be derived from the swap in terms of increased income, capital freed up from the trade, higher yield to maturity, or possible capital appreciation, and these should be weighed against possible additional amounts of capital required, a give-up in current yield or capital appreciation potential, and other disadvantages, in order to determine whether the swap should be done.

POINT 7: *What alternatives other than the proposed security to be purchased might be considered?* _____

COMMENT: Before swapping into a particular issue, the investor should review the current yields and other features of the securities listed in the figures in Chapter 12, to determine whether another security is more appropriate and/or available at a bargain price relative to his current and future investment objectives. The investor should ask his securities broker or commercial banker to present suggested investments to him for evaluation with this worksheet.

FIFTEEN

Sources of Further Information

To date, very little information on fixed-income securities investing has been oriented toward or made available to the individual investor. In this chapter, we have gathered a list of periodicals, books, magazine articles, and other literature which will be of interest and assistance to the investor who desires to learn more about both general and specific aspects of fixed-income securities. The value of care and thoroughness in researching possible investments cannot be overemphasized. All too often, the same individual who spends weeks deciding on which clothes to purchase will invest many times more dollars in a security based on hearsay, rumors, "tips," or because a neighbor or friend has bought the same issue. Investing should be approached with caution. The investor who takes the time to inform himself about important factors affecting interest rates and specific securities, and stay informed about them, will stand a much better chance of earning a consistent and above-average return on his money. An essential part of the investment process is the selection of a securities broker and/or a commercial bank to execute trades.

As mentioned earlier in the book, not all commercial banks or securities brokers deal in a wide variety of fixed-income securities, and commercial banks do not trade in corporate bonds and preferred stocks. The investor should select a securities broker and/or a commercial bank with an excellent reputation, a strong financial position, and an involvement in a broad range of fixed-income securities. It is sometimes a good idea to write to any or all of the following organizations to ask for a list of *full-line* securities brokers and commercial banks who deal in a relatively *complete spectrum* of fixed-income issues, within the investor's area of residence.

To find out about securities brokerage firms, write to
Securities Industry Association
490 L'Enfant Plaza East, S.W.
Washington, D.C. 20024

National Association of Securities Dealers
1735 K St., N.W.
Washington, D.C. 20006

New York Stock Exchange, Inc.
11 Wall St.
New York, New York 10005

To find out about commercial banks, write to
Board of Governors
Federal Reserve System
Washington, D.C. 20551

U.S. Comptroller of the Currency
c/o U.S. Treasury Department
Washington, D.C. 20220

After the investor has gathered a list of securities brokers and/or commercial banks, he should make an appointment with the officer in charge of the branch most convenient to him and meet personally with the individual who would be directly responsible for his account. This is very important, because if the investor's personality and investment philosophy do not match those of his broker or bank representative, he should search for another individual whose objectives and approach to investing are closely aligned with his own.

Another reason why it is vital to choose a strong securities brokerage firm and/or commercial bank is that many of them publish regular surveys of the economy and fixed-income markets, as well as swap ideas, while others do not offer this type of advice. The investor should write to several brokers and dealer banks, in order to request sample copies of these surveys, as well as any handbooks, glossaries, or investment kits describing areas of the fixed-income securities markets in which the investor has an interest.

Besides the commercial banks and securities brokers, an extremely useful source of information on fixed-income issues is the Federal Reserve System. Each of the 12 District Offices of the Federal Reserve can supply a list of free or inexpensive articles and pamphlets describing the implementation of monetary and fiscal policy, the fundamentals of various types of fixed-income securities, and numerous other subjects of value to the investor. In addition, several of the districts publish a *Monthly Review* containing many articles of current interest about fixed-income markets. The *Monthly Reviews* of the Cleveland, New York, and St. Louis Federal Reserve Districts are particularly useful. To obtain a list of publications and to subscribe to the *Monthly Review* of a specific district, the investor should write to any or all of the following addresses:

Publications Services
Division of Administrative Services
Board of Governors of the Federal
  Reserve System
Washington, D.C. 20551

Public Information & Education
Federal Reserve Bank of Boston
30 Pearl St.
Boston, Mass. 02106

Publications Section
Federal Reserve Bank of New York
33 Liberty St.
New York, N.Y. 10045

Bank and Public Relations Department
Federal Reserve Bank of Philadelphia
925 Chestnut St.
Philadelphia, Pa. 19101

Research Department
Federal Reserve Bank of Atlanta
Federal Reserve Station
Atlanta, Ga. 30303

Publications and Reports Section
Research Department
Federal Reserve Bank of Chicago
230 South LaSalle St.
Chicago, Ill. 60690

Research Librarian
Federal Reserve Bank of St. Louis
411 Locust St., Box 442
St. Louis, Mo. 63166

Public Information Director
Federal Reserve Bank of Kansas City
925 Grand Ave.
Kansas City, Mo. 64106

Research Department
Federal Reserve Bank of Cleveland
1455 East 6th St.
Cleveland, Ohio 44101

Research Department
Federal Reserve Bank of Dallas
Station K
Dallas, Tex. 75222

Bank and Public Relations Department
Federal Reserve Bank of Richmond
100 North 9th St.
Richmond, Va. 23213

Administrative Service Department
Federal Reserve Bank of San Francisco
200 Sansome St.
San Francisco, Calif. 94120

The annual reports of each of the foregoing Federal Reserve districts also contain much useful information. The investor should always seek to obtain from his commercial bank, securities broker, or directly from the issuer itself a copy of its most recent annual report and a prospectus or offering circular if available, *before* making a specific investment. While this basic requirement is often neglected by investors, it can assist greatly in understanding the operations and financial condition of the issuer behind the security. This enables the investor to avoid surprises and form a sounder judgment about the inherent value of the proposed investment.

In the following sections, readings and other reference sources have been grouped into three main categories: (1) information of general use in forecasting interest rates and investing in fixed-income securities (Chapters 2 through 5 in this book), (2) information on specific types of securities (Chapters 6 through 11), and (3) information about yield curve analysis and swapping activity (Chapters 13 and 14). Before purchasing or subscribing to any of the books and periodicals mentioned in these three sections, the investor should visit his local library to find out whether the book fits his needs, or he should write to the publisher of the periodical to obtain sample copies. Generally, only those sources which would be of value to the individual investor are included here. If additional sources are needed, the Federal Reserve and the investor's securities broker or commercial bank should be able to provide suggestions. Expenditures for books or periodicals to help the investor improve his portfolio performance are in most cases deductible for federal income tax purposes. If the investor has a question in this area, he should check with competent tax counsel or with the Internal Revenue Service.

Information of General Use

Although numerous magazines and financial publications such as *Barron's, Business Week, Forbes, Fortune,* and *The Wall Street Journal* are extremely useful to the investor for background information and occasionally for specific investment suggestions, the sources listed here are primarily oriented toward fixed-income investing.

Newspapers and periodicals One of the best sources for keeping abreast of all the various sectors of the fixed-income securities markets is *The Money Manager,* published weekly by *The Bond Buyer,* 1 State St. Plaza, New York, N.Y. 10004 (subscription price: $126 per year). This newspaper-style publication contains detailed reviews of current developments and trends in corporate bonds, U.S. government securities, agency issues, international securities, and tax-exempt notes and bonds of all types. In addition, articles on the economy, monetary policy, and government fiscal measures are frequently included. Two newsletters which are published weekly from Washington and which review Treasury financing operations and Federal Reserve actions are the *Bond and Money Market Letter,* published by Goldsmith-Nagan, National Press Building, Washington, D.C. 20004 (annual subscription price: $95), and the *Washington Bond Report,* published by J. Slevin, 1295 National Press Building, Washington, D.C. 20004 (annual subscription price: $98).

The debt rating services also publish weekly reviews of major developments, new offerings, ratings changes, and suggested investments for virtually every sector of the intermediate- and long-term fixed-income securities markets. Moody's Investors Service, Inc., 99 Church St., New York, N.Y. 10007, puts out the *Moody's Bond Survey* (annual subscription price: $250), which is very broad in scope. Standard & Poor's Corporation, 345 Hudson St., New York, N.Y. 10014, publishes *The Fixed-Income Investor* (annual subscription price: $275), which also treats a wide range of securities. Twice monthly, Fitch Investors Service, 12 Barclay St., New York, N.Y. 10007, publishes the *Fitch Corporate Bond Review* (annual subscription price: $120), as well as other types of reports on public utility bond issues and municipal securities.

Books In the past 25 years, there has been a dearth of pragmatically oriented books aimed at helping the individual invest in fixed-income securities. The two which are mentioned here have been widely utilized by professional investors, yet they can be of help to anyone. *Security Analysis: Principles and Technique* (McGraw-Hill, New York, 1962) by Benjamin Graham, David L. Dodd, and Sidney Cottle was originally published in 1932 and presents a very thorough, fundamental, and conservative approach to the valuation of debt, equity, and a corporation's financial statements. Although weighty and methodical in many sections, a careful reading of this work will prove invaluable to those investors who can devote the necessary time to this project. *Inside the Yield Book* (Prentice-Hall, Englewood Cliffs, N.J., 1972) by Sidney Homer and Martin Liebowitz contains numerous insights into the arithmetic aspects of fixed-income securities and their implications for investing.

Statistical information Once each year, the Economics Division of the Bankers Trust Company, P.O. Box 318, Church Street Station, New York, N.Y. 10015 publishes *Credit and Capital Markets,* which is available at no charge. This extremely helpful overview of the sources and uses of funds within the economy is usually available in late February, and it gives the outlook for interest rates, credit needs, and capital demands during the coming year. On a more specific level, the debt rating services publish monthly summaries of rating information, call features, sinking-fund provisions, historical and recent price and yield ranges, and other data on corporate bonds, international securities, convertible issues, and many other types of securities. In addition, these booklets contain charts and other historical yield data for various quality rating classifications within certain types of bonds (such as railroad, utility, and industrial issuers). *Standard & Poor's Bond Guide* (published by Standard & Poor's Corporation, 345 Hudson St., New York, N.Y. 10014) costs $43 per year, and *Moody's Bond Record* (published by Moody's Investors Service, Inc., 99 Church St., New York, N.Y. 10007) contains data on a broad range of securities and costs $60 annually. Fitch Investors Service, 12 Barclay Street, New York, N.Y. 10007, publishes the *Fitch Corporate Bond Ratings Book* on an annual basis, with monthly supplements (annual subscription price: $38). Another source of useful statistical information is the Financial Publishing Company, 82 Brookline Ave., Boston, Mass. 02215, which publishes a large number of different yield tables and basis books. By writing to them, the investor can obtain a free catalog and descriptive price list.

Pamphlets Although it was pointed out above that lists of pamphlets and articles about fixed-income securities could be obtained from the various Federal Reserve district banks, we specifically mention three of general interest here. *Modern Money Mechanics: A Workbook on Deposits, Currency, and Bank Reserves* (published by the Federal Reserve Bank of Chicago) describes in plain language how the money supply contracts and expands and reviews the effects of various governmental policies on the money supply. The Federal Reserve Bank of Philadelphia has published a very useful *Guide to Interpreting Federal Reserve Reports,* which provides two glossaries and other detailed explanations of the meaning of (1) the weekly statement of condition of large commercial banks and (2) the statement of condition of the 12 Federal Reserve Banks. Finally, *Open Market Operations,* published by the Federal Reserve Bank of New York, discusses the means by which the Open Market Desk implements the policy directives of the Federal Open Market Committee.

Information on Specific Types of Securities

For each of the specific types of securities discussed in Chapters 6 through 11, we have listed between three and five sources of further information. In all the sections which follow, books, pamphlets, periodicals, articles, and statistical services have been combined.

U.S. government and agency securities A newsletter which is devoted entirely to governmental issues is *Reporting on Governments,* published weekly by Reporting on Governments, Inc., 2 Fifth Ave., New York, New York 10011 (annual subscription price: $99). This report describes, in letter format, recent developments in monetary and fiscal policies, interest rate trends, and economic conditions. Another helpful resource is the *Guide to the Securities of Federal Agencies, Government-Sponsored Corporations, and International Institutions,* distributed by the Public Information Department of the Federal Reserve Bank of New York, 33 Liberty St., New York, N.Y. 10045. This free guide shows, for each major agency or institution, where additional information can be obtained and the issuance, collection, and payment services provided to each issuer by the Federal Reserve Banks.

Two articles in the monthly *Economic Review* published by the Federal Reserve Bank of Cleveland provide background information on U.S. government and agency securities. They are "U.S. Government Bonds as Capital Market Instruments," contained in the August 1971 issue, and "Federal Agency Issues: Newcomers in the Capital Market," in the February 1972 issue. A book by Ira O. Scott, called *The Government Securities Market* (McGraw-Hill, New York, 1965) also has a good deal of background material and explanatory information on this area. Finally, The First Boston Corporation, 20 Exchange Pl., New York, N.Y. 10005 publishes biennially a comprehensive *Handbook of Securities of The United States Government and Federal Agencies, and Related Money Market Instruments,* currently in its twenty-sixth edition.

Tax-exempt Securities The Securities Industry Association, 20 Broad St., New York, N.Y. 10004, has prepared a useful book entitled *Fundamentals of Municipal Bonds* ($6). It can also be obtained through SIA member firms, and is a very thorough yet simple review of practically every aspect of municipal securities investing. In addition, the August-September 1972 issue of the Federal Reserve Bank of Cleveland *Economic Review* contains a helpful overview article on tax-exempt securities called "The Market for State and Local Government Bonds."

For those investors who are actively involved in the municipal markets on a frequent basis, two rather expensive periodicals may be of use. *The Daily Bond Buyer,* published Monday through Friday by *The Bond Buyer* (see address given on page 318; annual subscription price: $636), is widely read by municipal bond traders, underwriters, and investors. It contains information on virtually every new tax-exempt offering and reviews current developments in all sectors of the municipal markets. *The Blue List*, published Monday through Friday by the Blue List Publishing Company, 345 Hudson St., New York, N.Y. 10014 (annual subscription price: $200), includes the names and prices of all types of municipal securities (as well as some federally sponsored bonds and corporate bonds) currently being offered by tax-exempt securities dealers.

Short-term money market instruments By far the best review of the various types of short-term money market instruments is a 116-page free booklet called *Money Market Instruments*, published by the Federal Reserve Bank of Cleveland. Numerous other brochures and information kits on these investments have been prepared by several securities brokerage firms and commercial banks. Two valuable books which devote attention to short-term money market instruments are *Inside the Money Market* (Random House, New York, 1972) by Wesley Lindow and *The Money Market and Monetary Management* (Harper & Row, New York, 1972) by G. Walter Woodworth.

Corporate securities Again, the September 1969 issue of the Federal Reserve Bank of Cleveland *Economic Review* includes an excellent article on corporate bonds entitled "Corporate Bonds 1960–1968." A practical booklet on corporate and other types of bonds called *The Bond Book* is available from Merrill Lynch, Pierce, Fenner & Smith, Inc., 165 Broadway, New York, N.Y. 10006. For investors who wish to perform ratio analyses on corporate financial reports, a very clear book which could be of assistance is *The Interpretation of Financial Statements* (Harper & Row, New York, 1964), by Benjamin Graham and George McGobrick. In the preferred stock area, Kidder Peabody & Co. Inc., 10 Hanover Square, New York, N.Y. 10004 has prepared *A Guide to Preferred Stocks*, which describes some of the factors affecting the yields and prices of preferred stocks.

Two firms publish weekly statistical surveys of the convertible securities area, with information on bond conversion values, yield differentials, and other data. Kalb, Voorhis & Co., 27 William St., New York, N.Y. 10005 distributes the *KV Convertible Fact Finder* (annual subscription price: $90), and Arnold Bernhard & Co., Inc., 5 East 44th St., New York, N.Y. 10017 produces the *Value Line Convertible survey.* Value Line has also published a 132-page booklet on convertible securities called *More Profit–Less Risk.*

International securities Two weekly publications published in London contain information on currency movements and international bonds denominated in dollars and in other currencies. One is called the *Financial Times Euromarket Letter,* distributed by the Financial Times Limited, Bracken House, Cannon St., London EC4P 4BY, England (annual airmail subscription fee: $360), and the other is named the *International Insider,* published by William F. Low, Gillett House, 55 Basinghall St., London EC2V 5EL, England (annual airmail subscription fee: $215). Both are quite informative. The monthly magazine *Euromoney,* published by Euromoney Publications Limited, 14 Finsbury Circus, London E.C.2, England (annual airmail subscription fee: $50) contains numerous articles of interest to the investor in international securities. An estimable background article is contained in the May 1971 issue of the Federal Reserve Bank of Cleveland *Economic Review,* entitled "Eurobonds and the Eurobond Market." Several of the large New York City banks have also prepared descriptive booklets on the international money and capital markets.

Information on Yield Curve Analysis and Swapping Activity

Very little material has been written to help individual investors utilize yield curve analysis and swapping techniques in the management of their portfolios. *The Term Structure of Interest Rates* (Prentice-Hall, Englewood Cliffs, N.J., 1962) by David Meiselman, and Burton Malkiel's book *The Term Structure of Interest Rates–Expectations and Behavior Patterns* (Princeton University Press, Princeton, N.J., 1966) present the yield curve concept in great detail, but it is often left up to the reader to relate the principles in these books to his investment strategy. In the area of swapping, certain chapters of *Inside the Yield Book* by Sidney Homer and Martin Liebowitz (Prentice-Hall, Englewood Cliffs, N.J., 1972) may be useful. Generally, the investor should draw upon the ideas presented in this book, the recommendations and resources of his securities broker or commercial bank, and his own research, ingenuity, and common sense in developing swap ideas.

Index

FHLMC (*see* Federal Home Loan Mortgage Corporation)
FICB (*see* Federal Intermediate Credit Banks)
Financial Publishing Company, 27, 211, 320
Financial Times Euromarket Letter, 323
First Boston Corporation, 107, 275, 321
First National Bank of Chicago, 107
First National City Bank, 107
First Pennco Securities, Inc., 107
Fiscal agent, 159
Fiscal policy, 80, 102
Fitch Corporate Bond Ratings Book, 319
Fitch Corporate Bond Review, 318
Fitch Investors Service, 318, 319
  commercial paper ratings, 181
Fixed-Income Investor, The, 318
Fixed-income securities, 2–5
  individual investors' interest in, 3
  paradoxes inherent in, 3–4
Flat, definition of, 214
FLB (*see* Federal Land Banks)
Floating rate notes (*see* Variable rate notes)
Flow of funds analysis, 85–86
Flower bonds (U.S. Treasury issues), 5, 135
Fluctuations (*see* Price fluctuations)
FNMA (*see* Federal National Mortgage Association)
FOMC (Federal Open Market Committee), 64, 161
  (*See also* Open-market operations)
Forbes, 318
Ford Motor Company, 182, 261
Foreign bonds:
  external, 261, 282
  indigenous, 261, 282
  (*See also* International securities)
Foreign currency (*see* Currency)
Formulas:
  aftertax equivalent yield of a preferred stock for a corporation, 245
  approximate return on Treasury bills, 112
  bond equivalent yield of a Treasury bill, 122
  comparing aftertax yields of Treasury securities with other issues, 134
  discounts on bankers' acceptances, 172
  dollar price of a Treasury bill, 119
  fully taxable equivalent yield of a tax-exempt security, 194
  yield to-maturity for security purchased at discount or premium, 231
Fortune, 318
Forward calendar:
  of agency borrowing, 92–93, 102
  of corporate borrowing, 97, 102

Forward calendar (*Cont.*):
  of state and local government borrowing, 94, 102
  visible supply (*see* of state and local government borrowing *above*)
Forward cover, 261
Forward exchange, 258, 265
  (*See also* Currency)
Forward exchange contract, 258, 265
France, 264
Freddie Mac (*see* Federal Home Loan Mortgage Corporation)
Full employment budget, 90
Full faith and credit, securities backed by:
  of state or local government, 200
  of the United States government, 103
Funds:
  cash management, 184–185
  closed-end, 242
  corporate bond, 241–244
  federal (*see* Federal funds)
  government securities mutual funds, 139
  money market (*see* cash management *above*)
  open-end, 241–242
  pension, 84
  tax-exempt bond, 218–220

General Electric, 182, 239
General Motors Acceptance Corporation, 182–183, 225
General obligation bonds, 198–199
Germany, 157, 260–261, 264–266
Ginnie Mae (*see* Government National Mortgage Association)
GNMA (*see* Government National Mortgage Association)
GO (*see* General obligation bonds)
Goldman, Sachs & Co., 67, 107, 275
Goldsmith-Nagan, 318
Government agencies:
  exemption from SEC registration, 141
  total debt outstanding, 140–141
  yields compared to corporate and Treasury issues, 141
  (*See also* Federal Agencies; Government-sponsored enterprises)
Government National Mortgage Association (GNMA), 5, 91, 149, 152–154
  modified pass-through certificates, 152–154, 280
  mortgage-backed securities, 152, 280
  participation certificates, 152, 280
Government securities (*see* United States Treasury)

Local public agencies (*see* Tax-exempt
   securities, project notes)
London stock exchange, 262
Los Angeles Airports Department bonds, 200
Los Angeles Department of Water and
   Power, 194–195
Low, William F., 323
Luxemburg stock exchange, 262

M₁, 99
   (*See also* Money supply)
M₂, 99
   (*See also* Money supply)
McGobrick, George, 322
Malkiel, Burton, 323
Margin, 12, 136–138
Margin requirements on borrowing, 77, 195
Marketability (*see* Liquidity)
Marketable time drafts (*see* Bankers'
   acceptances)
Matched sale-purchase (*see* Reverse
   repurchase agreement)
Matsushita Electric, 262
Maturity:
   influence on price fluctuations, 29–30, 56
   influence on yield of securities, 37
   (*See also* Yield curves)
   objectives, 12–13
   structure, 284
Meiselman, David, 323
Merchant Marine bonds, 155
Merrill Lynch, Pierce, Fenner & Smith, Inc.,
   107, 275, 322
MGIC Indemnity Corporation, 206
MGIC Investment Corporation, 206
Monetary base, 99
Monetary policy, 80
   (*See also* Federal Reserve System)
Money in circulation, 68, 99
   (*See also* Credit)
Money Manager, The, 318
Money market, 63, 165
   indicators, 70
   instruments, 165–166
      yields compared with other securities,
      167–168
Money Market and Monetary Management, The
   (Woodworth), 322
Money market funds (*see* Funds, cash
   management)
Money supply:
   definitions of, 71
   expansion of, 64–65, 76
   growth rate of, 71–72

Moody's Bond Record, 319
Moody's Bond Survey, 318
Moody's Investors Service, Inc., 318, 319
   commercial paper ratings, 181
   corporate bond ratings, 237–238
   municipal bond ratings, 206, 207, 209–210
   preferred stock ratings, 246–247
   short-term municipal ratings, 215
Moral obligation for revenue bonds, 200–201
Morgan Guaranty Trust Company of New
   York, 107, 275
Municipal Bond Insurance Association, 206
Municipal securities (*see* Tax-exempt
   securities)
Mutual funds (*see* Funds)

National Association of Securities Dealers,
   315
National income accounts budget, 90
Negative carry, 107
Negotiated offering, 160, 203
Net asset value, 242
Net borrowed reserves, 67–69, 98
Net free reserves, 67–70, 99
Netherlands, the, 157, 260, 264
New money preferreds, 245
New York City, 134–135, 194–195
New York Hanseatic Corporation, 107
New York Stock Exchange, 106, 149, 187,
   239, 244, 315
90-day Treasury bill rate, 66, 70, 99
   graph, 67
No-load funds, 184
Non-interest-bearing securities, 18, 53, 112
Nonnegotiability of certificates of deposit,
   174–175
Nonredemption period, 227
Northern Trust Company, 107
Notes:
   corporate, 225–226, 280
   government (*see* United States Treasury)
   municipal (*see* Tax-exempt securities)
   U.S. (*see* United States Treasury, bonds and
      notes)
Nuveen, John, & Co., Incorporated, 107

Objectives:
   investment, 9–17
      capital position, 14–16
      income, 10–11
      maturity, 12–13
      money inflow, 14–16
      need for, 9–10